PAUL SELIGSON
LEANNE GRAY
RICARDO SILI
NICOLA MELDRUM
EDUARDO TRINDADE

2nd edition

English ID

Teacher's Book
Starter

Richmond

58 St Aldates
Oxford
OX1 1ST
United Kingdom

ISBN: 978-84-668-3047-8
Second reprint: 2024
CP: 944337

Publishing Director: Deborah Tricker
Publisher: Luke Baxter
Media Publisher: Luke Baxter
Managing Editor: Laura Miranda
Editors: Hilary McGlynn, Laura Miranda
Design Manager: Lorna Heaslip
Cover Design: Lorna Heaslip
Design & Layout: emc design Ltd, Jon Fletcher, Dave Kuzmicki
Photo Researcher: Victoria Gaunt, Emily Taylor (Bobtail Media)
Audio Production: John Marshall Media Inc.
ID Café Production: Mannic Media

We would like to thank all those who have given their kind permission to reproduce material for this book:

Illustrators: Alexandre Matos, Klayton Luz, Laurent Cardon, Leonardo Teixeira, Marcelo Costa, Rico

Photos: ARCHIVO SANTILLANA; COURTESY OF PEST CONTROL OFFICE, BANKSY, LONDON, 2004; A.G.E. FOTOSTOCK/ David Nunuk; ALAMY STOCK PHOTO/Acorn 1, Aliaksandr Barouski, A. Astes, AF archive, Allstar Picture Library, Antonio Guillem Fernández, Beatrice Preve, Cheryl Moulton, Cultura Creative (RF), Cristian M. Vela, David Wall, Dejan Jekic, Dmytro Zinkevych, Eduard Zajonchkovski, Edward Westmacott, Eugene Sergeev, Everett Collection Inc, Foto Arena LTDA, Hannu Liivaar, imageBROKER, Islandstock, James Boardman, John Kellerman, Juice Images, Kari, Katy Blackwood, Lena Kuhnt, Mim Friday, Mode Images, ONOKY – Photononstop, Papilio, Panther Media , Paul Thompson Images, Paul Williams, Pixel-shot, Pongphan Ruengchai, Realimage, Richard Sheppard, RobertHarding, ScotStock, Serhii Kucher, studiomode, Tetra Images, xelf, Wavebreak Media, Wing Lun Leung; GETTY IMAGES SALES SPAIN/Abezikus, Akabei, Aku Siukosaari, Alberto Guglielmi, Alex, Alex Pantling, aluxum, Andreas Koerner, Andrey Eremin, Anthony Paz, Anwar Hussein, Apomares, Alxpin, Amanda Edwards, Amesy, Anopdesignstock, AntonioGuillem, Artpipi, Ash Donelon, ATU Images, AzmanJaka, bohemia8, BrankoPhot, Brian, Brian Hagiwara/FoodPix, Buena Vista Images, Caiaimag, Cameron Spencer, Carol Yepes, 2016 CBS Photo Archive, Chung Sung-Jun, Clive Streeter, CommerceandCultureAgency, Corbis RF Stills, CPQNN, Cristian Baitg Schreiweis , Cultura RF, Dan Dalton, Dean Mitchell, Dia Dipasupil, Diana Miller Photography, Dave King Dorling Kindersley, David Banks, David Becker, David M. Benett, David Ramos/Stringer, Deimagine, Digitalgenetics, Dmytro Aksonov, Donyanedomam, DougSchneiderPhoto, Dphotographer, Drew Angerer, Education Images, EvelynDutra, EyeEm, E+, fizkes, Flashpop, FoodPix, Fotostorm, Franckreporter, FRANCOIS GUILLOT, Frederic Prochasson, Golubovy, GoodLifeStudio, Gradyreese, Gresei, Grinvalds, Guenterguni, Hemera Technologies, Hero Images, Hill Street Studios, _HK_, Howard Shooter, Hoxton, Hybrid Images, Image Source, Industryview, Ira L. Black – Corbis, Images say more about me than words, Image Source, I love Photo and Apple, iStock, istockphoto, Ivanastar, Izusek, JackF, James Darell, James D. Morgan, James Woodson, jattumongkhon, Jeff Kravitz, Jeffrey Mayer, Jim Franco, Jim Spellman, John and Tina Reid, JoseIgnacioSoto, Jose Luis Pelaez Inc, JRL, Juan MABROMATA/AFP,

© Richmond / Santillana Global S.L. 2021

All rights reserved. No part of this book may be reproduced, stored in a retrieval system or transmitted in any form by any means, electronic, mechanical, photocopying, recording or otherwise, without the prior permission in writing of the Publisher.

Juanmonino, KatarzynaBialasiewicz, Kevin Mazur, Kevin Summers, Kevin Vandenberghe, Klaus Vedfelt, KOHb, Kritchanut, Ksenica, kupicoo, kurmyshov, Kutay Tanir, kyoshino, Lauri Patterson, LdF, lenalir, Leslie Banks, Lisovskaya, lukas_zb, Luis Alvarez, mangpor_2004, ma-no, Maskot, MarcoGovel, Markus Cuff/Corbis, matsabe, Mike Harrington, Mizoula, Monkey Business Images, Morsa Images, Nadalin Fotografia, NADOFOTOS, Natalia Ganelin, Nattakorn Maneerat, NataliaKul, Nattakorn Maneerat, master1305, Michael Cogliantr, Morsa Images, Newton Daly, Nikada, NoDerog, northlightimages, OlegAlbinsky, ozdigital, Pacific Press, Paul Bradbury, Paul Johnson, PeopleImages, Peter Adams, Petar Chernaev, Perets, Phant, Photolibrary RM, Piriya Photography, pixelfit, piyaset, Pogonici, quavondo, Riccardo Omar Martinez Roa, RichLegg, Ridofranz, Robin Lynne Gibson, Rodrigo Varela, RTimages, RudyBalasko, Ryan Pierse, Santypan, SeventyFour, Shootdiem, Shunyufan, Stefano Oppo, Stevanovicigor, Steve Brown Photography, Stockfood, Tamara Staples, Tara Moore, TF-Images, Thinkstock, Thomas Barwick, Tim Grist Photography, Tim P. Whitby/Stringer, Tom Werner, Unalozmen, TracyHornbrook, VALENTYN VOLKOV, Vaughn Ridley/Stringer, Virojt Changyencham, Visions Of Our Land, Visualspace, Vitalliy, vitalssss, vitmark, Wavebreakmedia Ltd, WendellandCarolyn, Westend61, Wojciech_gajda, Wundervisuals, Xavier Arnau, Xavi Torrent/Stringer, Xijian, Yuri_Arcurs, Zakokor, Zen Rial, Zhengxin, 10'000 Hours; SHUTTERSTOCK/ Andrew Zarivny, Africa Studio, Ahturner, AllyTroops, ArchMan, Anyaivanova, Azure1, Bas Meelker, BFI Film Fund/Kobal, Blackzheep, Boneboyz, Broadimage, 20th Century Fox/Kobal, charnsitr, Chelsea Lauren, Chere, Cosmic_Design, Daniel_Dash, Davydenko Yuliia, de2marco, Denys Prykhodov, Dimedrol68, Dmitrij Skorobogatov, Elena Schweitzer, ESB Professional, Eva Bocek, Evikka, Fenton one, FotograFFF, Francois Mori/AP, Frank Augstein/AP, Golden Sikorka, graphic-line, Gregory Pace, guruXOX, Hybrid Gfx, Julia Lemba, Katerina Bend, Kristina Bumphrey/StarPix, indranilc, Jan Havlicek, Jiggo_Putter Studio, Leeview Ponkun, Lemon Lab, Leonard Zhukovsky, leungchopan, Lukas Coch/EPA, Lukasz Stefanski, Maks Ershov, MaraZe, margouillat photo, Maridav, Martina Ebel, Maks Narodenko, Maximumvector, Mazurkat, Maxx-Studio, Mega Pixel, Melica, Michael Buckner/ TVLine, Michael Buckner/Variety, Millenius, Mmkarabella, Monkey Business Images, Natalia Bratslavsky, nadiya_sergey, Nattika, nelik, Nerthuz, Nicram Sabod, Null Marvel/Disney/Kobal, Oakenman, Oleksandra, Patrice6000, Patrick Lewis/Starpix, Petlia Roman, Peter Kotoff, Photoongraphy, Photoonlife, PinkBlue, Piyaset, Railway fx, Rawpixel.com, Robert Kneschke, Robyn Mackenzie, Rob Latour, Ruben Albarran, Ruslan Kudrin, Sara Jaye Weiss, Sasha Ka, Sezer66, Sheila Fitzgerald, s_bukley, 5 second Studio, Shukaylova Zinaida, Simm49, Sirius1, Sorbis, SpeedKingz, StillFX, Syda Productions, Tatiana Arestova, TheHighestQualityImages, TNShutter, Tukunen, Universal/ Kobal, Urfin, Various photo, VasiliyBudarin, Vecarla, Vectorshape, Voravuth Chuanyou, VVadyab Pico, WAYHOME studio, Who is Danny, Wondervisuals, Yeti studio, Yuri_Arcurs, Zerbor, Zhigulina Oksana; 123RF/ccat82, stylephotographs; ARCHIVO SANTILLANA.

The Publisher has made every effort to trace the owner of copyright material; however, the Publisher will correct any involuntary omission at the earliest opportunity.

Printed in Brazil by Forma Certa
Lote. 800397

Contents

ID SB Language Map	4
Introduction	6
Features Presentation	
Unit 1	24
Unit 2	48
Review 1	72
Unit 3	76
Unit 4	100
Review 2	124
Unit 5	128
Review 3	152
Starter SB Grammar	156
Sounds & Usual Spellings	166
Audioscript	168
Songs	176

ID Language map - Student's Book

	Question syllabus	Vocabulary	Grammar	Speaking & Skills
1				
1.1	What's your name?	Opening greetings Numbers 1–12		Introduce yourself Say numbers
1.2	Where are you from?	Classroom language		Introduce a friend
1.3	What's this in English?	Classroom items Familiar items	*a* and *an* Verb *be* ⊕ ⊖ Contractions: you're, it's, isn't, what's	Name items in English
1.4	What's your phone number?	The alphabet	Verb *be* ❓	Spell names Ask for & give personal information
1.5	What's your email address?	Cognates Email		Recognize cognates
	How are you today?	Greetings		Complete a personal information form
	Writing 1: An introduction to an online group	**ID Café 1:** First class		
2				
2.1	Are you a student?	Countries and nationalities Numbers 13–20 and plurals	I am / you are ⊕ ⊖ and personal pronouns	Ask & answer about people Say numbers & plural items
2.2	Who's your favorite actor?	Opinion adjectives	he / she / it is ⊕ ⊖ Contractions	Talk about preferences Do a quiz about people & nationalities Ask for and express opinions about favorite people & things
2.3	Is ceviche Mexican?	Numbers 20–100+	Is he / she / it ❓	Express opinions Say numbers & plural items Talk about age & years
2.4	Where are your two favorite places?	Adjectives	you / we / they are ⊕ ⊖ ❓ Contractions	Write an online chat about a vacation
2.5	Is English essential for your future?	Cognates		Read for general comprehension Complete a form about a classmate
	How old is Ariana Grande?			Share information about other people
	Writing 2: A blog post	**ID Café 2:** People, places, passports!		**Review 1** *p.30*
3				
3.1	What do you do?	Jobs Job suffixes	*a* and *an* + jobs Plurals	Ask & answer about jobs
3.2	Do you have brothers and sisters?	Family	Simple present: I / you / we / they ⊕ ⊖ ❓ Possessive adjectives	Talk about family
3.3	Do you have a job?	Places of work	Simple present ❓	Ask & answer about jobs & places of work
3.4	Where does your mother work?		Simple present: he / she / it ⊕ ⊖ ❓	Ask & answer about family
3.5	Do you live near here?			Listen for specific information
	Where do you study?			Exchange personal information
	Writing 3: A personal profile	**ID Café 3:** Job interviews		
4				
4.1	Is there an ATM near here?	Personal items Colors	*There + be*	Identify items
4.2	Are those your books?		this / that / these / those	Say the names of personal items & colors
4.3	What things do you lose?	Plural nouns Telling the time		Agree / Disagree with text Describe items & quantity
4.4	What time do you get up?	Typical days	Simple present review	Ask & answer about your typical day
4.5	How do you pronounce *meme* in English?	Information technology		Pronounce & spell cognates
	What color is your wallet?			Ask about lost property
	Writing 4: A description	**ID Café 4:** In the bag		**Review 2** *p.56*
5				
5.1	Do you drink a lot of coffee?	Meals, food and drinks		Express opinions about food & drinks Talk about eating habits
5.2	What's your favorite food?	Food	like / love / don't like / hate	Make a list of food & drinks Talk about things you like / don't like
5.3	What do you usually do on Friday evenings?	Days of the week Weekend and free-time activities	Frequency adverbs	Ask & answer about, & compare weekend activities
5.4	Do you like Rihanna's music?		Possessive 's Object pronouns	Guess classmates' possessions Ask for & share opinions about celebrities and brands
5.5	Do you eat a lot of fast food?	Fast food		Notice sound–spelling combinations
	Anything to drink?	Opposites		Order food
	Writing 5: A reply to a social media post	**ID Café 5:** It's about taste		**Review 3** *p.70*

Grammar p. 72   Sounds and usual spellings p. 82   Audioscript p. 84

ID Language map - Workbook

	Question syllabus	Vocabulary	Grammar	Speaking & Skills
1 1.1	What's your name?	Opening greetings Numbers 1-12		Introduce yourself Write numbers
1.2	Where are you from?	Classroom language		Ask & answer personal questions
1.3	What's this in English?	Classroom items Familiar items	*a* and *an* Verb *be* ➕➖ Contractions: *you're, it's, isn't, what's*	Name items in English
1.4	What's your phone number?	The alphabet	Verb *be* ❓	Write your profile
1.5	What's your email address?			Complete a form
2 2.1	Are you a student?	Countries and nationalities Numbers 13–20	*I am / you are* ➕➖	Ask & answer about people
2.2	Who's your favorite actor?	Opinion adjectives	*he / she / it is* ➕➖ and personal pronouns Contractions	Express opinions
2.3	Is ceviche Mexican?	Numbers 20–100+	*Is he / she / it* ❓	Write numbers Do a quiz
2.4	Where are your two favourite places?		*you / we / they are* ➕➖❓ Contractions	Give personal information
2.5	Is English essential for your future?	Personal information		Share information about other people
3 3.1	What do you do?	Jobs	*a* and *an* + jobs Plurals	Ask & answer about jobs
3.2	Do you have brothers and sisters?	Family	Simple present: *I / you / we / they* ➕➖❓ Possessive adjectives	Ask & answer about family
3.3	Do you have a job?	Places of work	Simple present ❓	Complete a survey
3.4	Where does your mother work?		Simple present: *he / she / it* ➕➖❓	Read an email
3.5	Do you live near here?			Compare people's interests
4 4.1	Is there an ATM near here?	Personal items	*There + be*	Identify items
4.2	Are those your books?	Colors	*this / that / these / those*	Say the names of personal items
4.3	What things do you lose?	Plural nouns Telling the time	*There + be*	Identify items Tell the time
4.4	What time do you get up?	Typical days	Simple present review	Talk about a typical day
4.5	How do you pronounce *meme* in English?	Information technology		Read and talk about social networks
5 5.1	Do you drink a lot of coffee?	Meals, food and drinks		Talk about eating preferences
5.2	What's your favorite food?	Food	*like / love / don't like / hate*	Talk about eating habits
5.3	What do you usually do on Friday evenings?	Days of the week Weekend and free-time activities	Frequency adverbs	Talk about your week & weekend activities
5.4	Do you like Rihanna's music?		Possessive *'s* Object pronouns	Talk about famous people
5.5	Do you eat a lot of fast food?	Fast food		Read an email Talk about favorite food & drink

Audioscript p. 114 Answer Key p. 116 Phrase Bank p. 118 Word List p. 120

Introduction

This is the 2nd edition of Richmond's four-level American English course for monolingual adult and young adult learners whose mother tongue is Spanish or Portuguese. Together with iDentities 1 and 2, it forms the first six-level course purpose-built for Latin America, taking learners from Beginner to a strong C1 level.

With the right focus, embracing and celebrating familiar language while anticipating inevitable transfer errors, speakers of Spanish and Portuguese ought to learn to be both fluent and accurate in English more quickly than most.

This unique, highly original course, with a brand-new eye-catching design, motivating topics and constant opportunities for personalization, helps learners to express who they are—their personality, culture, their identity—in English. English ID helps you learn to be yourself in English.

What do Romance-language speakers most expect and need from an English course?

You might want to note down your own answers before you read on.

Our research suggests that, above all, learners expect:

- to become fluent listeners and speakers as quickly as possible;
- confidence building—to know the L1 equivalent of new language items quickly so that they can overcome their fears and speak meaningfully in class;
- quick results, and a strong sense of progress;
- contemporary, locally pertinent, interesting content, tailored to their likely interests and linguistic needs. Real-life, adult, local relevance, with lots of personalization;
- overt teaching of grammar and vocabulary, a systematic approach to pronunciation, plenty of skills practice;
- specific help with writing and spelling;
- an appropriate, adult teaching style combined with strong self-study elements, including autonomous learning tools to speed up their learning: we provide keys to most of the material, audio for all longer texts, and all the listening and video activities are available on the Richmond Learning Platform for self-study;
- value—both for the time they invest and the money they spend.

Methodology

English ID is in every sense a communicative course, teaching learners to speak in as short a time as possible and focusing on both fluency and accuracy.

Fluency: notice the multiple exchanges modeled throughout lessons in speech bubbles, or the number of Latinate cognates included in every text, with word stress marked in pink to give sts confidence to try to say them.

Accuracy: via the **Common mistakes** (anticipating likely L1 transfer errors that should be avoided) presented in each lesson, or the Notice tasks in the **Audioscript** to provide genuine contextualized help with pronunciation and spelling.

Learners need to be given opportunities to express their thoughts. English ID and, later, iDentities progressively adapt as the series evolves to reflect the best learning practices at each of the learner's advancing levels. Initially, English ID Starter relies on lots of short question-and-answer exchanges supported by lots of drilling in the *Student's Book*, to be done in class. Then, at subsequent levels, such drills become more discretionary, moving into both *Workbook* and *Teacher's Book*. At advanced levels, there is an increased focus on levels of formality, as a student's need to master various registers gradually increases.

The same goes for the lexis—where the initial simple task of matching vocabulary to pictures in the early levels of English ID becomes more abstract and contextualized—and grammar, where spoon-feeding is reduced and inductive learning increased, as learners' confidence and foreign language learning experience grow.

English ID provides the tools to allow you, the teacher, to incorporate your own pedagogical identity into the course, as well as to emphasize what you think will be more relevant for your learners.

Advantaging Monolingual Classes

Globally, most classes are monolingual. English ID was conceived to facilitate monolingual classroom learning. The frequent lack of opportunity to speak English locally means teachers need to maximize fluency practice, getting the students to use the language as much as possible in class.

In monolingual classes, learners share the same L1 and most aspects of a culture, which a teacher can exploit. They share similar advantages / difficulties with English too, which should be a unifying "strength" for anticipating problems and errors. Accelerating through what is easier for learners, and spending more time on what is difficult, "sharpens" classes to maximize the learning potential.

Adults need a radically different approach from children, whose mother tongue is not yet established, and who learn like sponges, absorbing all the English you throw at them. Young adults' and adults' minds are different: they cannot help but translate—mentally at least—and immediately

Introduction

resort to the mother tongue when they cannot find the words to express their thoughts in English. Rather than running against nature, English ID avoids this trap by gently embracing similar items when appropriate, but without ever forcing active use of L1, leaving that option up to you.

Paraphrasing Ur (2011), "teachers should choose procedures that lead to best learning by whichever students they're teaching" (extracted from *Vocabulary Activities*, Penny Ur, Cambridge University Press, 2011). We believe English ID's formula can really help native speakers of Spanish and Portuguese learn both more comfortably and more efficiently.

English ID embraces students' linguistic strengths. It helps students to use what they know and helps you, the teacher, to foresee these automatic transfers and focus appropriately on them. With English ID, students can easily enjoy what is easy and, at the same time, the more complex issues can be made clearer for them.

Flexi-lessons

Each English ID lesson is linear, and can be taught directly from the page, with our interleaved *Teacher's Book* lesson plans reflecting and fully supporting this.

However, as we appreciate that all teachers and classes are different, English ID also provides multiple entry points for each lesson for you to choose from.

You can begin with:

- the suggested **warm-up** activity in most *Teacher's Book* lesson plans;
- the *Teacher's Book* books-closed presentation (either of main lexis or grammar);
- the **lesson title question**. Return to it at the end of class for sts to answer it better—a "test–teach–test" route through the lesson;
- a **Make it personal** from the page in the same test-teach-test way;
- the lesson's **song line**;
- the **Common mistakes** —board them corrected or focus on them on the page at the start of class to highlight what to avoid and thus maximize opportunities to get things right throughout the class;
- the **Grammar** pages for a more traditional, deductive presentation.

In addition, you can choose from these lesson routes for monolingual Spanish / Portuguese learners as monolingual classes allow you to be more proactive, and offer opportunities for more tailored, accelerated pedagogy:

- Divide lexical presentations into two phases: first, focus on cognates, then the other words. Have sts guess the pronunciation of the words they recognize.
- Read the lesson text (on-page reading or listening from the **Audioscript** section). In pairs, sts try to pronounce the pink-stressed words. Teach the class as usual, then come back to the words at the end of the class, and have sts pronounce them better.
- Underline the words which look the same (or similar) in Spanish or Portuguese, then check as the lesson evolves whether they are or are not true cognates, and how to pronounce them. This is especially good for weaker learners, as it helps them get familiar with texts in a non-threatening way.
- Do the same as above with suffixes.
- Speed up or avoid inductive presentations, by, e.g. the **Common mistakes** route above.
- Compare word stress, as in the presentation of the months in *Student's Book 1* on p. 35, ex. 3A.

Key concepts

English ID promotes the three "friendlies": It is language-friendly, learner-friendly, and teacher-friendly.

1. Language-friendly

English ID is not just another international series. It is a language-friendly series, which embraces sts' existing language knowledge—a fundamental pillar of all foreign language learning through, e.g. exploiting cognates, familiar structures, famous song lines, and local cultural background—to help them better understand how English works.

2. Learner-friendly

English ID respects the learner's need to be spoken to as an adult, so sts explore a full range of topics requiring critical thinking. It also helps sts to negotiate and build their own new identity in English.

In addition, English ID:

- supports sts, helping them avoid obvious errors in form, word order, and pronunciation;
- motivates sts, as they discover they can recognize a lot of English, which they already have "inside themselves";
- offers a vast range of activities, resources and recycling in order to ensure sts have enough practice to finally learn to speak English.

Introduction

3. Teacher-friendly

English ID respects each teacher's need to teach as he or she wants to. Some wish to teach off the page with minimal preparation, others dip in and out, while others largely follow the *Teacher's Book*. All these options have been built into English ID from the start.

The flexi-lesson structure helps teachers to individualize, personalize and vary classes, as well as focus on what is important for them.

Key features

1. A 30-question syllabus

Every lesson begins with a question as the title, which serves as a natural warm-up activity to introduce and later review each lesson topic.

These questions offer:

- an introduction to the lesson topic, an essential component for a good lesson, as, in some cases, topics may be new to sts;
- a ready-made short lead-in to create interest, paving the way for the integration of skills, grammar, and content;
- an opportunity for sts to get to know and feel comfortable with each other before the lesson begins, facilitating pair and group work;
- an instant review or speaking activity, whenever you need one: sts in pairs can look back at the map of the book and ask and answer questions;
- a wonderful expression of syllabus;
- a useful placement test. Asking some of the 30 questions when sts are being level-tested is a good way to help place them appropriately.

2. A balanced approach to grammar

Our rich grammar syllabus offers an eclectic approach to meet the needs of all sts. It offers an innovative combination of:

- inductive grammar, with students discovering patterns and completing rules for themselves in and around the lesson-page grammar boxes;
- deductive grammar—the 10-page **Grammar** section, which regularly encourages sts to contrast English with their L1 and notice where English is easier, in order to motivate. This can be done in class for quick diagnostic work if sts are making lots of mistakes, or assigned as homework as a form of "flipping"—sts complete the grammar exercises before the forthcoming lesson, in order to speed up input and give more time for practice;
- implicit, contrastive grammar analysis, by showing what not to say via **Common mistakes**;
- a wide variety of extra grammar practice in Reviews, the *Workbook*, and on the Richmond Learning Platform, as well as suggestions for extra contextualized writing in the *Teacher's Book*.

3. It has to be personal

Not only the 30 lesson question titles, but each phase of every lesson (and most *Workbook* lessons) ends with **Make it personal** activities: real, extended personalization—the key stage in any language practice activity. Sts expand all topics and main language items into their own lives, opinions, contexts, and experiences. This is how sts continue to construct and consolidate their English identity. Successfully "making it personal" is what makes sts believe that they can be themselves in English.

4. Avoid common mistakes to speak better, more quickly

Most lessons include **Common mistakes**, a flexible resource to foster accuracy. We highlight what to avoid before, during, and / or after any lesson. **Common mistakes** helps maximize self- and peer-correction too. Sts are enabled to help and teach themselves, by anticipating and therefore more quickly avoiding, reviewing, and remembering typical learner errors.

If short of time, as teachers so often are, **Common mistakes** can help you cut through a longer, more inductive presentation and get to the practice activity more quickly. They are flexible, too: you can refer to them at any time in the lesson, usually the earlier the better.

5. Integrated skills

The fifth lesson in each unit is an integrated skills page, which gives sts the opportunity to immerse themselves in a highly engaging, contemporary topic and practice all four skills in real-world activities.

6. Classic song lines to "hook" language

English ID uses music in exercises, cultural references, images, and, most obviously, the authentic song lines in each lesson. In addition, music as a theme features prominently in several lessons.

Why music? Songs are often the most popular source of authentic listening practice in and out of class. Most sts have picked up a lot of English words through songs, ads, TV theme tunes, movie soundtracks, etc. But often they don't realize they know them or the exact meaning of what they're singing.

Introduction

The song lines empower both teachers and sts by offering useful language references and pronunciation models; and an authentic source of student-friendly input to elicit, present, practice, personalize, extend, and "hook" almost anything.

Unique to English iD and iDentities, the song lines have a direct link to each lesson, whether to illustrate grammar, lexis, or the lesson topic, and are designed to provide an authentic hook to help sts remember the lesson and the language studied. Looking for the link provides an additional fun, puzzle-like element to every lesson.

English iD *Teacher's Book* offers a highly original useful **Songs** bank of cultural, background, and procedural notes for every song line, including the artist's name, suggestions on exactly where and how to exploit it, and optional activities. You can find this useful resource on pages 176–184.

Tip Of course, we don't suggest you use these songs in full, just the extract we've chosen. Besides, many aren't actually appropriate when you look at the complete lyrics, but the lines we've chosen are globally famous and should be easy to identify, find on the Internet, and be sung by at least some sts. Obviously, with your own classes you can exploit the song lines in a variety of ways.

Some ways to use song lines in English iD:

- play / show (part of) the song as sts come into class;
- sing / hum the song line and / or look for links to the song at an appropriate time during the class to help sts remember the lesson later;
- read and guess the artist's gender, message, etc.;
- analyze the song for pronunciation: rhyme, repeated sounds, alliteration;
- expand. *What comes before / after this line? What's the whole song about?*;
- change the tense or some words to make it more or less formal and see how it sounds. *Why did the artist choose this tense?*;
- provoke discussion around a theme / issue;
- ask *What do you associate the song with?*, e.g. a moment, vacation, dance, movie;
- search online for other songs that connect to the lesson in some way;
- use sections of the song as a class warm-up, review, listening for pleasure, an end of the lesson sing-along, etc.;
- board or dictate the line but add, subtract, or change some words for sts to correct it (similar to **Common mistakes**).

Course structure and components

English coursebooks have often been too long, too repetitive, or inflexible, meaning teachers have either to rush to get through them—denying sts the practice they need to achieve an adequate degree of fluency—or start omitting sections, often leaving sts feeling frustrated. English iD was designed to be flexible, so you can tailor it to fit your schedule.

English iD Starter has …

- five core units, each comprised of five approximately one-hour lessons, followed by an integrated **Writing** lesson and an iD **Café** video lesson;
- 10 pages of grammar reference with corresponding exercises;
- selected audioscripts that encourage sts to focus on specific listening points;
- *Workbook*: one page of review and extra practice material per lesson;
- Richmond Learning Platform for English iD, which can be accessed using the code on the inside front cover of the *Student's Book*;
- *Digital Book for Teachers*: IWB version of the *Student's Book*.

Vocabulary

Vocabulary teaching is a particularly strong feature of English iD because of the variety of input and review options.

1. Picture Dictionary

The most popular way to teach / learn vocabulary is through some kind of "picture + key" approach, where students can work out the meaning from the visual, without the need to translate, and then cover and test themselves.

Every English iD unit begins with a contextualized, lesson-integrated picture dictionary. Core vocabulary is presented through various combinations of this basic four-step approach:

1. Match words / phrases to pictures.
2. Guess pronunciation (from the pink stress / sts' own linguistic experience, and growing knowledge of English).
3. Listen to the words in context and check / repeat as necessary.
4. Cover and test yourself / a partner, either immediately or any time later for review.

Introduction

All **Reviews** begin by sending sts back to the picture dictionary elements in each unit to review and remember words. Almost all of the images in English ID are contextualized and used to present, review, and test vocabulary.

2. A cognate-friendly approach

Thousands of words with cognate relationships are common to English and most Latin languages. Over 1,500 of these are very common. There are also thousands of recognizable cognate-rooted words. By systematically building them into English ID, we feel we have created a unique opportunity for students to progress more quickly and more comfortably with English. Put simply, they can both understand and produce more language—and more interesting adult language—faster.

Throughout their learning process, students make cross-linguistic connections, so we have chosen to nurture this strategy systematically throughout English ID. It enhances both their language awareness and their English lexical knowledge, and makes learning more efficient.

English ID prides itself on helping students to expand their vocabulary quickly. Lexical presentations often separate what is "known / easy"—whether from "international" English, words already seen in the course, or near cognates—from "what is new / unfamiliar," to help students focus better.

Familiar words mainly require attention for pronunciation and spelling, whereas the unfamiliar require a lot more effort to learn meaning too. This provides a valuable additional "hook" into the student's memory.

Significant stress or word-formation patterns are regularly highlighted to enable "learning leaps."

English ID consciously works on developing the confidence the students need to begin to guess how words might be pronounced or spelled in English. Guessing—being willing to take a shot, bringing in words that you already know which might work well in English—is a key learning strategy, often ignored elsewhere.

Embracing cognates also allows much more interesting, more adult speaking, and listening tasks too, e.g., asking *Any coincidences / similarities / pronunciation surprises? What do you have in common? Who is more assertive?*, etc.

Tip We do not suggest you drill all these words nor try to make them all into active vocabulary. In most cases, cognates are there just as passive vocabulary, actually helping sts understand more. We see no point in hiding words from sts when they can cope with them, and indeed usually enjoy doing so. The words which become active differ greatly from group to group and will always be your choice, not ours. We are simply trying to give sts access to more adult language more quickly.

Skills

Speaking

English ID teaches spoken English and prioritizes oral fluency. Fluency naturally precedes accuracy, and this is why English ID gives sts plenty of cognates to express themselves quickly, leading to accuracy sooner.

In order to learn both quickly and well, sts should be given every opportunity to try to express their ideas and opinions in comprehensible English at every stage of every lesson. After all, practice and personalization are the best way to improve and self-correct, and whatever method you use, accuracy will always be the last element of competence learners will acquire. In English ID, every lesson, be it a listening, vocabulary, grammar, reading, or writing focus, is full of controlled oral practice and personalized speaking opportunities, clearly marked and modeled by multiple speech bubbles on every page.

Listening

English ID has a huge amount of recorded material, in both the *Student's Book* and the *Workbook*, which is all available on the Richmond Learning Platform.

Listening homework should be set as often as possible, as what sts most need is to spend the maximum time in the company of English in order to become truly confident when expressing themselves in English. These days this is relatively easy—they can listen while doing other things, at home, traveling, at the gym, etc.

In addition to the material included in the course itself, teachers may find some of the following suggestions helpful, either in or out of class:

- have sts create their own listening practice at this level—listening to music or podcasts, watching TV or movies, using bilingual websites to figure out what words mean, sending each other recordings in English via, e.g. WhatsApp;
- dictogloss short sections of any listening activity—listen and remember (or write down) all you can, then compare in pairs;
- pause at any time in any listening to check comprehension: *What do you think was said?* after any short section is a key question in trying to teach rather than keep testing listening.

If time permits …

- sensitize sts to how words blur and have a variety of sound shapes in connected speech and elicit / explain how pronunciation changes;

Introduction

- expose sts to "the difficult," e.g. phoneme variations in connected speech; dictate multiple examples of phrases containing the same weak forms;
- model processes used by L1 listeners: decoding sounds into words / clauses and building larger scale meaning;
- transcribe elision as they hear it: old people = *ole people*, a blind man = *a bly man*, etc;
- study and interpret, e.g. pairs: *He said he called* vs. *He said he'd call.*

The following are some ideas for listening homework that you could set your sts:

- listening to recordings of the class itself (flipped)—instructions, stories, pair work, role-play, etc.;
- web-based listening: songs, podcasts, searching online for the huge number of online lessons available now, YouTube, radio, audiobooks, TV (with subtitles in L1 & L2);
- homework partners—call / record messages, check answers with partner, dub favorite movie scene, etc.

Reading

English ID provides substantial reading practice in terms of the amount available, and the complexity of cognate-rich texts, building on sts' existing language knowledge to gain fluency more quickly. We strongly suggest you break up longer texts, giving short tasks.

- Keep tasks to 2 or 3 minutes, then have sts share what they remember, and predict what comes next before reading on.
- Sts in pairs each read a different paragraph to create an information gap, then tell each other what they read.
- Give sts (via the digital board, cut up slips, or let them choose) random samples of the texts—a couple of lines from different paragraphs, or the first and last line of each paragraph, etc., to share what they understood and speculate about what else they will read.
- With any text, you can get sts to cover it with a sheet of paper, read one line at a time, guess what comes next in pairs, then unveil the next line to see if they were right. They then do the same with the next line, and so on.
- Make each st in a group responsible for finding the answer to one of the questions, then share with the group.
- Help sts experience different reading skills: skimming, scanning, etc., even within the same text, by setting different tasks, and perhaps giving them reading role-cards for different paragraphs or columns of text: *A) Read and translate the text word by word.; B) Read the text in order to memorize as much of the information as you can.; C) Read the text for the general idea.; D) Read the text quietly to yourself at a comfortable speed.*

These ideas and many more you will find expanded in the *Teacher's Book* notes.

Writing

Our writing syllabus is primarily covered by the integrated **Writing** lesson at the end of each unit. Here sts are given a clear written model, a variety of tasks to analyze it, specific writing tips and a structured model to draft, check, then share with a classmate, before finally submitting it to you or posting on the class learning platform / wiki. The intention is to protect you, the busy teacher, from having to dedicate time to excessive marking of avoidable mistakes, as well as to help sts be more in control of their own writing.

Pronunciation

The English ID **Audioscript** section is not just a script to be read or listened to with no clear focus. It's designed to provide real training with listening and pronunciation.

It aims to help sts learn to listen better as the course progresses by focusing on features of pronunciation:

- noticing sounds, stress, aspects of connected speech, intonation and spelling relationships;
- spoken language (e.g. noticing discourse signals such as fillers, pauses, repetition, self-correction, and interruptions);
- sub-skills of listening, like inferring, predicting, identifying main points in discourse, understanding attitudinal meaning and all aspects of listening.

Again, it is flexible and both teacher- and learner-friendly. All the tasks are "noticing" tasks. The tasks are always "highlighted," making them all free-standing, to avoid the need for teacher intervention, unless, of course, you wish to spend time here. So, you can choose to do them in class, or sts can do them on their own.

It is a good idea for sts to listen, read, and notice the audioscript tasks as extra preparation before a role-play. Rather than just listening (and reading) again and again, trying to memorize dialogues before role-playing them, these tasks give a clear focus for additional listening and pre-role-play pronunciation practice.

All new polysyllabic words are introduced in context, with the stress highlighted for students in pink. Regularly marking stress on new words (in the book and on the board) means you progress from just teaching form and spelling, on to really prioritizing teaching, modeling, and recording spoken language. Word stress is shown in pink only the first time a word appears. To include it each time would give no sense of syllabus or progress to sts.

The **Sounds and Usual Spellings** chart is another excellent resource. This gives two illustrated model words for each of the 40 sounds in U.S. English, and access to the phonetic symbol.

Introduction

Knowing all the potential sounds in a language sets a ceiling on their guesses and builds confidence. If sts can learn those two words per sound, they should be able to have a reasonable guess at the pronunciation of words in a dictionary and begin to get comfortable with using phonetics. Remember, learning to guess pronunciation of new words is a key skill.

The table also provides model words to illustrate the usual spelling patterns for each sound. Sensitizing sts to sound–spelling combinations is a key part of learning to read, write, and pronounce with confidence.

To the extent that you choose to work on pronunciation, any of the following ideas may be helpful.

- Emphasize the relevance of the pronunciation tasks to improve listening comprehension and increasingly natural-sounding English.
- Make sure sts understand that their pronunciation does not need to be "perfect" or "near native," but it does need to be clear and facilitate communication. To that end, focus on features that most impinge on international communication with your particular learners.
- Explore what sts already know, e.g. from song lines, TV, their travels, etc., and have them record and listen to themselves imitating texts they like or wish to deliver better.
- Model new words in context rather than in isolation, e.g. in a phrase: *the environment* not just *environment*, so they get used to stressing and reducing. In this way, the focus on intonation, phrase or sentence stress, word boundaries, etc. increases.
- Respond naturally to incorrect models or effects of "wrong" intonation and encourage repetition to say it better, e.g. say *Excuse me?* in response to incorrect pronunciation or flat intonation.
- Highlight linking (a line between words: *an_orange*), pauses (/ = short pause, // = longer pause) and sentence stress shift (eliciting different meanings according to which words are stressed).
- Work on transcripts, e.g. shadow read text and sub-vocalize to self; notice and underline most stressed words / pauses / links. Turn any audioscript into a proper listening / pronunciation teaching vehicle.
- Spot the "music", e.g. help them hear changes of pitch.
- Have sts track, shadow, rehearse, imitate, repeat, and record themselves.

Reviews

There is ample opportunity for review and recycling throughout the book via the six review lessons. These include many additional activities focusing on speaking, grammar, listening, reading, writing, self-test (error-correction), and point of view (debate). Some skills alternate across the review units, but all are thoroughly covered. Don't forget, you can always look back at the song lines and re-use the lesson question titles, too!

Learner autonomy

English ID offers a clear layout, lessons that progress transparently, and many language explanations. While these features greatly facilitate classroom teaching, they also allow for easy review and autonomous learning. Depending on the classroom hours available, many activities in the course (e.g. selected vocabulary, grammar, reading, and writing tasks) could be assigned for homework. The student-friendly grammar boxes, with additional explanation in the **Grammar** section, also allow for easy review. The Reviews themselves can be assigned for homework also.

If it seems feasible, you may wish to consider "flipping" more of your classes, too. Before any major presentation or review activity, have sts search online for material to support the next lesson. This is especially useful for weaker sts, who might be struggling to keep up, but also works for stronger sts, who might even be able to lead the next class themselves.

Sts who regularly have to miss classes should be trained to use these routes to catch up. For example, how to:

- use the picture dictionary pages to cover the words and test themselves;
- listen again to texts which they have read in class via the audio on the Richmond Learning Platform;
- work on their own pronunciation using the pink word stress for all new polysyllabic words;
- do the audioscript tasks and use the **Sounds and Usual Spellings** chart;
- use the word list and phrase bank from the Richmond Learning Platform for constant review, e.g. by recording, listening to, and repeating the phrase bank on their phones, in their cars, etc.;
- ask and answer the question titles, plus follow-up questions;
- look at and avoid the **Common mistakes**;
- investigate and sing the song lines via the Internet, etc.;
- enjoy all the features of the Richmond Learning Platform. We suggest you spend some class time taking them through each of these features, and regularly reminding them how much they can do on their own.

Introduction

Richmond Learning Platform for English ID

This extremely useful and user-friendly blended learning tool has been developed in parallel with the series and combines the best of formal and informal learning to extend, review and test core lesson content. The full range of resources is available to teachers and sts who adopt any of the levels of English ID.

The Richmond Learning Platform content for English ID includes:

- Extra Practice Activities that cover all language points in the *Student's Books*. New activities have been added to accompany the 2nd edition. Sts can now record themselves interacting with the characters from ID **Café**, practice their pronunciation using the **Sounds and Usual Spellings** chart, and identify **Common mistakes**;
- Richmond Test Manager contains tests specifically created to review the content of English ID. Teachers can choose what to include in their tests and can choose between digital versions of the tests or printable versions;
- Skills Boost: extra reading and listening practice available in both interactive and PDF format;
- Resources for teachers, including sets of photocopiables for practice and reference;
- Complete downloadable audio and video.

The Richmond Learning Platform's key features and tools include:

- Class Materials, where teachers and sts can find all content related to the level of English ID they are using in class;
- Assignments—a tool that allows teachers to assign digital and non digital content for sts to complete by a specified date;
- Test Manager, where teachers can find all the test content for English ID, and build their own tests to be delivered in the format that suits their teaching. Once generated, tests can be assigned to the whole class or specific sts, to be completed by a specific date and time;
- Markbook allows sts to access their own scores, while teachers can view the scores of the whole class and have a number of options to view the details of their sts' progress;
- Forum is a tool for communication between members of the class and can be used to bring writing activities to life.

Workbook

In the *Workbook*, a single page corresponds to each *Student's Book* lesson, designed to consolidate and reinforce all the main language. Exercises can be used in class, e.g. for fast finishers, or extra practice of specific areas.

The *Workbook* includes:

- a variety of exercises, texts, and puzzles to scaffold, continue practicing, and extend the main grammar and vocabulary of each lesson;
- Skills Practice: several listening activities per unit to continue practicing the most important skills outside class, plus plenty of short, enjoyable reading texts.

Interleaved Teacher's Book

English ID offers a rich, complete, teacher-friendly, lesson plan for every left- and right-hand page of each lesson. It provides a complete step-by-step lesson plan from beginning to end, offering:

- lesson overviews and aims;
- an optional books-closed warm-up for every lesson;
- an alternative books-open warm-up based around the question title;
- step-by-step notes and suggestions for each on-page activity, including background information and language notes where appropriate;
- help with identifying the focus of each activity and any new language being presented, including additional help (where relevant) on presenting increasingly complicated grammar;
- language tips specifically highlighting areas that may be problematic for Spanish / Portuguese speakers;
- teaching tips to vary and hone your teaching skills;
- suggestions for multi-level classes (ideas for both stronger and weaker sts);
- a complete answer key and audioscript;
- a bank of original ideas for exploiting each song line in a different way, as well as background information and step-by-step teaching notes for the song lines.

Digital Book for Teachers / IWB

The *Digital Book for Teachers* is a separate medium containing all the pages of the *Student's Book*. Teachers can use this resource to promote variety in their classes, at all stages of any lesson, so that sts can see the images on the IWB instead of looking at the book. It's particularly useful for operating the audio, zooming images, and adding zest and color to your classes!

On the next pages, you will find detailed information about all the features of English ID.

Welcome to English ID!

Finally, an English course you can understand!

Famous **song lines** illustrate language from lessons.

Lesson titles are questions to help you engage with the content.

Contextualized picture dictionary to present and review vocabulary.

Word stress in pink on new words.

Focus on **Common mistakes** accelerates accuracy.

Introduction

Stimulating **grammar** practice.

Make it personal: personalized speaking tasks to help you express your identity in English.

Speech bubbles: models for speaking.

ID Skills: extra reading and listening practice.

ID in Action: communication in common situations.

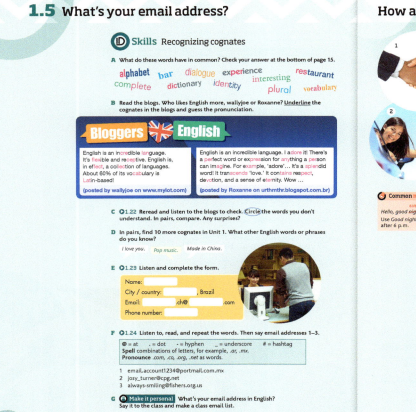

Introduction

Writing lessons integrated into each unit, with clear models and careful scaffolding to increase writing confidence.

ID Café: sitcom videos to consolidate language.

Reviews systematically recycle language.

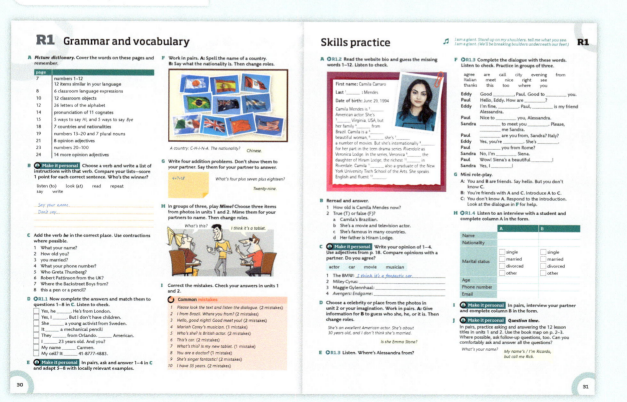

A complete **Grammar** reference with exercises. A full answer key can be found on the Richmond Learning Platform.

Grammar Unit 1

1A *a / an* and *the*

Dora is **a** teacher.   She's **an** excellent teacher.
D is **a** book.   It's **an** English book.
New York is **a** city.   It's **a** big city.

Use **a / an** for a non specific person, place, or thing = "one."
Use **a** before a consonant sound:
- **a** man, **a** chair, **a** book.

Use **an** before a vowel sound:
- **an** apple, **an** email, **an** icon, **an** opera, **an** urgent email.

Exception:
- **a** university, **a** uniform (the u is pronounced with a consonant sound /juː/)

a / an = singular = a tablet.

The teacher is Dora.   Where is **the** elevator? (singular)
Welcome to **the** New ID School of English.   **The** museums in DC are fantastic. (plural)

Use **the** for:
- a specific noun: **the** President, **the** capital city
- singular or plural: **the** Natural History Museum, **the** museums.

1B Verb *be*

The verb *be* has three forms: *am, is, are*.

⊕		Contractions	
I **am** single.		I'm single.	
You **are** married.		You're married.	
It **is** a problem!		It's a problem!	

⊖		Contractions	
I **am not** married.		I'm not married.	
You **are not** single.		You're not / aren't single.	
It **is not** good.		It's not / isn't good!	

You = singular and plural
You're a student = one
You're students = two or more

Use contractions when you speak or write informal texts.
Note: Don't contract *am + not*. Remember the subject.
I'm not. NOT *I amn't.*
I'm Mexican. NOT *Am Mexican.*

1C Verb *be*

Yes / No questions & Short answers

⊕ Be + Subject	⊕ S + be	⊖ S + be + not
Are you married?	Yes, I am.	No, I'm not.
Is it a 5G phone?		No, it's not. /
Is this your pen?	Yes, it is.	No, I isn't.

Invert the subject (S) and the verb (V) to form a question.
Are you Peruvian? NOT *You are Peruvian?*
Yes / No questions have a short answer.
Note: Don't contract ⊕ short answers.
Are you American? Yes, I am. NOT *Yes, I'm.*

Wh- questions

Wh-Question + be + S	Full Answer	Short Answer
Where are you from?	I am / I'm from Brazil.	Brazil.
How are you?	I am / I'm fine, thanks.	Fine, thanks.
What's your name?	It is / It's Marcos.	Marcos.
What's this?	It is / It's a tablet.	A tablet.

Form a *Wh-* question with *Wh-* question word + *be* + S.
Where are you from? NOT *From where are you?*
Answer *Wh-* questions with information.
Contraction: What's, Where's, How's.
Note: Don't contract *Wh-* questions + *are*.
Where are ...? or How are ... ? NOT *Where're ...? How're ...?*

Unit 1

1A

1 Circle the correct words.
1 Look at a / the photo in a / the book.
2 What's an / the eraser?
3 This is an / the apple. It's for a / the teacher.
4 "W" is a / the letter in an / the English alphabet.
5 Buenos Aires is a / the great city. It's a / the capital of Argentina.

2 Complete 1–5 with *a / an* where necessary.
1 This is _____ book.
2 Pedro and Mariana are _____ students.
3 Is this _____ credit card or _____ ID card?
4 I have _____ dog called Maya and _____ energetic cat called Luna.
5 Is this _____ letter "O" or _____ zero?

3 Correct the mistake in 1–5.
1 I'm student.   4 This is the my friend.
 I'm a student.   5 Shhhh! Teacher is
2 You're from U.S.   here.
3 I'm from the Brazil.   6 The parking lot is in the Terminal 2.

4 Write *the* where necessary.
1 _____The_____ book is on _____ table.
2 _____ teacher _____ is _____ in _____ classroom.
3 Look _____ at _____ photo _____ and _____ repeat _____ sentences.
4 What's _____ email _____ of _____ school?
5 This _____ is _____ President of _____ Colombia.

1B

1 Complete with *am*, *are*, or *is*.
1 ID _____ an English book.
2 I _____ from Peru. This _____ my friend from Italy.
3 You _____ a student.
4 This _____ my email address.
5 _____ this an eraser?

2 Make sentences 1–5 negative. Use contractions where possible.
1 This is a book.   _____
2 You're my friend.   _____
3 I'm from Europe.   _____
4 This is my car.   _____
5 You're my favorite teacher.   _____

1C

1 Match the questions and answers.
1 Are you single?   ☐ No, it's a tablet.
2 Is this an English class?   ☐ I'm from Egypt.
3 Where are you from?   ☐ Yes, it is.
4 Are you from France?   ☐ No, I'm not.
5 Is this a computer?   ☐ Yes, I'm from Paris.

2 Complete the dialogue 1–9 with the correct form of *be* (⊕ or ⊖).
Jorge Hi. I ¹_____ Jorge. Nice to meet you.
Linda My name ² _____ Linda. Nice to meet you too.
Juan Hello, Linda! ᵇ_____
Linda Hi, Juan. I ³ _____ fine, thanks.
Juan Cool!
Linda Juan, this ⁴ _____ Jorge.
Jorge Nice to meet you. ᶜ_____
Juan I ⁵ _____ from Mexico. And you? ⁶ _____ you from Spain?
Jorge Yes, I ⁷_____ I
Juan Cool! Hey Linda, ᵈ_____?
Linda It ⁸ _____ my flash drive. It ⁹ _____ for my documents.
Juan Cool!

3 Now write *Wh-* questions in the boxes to complete the dialogue. Use contractions where possible.

Introduction

Pictures to present and practice **pronunciation** with audio to accompany it on the Richmond Learning Platform.

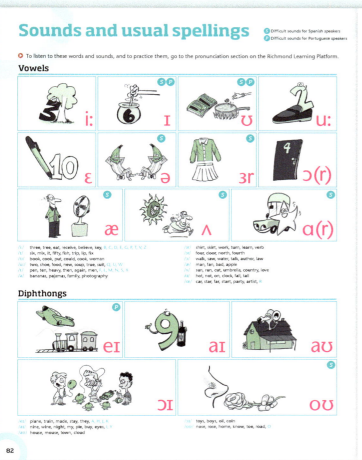
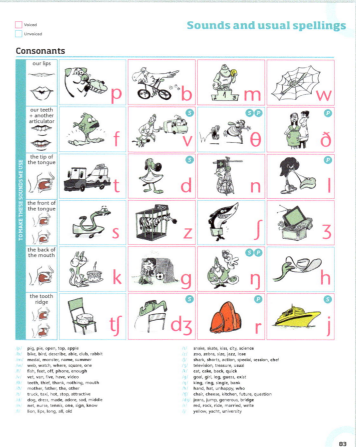

Audioscript activities to consolidate pronunciation.

Workbook to practice and consolidate lessons with complete audio on the Richmond Learning Platform.

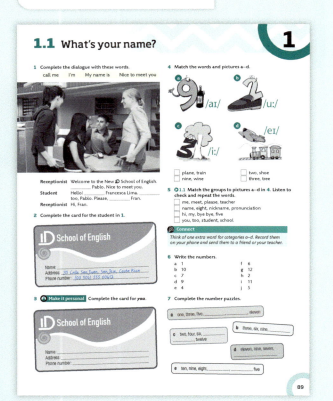

Phrase Bank to practice common expressions.

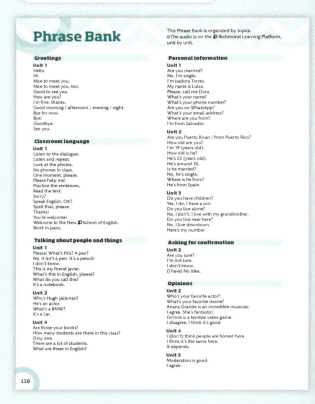

English ID 2nd Edition Digital

 Richmond *Learning* Platform

- Teachers and students can find all their resources in one place.
- **Richmond Test Manager** with interactive and printable tests.
- Activity types including pronunciation, common mistakes, and speaking.

New look

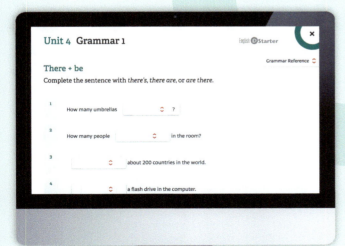

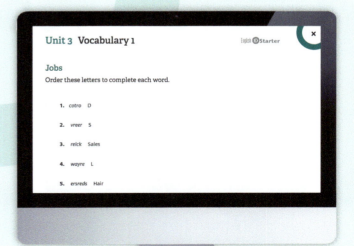

New activities

iD Café: Students watch the videos, do a language activity, and then record themselves taking part in a conversation with one of the characters from the video. Students can then download their conversation and share it with their teacher.

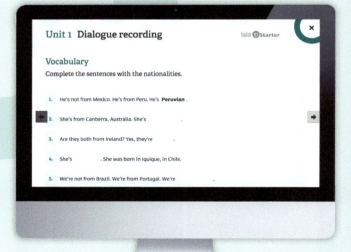

Introduction

Common mistakes: In order to revise this key feature of English ID, we have added a correct-the-mistakes activity for each unit.

Sounds and Usual Spellings: For the 2nd edition, we have brought the famous ID chart to life with a new activity for each sound in the chart. Students can listen to the sounds and the example words and then record themselves and compare their recordings to the examples. These recordings can then be downloaded and shared with their teacher.

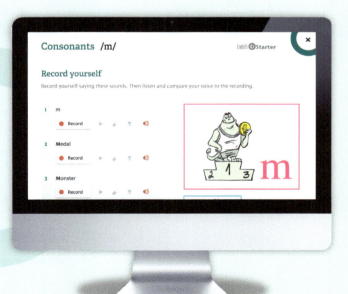

1

1.1 What's your name?

1 Listening

A ▶1.1 Listen and (circle) the correct words in the dialogue. Complete the teacher's ID card.

T Hello. Welcome to the New ID School of English. I'm Isadora, your **tea**cher / **stu**dent.
S Hi, Isadora.
T What / What's your name?
S My name is Luiza.
T Nice to meet you, Luiza.
S Nice to meet you too, Isadora.
T Please, call me **Isa.** / **Dora**.

B ▶1.2 Listen and repeat. In pairs, practice with your names.

I'm Isadora. What's your name?   *My name is Alejandro. Please, call me Alex.*

C ▶1.3 Read the students' ID cards and complete the dialogue. Listen, check, and repeat. Practice with your names.

M Hello, I'm Mariana.
P Hi, _____.
M Please, call me Mari. What's your _____?
P My name is _____.
M Nice to meet _____, Pedro.
P _____ to _____ you too, Mari.

Common mistakes

I Pedro. What your name?

D Read the information and pronounce the pink-stressed words from the dialogue in **A**.

Word stress is **ve**ry im**por**tant for good pronunci**a**tion. In ID, pink letters indicate stress.

E 🎤 **Make it personal** Introduce yourself to your classmates. How many names do you remember?

Hello. / Hi. I'm ... (Please call me ...)   *My name is ... Nice to meet you.*

6

1

Unit overview: In the context of meeting and greeting people and asking for / exchanging personal information, sts learn and practice singular forms of verb *be* ⊕ ⊖ ❓ in the simple present. They also learn numbers 1–12, and definite / indefinite articles to talk about familiar items, and the alphabet to spell names.

1.1 What's your name?

Lesson aims: Sts learn and practice introductions in the context of an English class and numbers 1–12.

Function
Listening to a teacher introduce herself.
Introducing yourself.
Noticing and practicing sentence and word stress.
Counting 1–12.

Language
Hello / Hi. I'm (Isadora). Please, call me (Dora).
What's your name?
My name is (Luiza).
Nice to meet you.

Vocabulary: Functional chunks (Hi! Hello I'm ... Please, call me ... Nice to meet you (too). What's your name?) Numbers 1–12

Grammar: Verb *be* ⊕ 1st and 3rd persons singular

Warm-up As sts walk into class, greet them with *Hi! / Hello!*, and see if they can respond in English. When everyone is sitting down, say: *My name is (your name).* and ask a student: *What's your name?* If necessary, prompt: *My name is ...* As you learn sts' names, present the chunk *Nice to meet you*. Write it on the board and draw the stress bubbles OoOo.

Tip With beginner levels, speak naturally but grade your language by using simple vocabulary and speaking more slowly. Be careful to use contractions and a natural rhythm. You can exploit simple phrases to teach sentence stress and other features of connected speech right from the start.

♪ **Song line:** Turn to p. 176 for notes about this song and an accompanying task.

① Listening

A If possible, display the **Digital Book for Teachers**. Point to the first name badge and say: *This is the teacher. What's her name?* Gesture to show you don't know. Point to the dialogue and tell sts to listen and read, using gestures to clarify. Play ▶1.1, then point to the circle and write *teacher / student* on the board. Ask: *What is correct? Teacher or student?* Play ▶1.1 again and tell sts to circle the correct words. Then tell sts to write the teacher's name on her badge.

▶1.1 Turn to p. 168 for the complete audioscript.

🔑 teacher, What's, Dora

B Point to the speech bubbles and say: *Listen and read*. Play ▶1.2 and make sure sts only listen. Say: *Listen and repeat.*, and gesture to clarify the instruction. Play ▶1.2 again for sts to repeat chorally. Point to the first speech bubble and say it, using your own name. Point to the second speech bubble and prompt a student to say it, using their own name. In pairs, sts practice the dialogue using their names.

▶1.2 Turn to p. 168 for the complete audioscript.

C Point to the two student badges and say: *What's her name?* (Mariana) *What's his name?* (Pedro) *Read and complete.* Gesture so sts know to write in the gaps. Monitor and check. Paircheck, then play ▶1.3 and say: *Listen and check answers*. Classcheck.

In pairs, sts role-play the dialogue using their names. Then have them change roles and role-play again. Monitor for accuracy and sentence stress.

✓ **Common mistakes** Show sts the Common mistakes feature, which appears throughout the book. Explain that Common mistakes focuses on typical errors that happen because of translation from L1 (Spanish or Portuguese). Read the Common mistakes box with the class and show them that the verbs are missing. Point out the corrections, and that the verb *am* is contracted to *'m* and *is* is contracted to *'s*.

Language Tip Remind sts that in English every correct sentence must have a verb. Make sure they don't forget to include a verb in questions and answers.

▶1.3 Turn to p. 168 for the complete audioscript.

🔑 Mariana, name, Pedro, you, Nice, meet

D Write *teacher* on the board and say: *What's the correct pronunciation? Is it TEAcher or teaCHER?* Mark the stress on the board by underlining the stressed syllable or drawing stress bubbles Oo. Point to the box and read the information. Tell sts that pink letters indicate stress. Show them this is a feature of the book by looking at other pages and pointing to words with pink letters. Drill the pink-stressed words in **A**.

E 👤 **Make it personal** Use the speech bubbles to model the activity. Say the first one with your name, then prompt a student to say the second one with their name.

Ask the whole class to stand up. Tell sts to walk around and introduce themselves to as many people as possible. Classcheck by indicating individual sts and asking the rest of the class: *What's his / her name?*

1.1

*Welcome to the new age,
Whoa, oh, oh, oh, oh, whoa, oh, oh, oh,
I'm radioactive, radioactive.*

② Vocabulary Numbers 1–12

A ▶1.4 Listen to the song extract, then use the pictures to sing it. Write the numbers 1–12 next to the correct words.

| seven ___ | eleven ___ | nine ___ | twelve ___ | four ___ | three ___ |
| one _1_ | ten ___ | five ___ | two ___ | six ___ | eight ___ |

B *Dictation!* In pairs, say five numbers for your partner to write. Then change roles.

Eight, three, eleven, two, nine.

C ▶1.5 Listen and say the number of the item you hear.

Bye bye.

*Number four …
The hospital.*

D 🔵 **Make it personal** In groups of three, race each other.
A: Say a number or item.
B and C: Race to say the correct answer. One point for the fastest each time.

7

2 Vocabulary Numbers 1-12

A This activity is based on the song *Rock Around the Clock* by the American rock and roll group Bill Haley and His Comets. Direct sts to the pictures showing numbers, clocks and guitars. Play ▶1.4 and then ask: *Do you know this song? Use the pictures to sing it!* Sing the song lines slowly, pointing to the pictures in turn as you sing the words, and gesture for sts to sing with you. Play ▶1.4 again and ask sts to write the numbers next to the correct words. Classcheck and draw attention to the pink letters, drilling the correct word stress. Play ▶1.4 again and ask sts to sing along.

▶1.4 Turn to p. 168 for the complete audioscript.

> 7, 1, 11, 10, 9, 5, 12, 2, 4, 6, 3, 8

B Make sure your sts have some paper or a notebook.

> **Tip** If possible, encourage the use of recycled paper or tell sts to bring a notebook to class. They will have opportunities to make notes on new language throughout the course.

Say: *Listen and write*. Dictate five numbers and gesture for sts to write them. Classcheck by writing the numbers on the board and asking sts to write the words. Put sts into pairs and tell them to dictate five numbers to each other. Direct them to the speech bubble for an example.

> **Tip** If you think they need extra practice, put sts in new pairs and tell them to repeat the activity.

C Point to the banana and ask: *What's this?* Elicit the names of the rest of the items, teaching any vocabulary they don't know and the correct pronunciation. Play ▶1.5 and pause after the first beep. Ask sts to say the number of the item to their partner. Continue with the rest of the track. Play the track again and classcheck.

▶1.5 Turn to p. 168 for the complete audioscript.

> 6, 4, 1, 5, 9, 3, 12, 10, 11, 7, 2, 8

> **Tip** Sts have problems with the pronunciation of many of these items, especially those which are cognates in their L1. Often the stress and vowel sounds are different in L1. Play the audio again and ask sts to listen and repeat the words, marking the stress.

D **Make it personal** Read through the instructions with the class. Demonstrate the activity with two students for two or three items until you are sure everyone knows what to do. Encourage sts to race by saying the answer as fast as they can. They get one point for being the fastest each time. Put sts into groups of three and tell them to do the activity. Find out who got the most points in each group.

> **Tip** There is a lot of new classroom language in this lesson. Review this by making the gestures you used for, e.g. *listen and repeat, write, listen and read*, and eliciting the language. Direct sts back to the photo of the class on p. 6. Go through the phrases on the wall, adding more gestures so sts will understand your signals throughout this course.
>
> You could ask sts to write similar classroom language on large pieces of card to stick on the walls of your classroom, or they can write the phrases in their notebooks.

1.2 Where are you from?

1 Vocabulary Classroom language

A ▶1.6 Listen to the teacher and complete instructions 1–6. Listen again and repeat.

read

listen to

look at

say

complete

repeat

> **Common mistakes**
>
> Listen ~~/~~ *to* the teacher.
> Look ~~/~~ *at* the photos.
> The is singular and plural.

1 _____ the **ex**ercise.
2 _____ the **di**alogue.
3 _____ the **pho**tos.
4 _____ the text.
5 _____ the words.
6 _____ the **sen**tence.

B ▶1.7 Listen and follow the model. Practice the sentences.

Listen to the dialogue. – The sentence.   *Listen to the sentence.*

C Do you know other classroom instructions? Make a list with your teacher.

Open your book.   *Work in pairs.*

D 🙂 **Make it personal** Play *Mime*! Take turns miming a classroom instruction for the class to guess.

8

1.2 Where are you from?

Lesson aims: Sts are presented with classroom language chunks, and practice giving and understanding instructions. They also learn and practice how to introduce a friend to others.

Function
Saying and understanding classroom instructions.
Listening to a person introducing two friends.
Asking and answering questions about where people are from.
Introducing a friend / Meeting people.

Language
Listen to the dialogue.
Look at the photo.
Repeat the sentence.
This is my friend Pedro. Pedro, this is Luiza.
Where are you from? I'm from Lima.

Vocabulary: Common classroom verbs (complete, listen, look, read, repeat, say) and nouns (dialogue, text, sentence). Phrases for introducing people (This is my friend. Where are you from?)

Grammar: Definite article *the*. Verb *be* ➕ ➖ ❓ singular forms.

Warm-up Books closed. Draw an ID badge on the board. Complete it with information about an imaginary character or a famous person and introduce yourself to one or two sts using your imaginary ID: *Hello. I'm (name). Nice to meet you. What's your name?* Elicit an answer from some sts.

Give sts some paper and tell them to make their own badges with false information. Explain they can invent a new name, or they can be a famous person.

Tell sts to stand up and mingle with classmates, introducing themselves to at least five people with their "new" identities.

1 Vocabulary

A Say: *Open your books* and gesture so sts understand. Point to the photos and drill the verbs below each photo (read, listen to, look at, say, complete, repeat). Make gestures (e.g. listen to – point to your ear) or mime actions (e.g. read – open an imaginary book) to convey meaning. Give commands to check sts' understanding, e.g. point to the board / door and say: *Look at the board / door.* Point to sentences 1–6 and ask: *What's number 3?* (Look at the photos.) Say: *Listen to the teacher and complete.* Play ▶ 1.6. Sts complete the sentences, then paircheck answers. Classcheck with answers on the board. Draw sts' attention to the pink letters, and drill pronunciation of the sentences, emphasizing the word stress. Then play the track again, pausing after each sentence for sts to repeat chorally.

▶ 1.6 Turn to p. 168 for the complete audioscript.

🔑
1 Complete
2 Listen to
3 Look at
4 Read
5 Repeat
6 Say

B This is a transformation drill exercise that is used throughout the book. Point to the speech bubbles and say: *Listen and follow the model.* Play ▶ 1.7 up to "Your turn," and the first pair of beeps, before and after the student prompt. Pause the track and elicit the response from the whole class (Listen to the sentence.). Get a few individual responses too.

Resume playing the track for sts to check the answer and listen for the next prompt. After each prompt, pick a different student to transform the sentence. Correct any errors, then play the track again for sts to practice.

Tip Write *Listen to* _____ on the board and ask sts to complete it with different things (e.g. me, the teacher, the sentence, the dialogue, the radio, music, this song).

Common mistakes Read with the class. Point out we listen *to* something and look *at* something. Remind them that *the* is used for both singular and plural items.

Language tip L1 Spanish and Portuguese speakers tend not to use a preposition with the verbs *listen* and *look*. Remind sts to use the correct prepositions with these verbs in English.

▶ 1.7 Turn to p. 168 for the complete audioscript.

C Read the question with the class and elicit more classroom instructions, writing them on the board. Tell sts to practice saying them in pairs to work on pronunication. Monitor and correct errors as you hear them. Leave the instructions on the board so sts can refer to them in **D**.

Tip Prompt self-correction by saying, e.g.: *Pronunciation* or *Preposition*, and using a facial expression to show there is an error. If sts cannot correct themseves, gesture for their partner to help.

D Make it personal Demonstrate the activity. Mime one of the classroom instructions in **A** for the whole class to guess. In pairs, sts take turns miming and guessing classroom instructions. Prompt / Offer help whenever necessary. Then invite pairs to mime for the class.

2 Listening

🎵 *Listen to the Mariachi play at midnight
Are you with me, are you with me?* **1.2**

A ▶ 1.8 Look at the photo and listen. What are the students' names? Where are they from?

Number 1 is ...

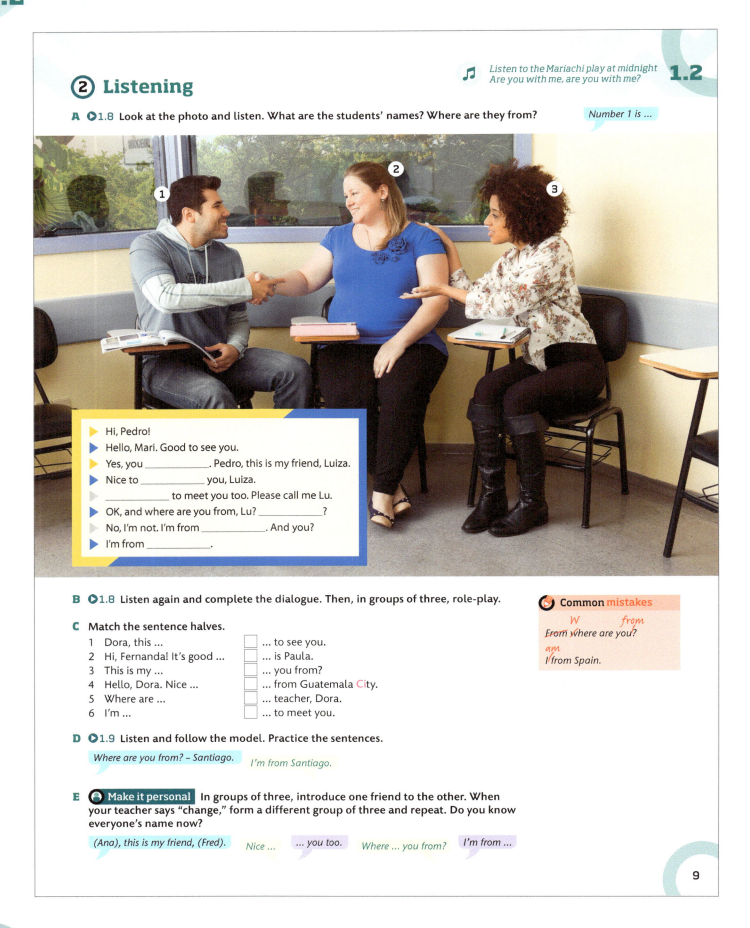

- Hi, Pedro!
- Hello, Mari. Good to see you.
- Yes, you _____. Pedro, this is my friend, Luiza.
- Nice to _____ you, Luiza.
- _____ to meet you too. Please call me Lu.
- OK, and where are you from, Lu? _____?
- No, I'm not. I'm from _____. And you?
- I'm from _____.

B ▶ 1.8 Listen again and complete the dialogue. Then, in groups of three, role-play.

C Match the sentence halves.

1. Dora, this ...
2. Hi, Fernanda! It's good ...
3. This is my ...
4. Hello, Dora. Nice ...
5. Where are ...
6. I'm ...

- ... to see you.
- ... is Paula.
- ... you from?
- ... from Guatemala City.
- ... teacher, Dora.
- ... to meet you.

Common mistakes

~~From~~ **W**here are you? → *from*
I ~~/~~ from Spain. → *am*

D ▶ 1.9 Listen and follow the model. Practice the sentences.

Where are you from? – Santiago.   *I'm from Santiago.*

E 🅐 **Make it personal** In groups of three, introduce one friend to the other. When your teacher says "change," form a different group of three and repeat. Do you know everyone's name now?

(Ana), this is my friend, (Fred).   *Nice ...*   *... you too.*   *Where ... you from?*   *I'm from ...*

1.2

② Listening

🎵 **Song line:** Turn to p. 176 for notes about this song and an accompanying task.

A Tell sts to cover the dialogue. Point to the photo and ask: *Are they students or teachers?* (students). Ask: *What are their names? Where are they from?* and play ▶1.8 for sts to listen and notice the names of the three people and the three cities they mention. Classcheck what the names are, and make sure sts have correctly identified Mari and Luiza by pointing at each of them in the photo and asking: *Who's this?* Then elicit the names of the three cities they hear (Sao Paulo, Curitiba, Santiago). Ask: *Where's Pedro from?* (Santiago) *Where's Luiza from?* (Curitaba). Then ask: *Do you know where Mari is from?* (No). Make sure sts understand that Mari doesn't say where she is from.

▶1.8 Turn to p. 168 for the complete audioscript.

🔑 Pedro: Santiago, Luiza: Curitiba, Mari: not known

B Point to the dialogue in **A**. Say: *Listen again and complete the dialogue.* Replay ▶1.8. Paircheck, then classcheck. Play the track one more time and pause after each sentence for sts to repeat. Then, have sts role-play the dialogue in groups of three.

🔑 too, meet, Nice, São Paulo, Curitiba, Santiago

C Do number 1 with the class as an example. Then have sts match the sentence halves. Paircheck. Classcheck and drill pronunciation of all sentences.

Common mistakes Read with the class. Briefly drill both the correct question and answer in the box, and have sts ask each other in pairs, "Where are you from?" "I'm from …"

Language tip L1 Portuguese or Spanish speakers often have trouble with questions that end with a preposition, because this never happens in their L1. Tell sts that, in English, the preposition always comes at the end of a question.

🔑
1 … is Paula.
2 … to see you.
3 … teacher, Dora.
4 … to meet you.
5 … you from?
6 … from Guatemala City.

D Transformation drill exercise. Say: *Listen and follow the model.* and point to the speech bubbles. Play ▶1.9 up to "Your turn" and the first prompt and beep. Say: *Where are you from? Santiago.* Then say: *I'm from Santiago.* and get the whole class to repeat. Ask a few sts to repeat individually too.

Resume ▶1.9 and pause after the next beep. Elicit the correct response from a student and continue playing the track after checking. Play the rest of the track and at each beep pick a different student to transform the sentence.

▶1.9 Turn to p. 168 for the complete audioscript.

E 🎧 **Make it personal** Put sts into groups of three, and refer them to the speech bubbles. Demonstrate the activity with two sts at the front of the class. Introduce the two sts to each other, and prompt them to respond. Tell all the groups to do the same. Circulate and help if necessary. Then say: *Change.* and have the sts make new groups of three. Tell them to repeat the activity. Do this until sts have spoken to everyone in the class. Check if they can remember everyone's name by asking one st to stand up and asking another st: *Who's this?* Encourage other sts to help if necessary. Continue to ask about all the sts' names.

Extra activity Ask sts to close their books and write a dialogue of three people introducing each other. Tell them to invent names or use the names of famous people. Monitor and help when necessary. They can bring these dialogues to the next class to act out with their classmates.

1.3 What's this in English?

1 Vocabulary Classroom items

A Name five items you can see in your classroom – in English!

B ▶1.10 Match items 1–12 to the words. Listen, check, and repeat.

- [2] a book
- [ ] a chair
- [ ] a desk
- [ ] a flash drive
- [ ] an eraser
- [ ] an interactive whiteboard
- [ ] a marker
- [ ] a notebook
- [ ] an online dictionary
- [ ] a pen
- [ ] a pencil
- [ ] a tablet

C ▶1.11 Listen to Dora and Pedro. Check the four items they mention in **B**.

D ▶1.11 Listen again and complete the dialogue.
Pedro Dora, what's this in English? Is it a pen?
Dora No, it isn't. It's a _____.
Pedro Ah, yes, thanks. And _____ this in English?
Dora It's an _____. What's _____?
Pedro I don't know.
Dora Let's look in the _____.
Pedro OK ... Ah, yes, it's a _____. Thanks.
Dora You're _____.

🟠 Common mistakes

~~This is the book.~~ → *a*
~~Is an apple.~~ → *It's*
~~Is a pencil?~~ → *it*
~~No, is a pen.~~ → *it's*
~~No know.~~ → *I don't*

2 Grammar *a* and *an*

A ▶1.12 Listen to and read the grammar box. Then complete 1–5 with *a* or *an*.

- Use **a** with consonant sounds.
  a book, a student, a teacher
- Use **an** with vowel sounds.
  an airport, an elephant, an ID card

➡ **Grammar 1A** p.72

1 A Macbook is _____ type of computer.
2 Write me _____ email.
3 Look, _____ Italian restaurant!
4 La Traviata is _____ opera.
5 This is _____ envelope.

What's number 9?
It's an eraser.

B Cover the words in **1B**. In pairs, look at the photos and remember.

C 🟢 **Make it personal** In pairs, test your partner's memory. Then change roles.
A: Put some of the classroom items from **1B** on your desk.
B: Look at the items for 10 seconds. Close your eyes and remember.

1.3 What's this in English?

Lesson Aims: Sts learn and practice indefinite articles in the context of asking about and naming classroom items. They also review verb be ❓ ➕ ➖ in singular forms.

Function
Naming and asking about classroom items.
Listening to a student talk to a teacher.
Playing a game / Testing a partner.

Language
What's this in English? Is it a pen? No, it isn't. It's a pencil.
I don't know.
What's number 9? It's an eraser. It isn't a pen.
I'm from Lima. You're not from Lima. You're from Brazil.

Vocabulary: Classroom items
Grammar: Indefinite article *a* / *an*. Verb *be* ❓ ➕ ➖ singular forms.

Warm-up Review introducing people. Play some background music and ask sts to stand up. Say: *We're at a party!* Walk around the class with a student, introducing them to other sts. Use the dialogue below. Put sts in pairs. They walk around, greet classmates, and take turns introducing their partners to friends.

> **Weaker classes** Write the dialogue in **2C** on SB p. 9 on the board as a model.

1 Vocabulary

A Books closed. Use realia to present or elicit the names of some items in your classroom. Hold up / point to the item, e.g. a pen, and ask: *What's this?* Say: *It's a pen.* and have sts repeat after you. Repeat the procedure with four more items.

B Books open. Point to the photos or display them on the IWB. Point at number 1 and ask: *What's this?* (a tablet). Tell sts to complete the exercise. Paircheck, then play ▶1.10 so sts can check their answers. Play ▶1.10 again and tell sts to listen and repeat. Draw their attention again to the pink letters showing word stress.

> 1 a tablet   7 a pen
> 2 a book   8 a marker
> 3 a pencil   9 an eraser
> 4 an interactive whiteboard   10 a notebook
> 5 an online dictionary   11 a chair
> 6 a flash drive   12 a desk

C Ask sts: *Who's Dora?* (the teacher). Tell sts to listen to Dora and Pedro (a student) and check the items they hear. Play ▶1.11. Paircheck, then classcheck.

> a pen, a pencil, an eraser, a marker (*dictionary* is also mentioned as a means to check the word *marker*.)

D Tell sts to read the dialogue and try to remember the missing words. Play ▶1.11 again so sts can read, listen, and complete. Paircheck, then classcheck. Make sure sts understand the meaning of *I don't know*. Ask sts to work in pairs and read out the dialogue, taking turns being Dora.

▶1.11 Turn to p. 168 for the complete audioscript.

> pencil, what's, eraser, this, dictionary, marker, welcome

Tip Tell sts to close their books after two or three minutes and role-play the conversation from memory. They can use different items in the class to improvise.

2 Grammar *a* and *an*

A Write *a book / an eraser* and *a dictionary / an online dictionary* on the board and ask: *Why a or an?* Elicit some ideas (accept explanantions in L1 if sts are in a monolingual class), and then play ▶1.12 and read the rules. Sts complete 1–5 with *a* or *an*. Paircheck, then classcheck.

> **Common mistakes** Read with the class. Remind sts this feature shows typical errors made by speakers of their L1.

> **Language tip** The errors in Common mistakes are often made by L1 Spanish and Portuguese speakers. In their L1, they use the equivalent form of verb *be*, but not the subject (*it*). Explain that English sentences must contain a subject.

> 1 a   2 an   3 an   4 an   5 an

B Tell sts to cover the words in **1B**. Demonstrate the activity by pointing at the photos in **1B** and asking: *What's number 9?* Elicit "It's an eraser." Refer sts to the model in the speech bubbles and have them ask and answer about the items in pairs. Monitor and correct any problems with pronunciation or the use of *a* / *an*.

C **Make it personal** Put some items on your desk and ask a volunteer to come to the front of the class. Give them 10 seconds to look at the items, then tell them to close their eyes. Ask: *What's on my desk?* The student remembers as many items as they can. Then tell them to open their eyes and check. In pairs, sts to do the same using items from the classroom or their bags.

3 Grammar Verb be ➕ ➖

Oh-oh, I'm an alien, I'm a legal alien, I'm an Englishman in New York.

A ▶1.13 Read the grammar box and complete dialogues 1–4 with *'m, are, is, 's* or *isn't*. Listen, check, and repeat.

Questions ❓	Positive ➕	Negative ➖
Where **are** you from?	I**'m** from Lima.	I**'m not** from Arequipa.
	You**'re** from Bogotá.	You**'re not** from Baranquilla.
What**'s** this?	It**'s** a flash drive.	It**'s not** an eraser.
Are you a teacher?	Yes, I **am**.	No, I**'m not**.
Is it a tablet?	Yes, it **is**.	No, it **isn't**.

Contractions
you're = you are   it's = it is   isn't = is not   what's = what is

➡ **Grammar 1B** p.72

🔴 **Common mistakes**
~~'m~~
I̶ from Santiago.
it is
Yes, it̶'̶s̶.

1. **A** Hello, José. Where _____ you from?
   B I _____ from Bogotá.

2. **A** What _____ this in English? _____ it a pen?
   B No, it _____ a pen. It _____ a marker.

3. **A** _____ you Dora, the teacher?
   B No, I _____ not. I _____ a student too.

4. **A** _____ you from Brazil?
   B Yes, I am. I _____ from Salvador.

B ▶1.14 Listen and follow the model. Practice the sentences.

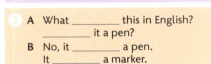
What's this in English? – A pen.   It's a pen.

🔴 **Common mistakes**
~~What~~
H̶o̶w̶ is this in English?
~~What~~
H̶o̶w̶ do you call this?

C 🟢 **Make it personal** *Familiar items* In pairs, speculate about photos 1–10. Do you recognize all the items?

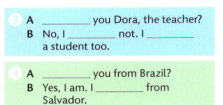
What's number 1? I don't know.
Is it a games console?
No, I think it's a computer mouse.
Oh, yes, you're right.

3 Grammar Verb *be* ➕ ➖

🎵 **Song line:** Turn to p. 176 for notes about this song and an accompanying task.

A Read the grammar box with sts and prompt / elicit real examples, e.g. "I'm from Quito. I'm not from Caracas.", "You're from Buenos Aires.", "It's a book. It isn't a notebook." Write the full forms / contractions on the board. Sts complete dialogues 1–4. Play ▶ 1.13 and tell sts to listen and check. Classcheck. Play the track again and tell sts to listen and repeat.

🌿 **Common mistakes** Read with the class. Remind sts to use the auxiliary verb *be* to describe nationality. Also point out that we cannot contract *it is* in short answers.

▶ 1.13 Turn to p. 168 for the complete audioscript.

🔑
1 are, 'm
2 's, Is, isn't, 's
3 Are, 'm, 'm
4 Are, 'm

🔑
1 a computer mouse
2 a car
3 a dog / dog's tongue
4 a taxi
5 a hotel
6 a cat
7 a computer / laptop keyboard
8 a burger
9 a banana
10 a public restroom sign

B Transformation drill. Refer sts to the speech bubbles and say: *Listen and follow the model*. Play ▶ 1.14 up to "Your turn," then pause after the first prompt and beep. Say: *What's this in English? A chair.* and elicit the correct answer from the whole group. Continue playing ▶ 1.14 to check the answer. Play the rest of the track and, after each beep, pick a different student to answer. Pause the track after each answer and have sts repeat chorally, so the whole group can practice the sentences / vocabulary.

🌿 **Common mistakes** Read with the class. Explain we use the question word *What* (not *How*) in these sentences.

▶ 1.14 Turn to p. 168 for the complete audioscript.

C 👤 **Make it personal** Show / Point to an object you think sts are unlikely to know the name of in English and ask: *What's this in English?* Write *I don't know.* on the board and gesture to convey meaning. Tell sts to look at photo 1 and encourage them to guess what it is, using L1 if necessary. Then refer them to the speech bubbles. Read them aloud, then model the activity with a student. In pairs, sts take turns asking / guessing about the items in the photos. After they have finished, ask *What's number ...?* about all the photos and elicit different ideas. Confirm the correct answers. Teach any unknown vocabulary, writing it on the board and correcting pronunciation.

Tip Review language from the lesson to help sts remember new vocabulary. Tell sts to write the words they remember from today's lesson in their notebooks. Then have them work in pairs and read their lists to each other. Encourage them to correct and praise each other's pronunciation. Monitor and offer support and praise. Tell them to write the words on sticky notes when they get home and put them around their house so they see, remember, and practice saying them.

1.4 What's your phone number?

1 Pronunciation The alphabet

```
    A  H J K 8
    _  C D E G P T V Z 3
    _  L M N S X 7
       _  Y 5 9
       Q _ W 2
```

A ▶1.15 Listen to and complete the doctor's chart. Which two letters of the alphabet are missing?

B ▶1.16 Listen to and repeat the letters.

C ▶1.17 Listen to and read the information. In pairs, say the alphabet in order.

> English has 26 letters: 21 consonants and five vowels, A, E, I, O and U.
> Memorize the letters in the five sound groups in the chart.
> Remember O and R too.

D Say these acronyms in English. Then in pairs, write one for your partner to say.

E 🎧 Make it personal *Spelling tennis* In groups of three, one person says a word and the other two spell the word with alternate letters.

Spell "door."   *double o*
       d   *r*

2 Listening

A ▶1.18 Listen and match parts 1 and 2 of the conversation to the pictures. Are Angela and Daniel classmates or friends?

12

1.4 What's your phone number?

Lesson aims: Sts learn the alphabet by listening to a doctor's eye-test, saying acronyms, and spelling names. Sts practice saying phone numbers and also use verb *be* to ask for and give personal information.

Function
Saying the letters of the alphabet.
Listening to a couple getting to know each other.
Spelling names and saying phone numbers.
Asking and answering personal information questions.

Language
What's your phone number?
Can you spell that, please? S-E-double B-Y.
Are you married? No, I'm single.
How are you today? I'm fine, thanks.

Vocabulary: The alphabet. Marital status (single, married, divorced, separated). *Oh* for zero, double 6. How are you? I'm fine, thanks. Spell that, please?

Grammar: Verb *be*

Warm-up Put some classroom items on your desk or display photos on the board. Point to individual items and ask: *What's this?* and review vocabulary from lesson 1.3. Then, for one of the items, ask *What's this? How do you spell it?* Elicit the spelling and write the word on the board, correcting pronunciation.

♪ **Song line:** Turn to p. 176 for notes about this song and an accompanying task.

1 Pronunciation

A Point to the doctor's chart and ask: *Where do you see this? What is it?* Elicit it is a doctor's chart to test your eyesight. Play ▶1.15 and say: *Listen and complete*. Paircheck, then play the track again and classcheck. Ask: *Which two letters are missing?* Have sts work in pairs to go through the alphabet and work out which letters are missing from the chart. Invite a pair to answer, and ask the other sts if they agree.

▶1.15 Turn to p. 168 for the complete audioscript.

> B F I U
> The two letters missing are O and R.

B Play ▶1.16 and ask sts to listen and repeat. Ensure sts notice that letters with similar pronunciation (same vowel sound) are grouped together. Write the vowel sounds on the board and drill them in isolation.

> **Tip** Use gestures or common words to help sts remember the sounds, e.g. /eɪ/ *Hey!* (waving to say hello); /iː/ *Sí!* (nodding, as in "yes" in Spanish); /ɜ/ *Yes!* (thumbs up); /aɪ/ *Why?* (raising your shoulders); /uː/ *You!* (pointing to someone); /oʊ/ *Oh!* (looking surprised); /ɑr/ *car* (mime driving).

Classcheck and encourage sts to pronounce each vowel sound in isolation and then the letters of the same group, e.g. /eɪ/ A-H-J-K.

▶1.16 Turn to p. 168 for the complete audioscript.

C Play ▶1.17 and have sts listen and read the information in the box. Write the five sound groups on the board and drill their pronunciation. Test sts by pointing at letters randomly and eliciting the correct sounds. In pairs, sts take turns saying the letters of the alphabet in order. Classcheck.

> **Tip** If possible, search for "eye-test charts" online. Select a simple chart (with fewer letters) and have sts role-play an eye test in pairs. Have sts sit opposite each other: **A** facing the IWB, **B** with his / her back to it. **A** reads the chart aloud, **B** writes the letters he / she hears on a piece of paper. At the end, **B** looks at the board and compares his / her notes to the original chart. Then, sts change roles and play the game again.

D Point to the first acronym and elicit the pronunciation. In pairs, sts take turns saying the acronyms. Classcheck. Then sts write an English acronym for their partner to say. Monitor and help with pronunciation. (Note: DVD = Digital Versatile Disc; SMS = Short Message Service; ATM = Automated Teller Machine; DIY = Do It Yourself, usually applied to doing building work, decorating, or repairs in the home.)

E 🔵 **Make it personal** Ask for two volunteers and tell them to stand up so the class can see them. Write *doctor* on the board and ask: *How do you spell "doctor"?* Ask one st: *What's the first letter?* (d) Ask the other st: *What's the next letter?* (o). Continue until they have spelled the word. Puts sts in groups of three and refer them to the model in the speech bubbles. Have them take turns saying a word for the other two to spell.

> **Tip** Tell sts to look through the vocabulary sections in lessons 1.1–1.3 for words to spell.

2 Listening

A Tell sts to look at the pictures and ask: *Where are they? Are they friends or classmates?* Encourage sts to speculate or say "I don't know." Play the first part of ▶1.18 and ask: *Is this picture a or b?* Don't confirm the answer yet. Play the second part and ask which picture it is. Classcheck.

▶1.18 Turn to p. 168 for the complete audioscript.

> 1 b 2 a
> They are classmates.

1.4

B ▶1.19 Match questions 1–6 to the answers. Listen, check, and repeat.

*A B C, it's easy as 1 2 3,
As simple as do re mi,
A B C, 1 2 3
Baby you and me girl.*

1 Are you in my English class?
2 How are you?
3 What's your phone number?
4 What's your name?
5 Can you spell that, please?
6 Are you on WhatsApp?

☐ It's 78190366.
☐ O-C-H-O-A. It's a Mexican name.
☐ Yes, I am. Message me.
☐ It's Angela Ochoa.
☐ I'm fine, thanks.
☐ At the New ID school of English? Yes, I am.

C Read the information.
A: Spell a name from the Contact list.
B: Say the person's phone number.

In phone numbers:
0 (zero) = oh
66 = double 6
007 = double oh seven

In names:
LL = double L

In acronyms:
BBC = B-B-C (not double B-C)

R-E-I-S. *7-8-1-5-oh-2-double 9.*

Contact list 14:10

Name	
Reis	7815 0299
Henn	9087 6543
Quiroga	3568 9975
Debby	3517 2200
Flamel	8055 5644
Vargas	2171 6230

D 🎧 **Make it personal** 📶 Search online for some useful numbers. In pairs, dictate them to your partner.

The local hospital is 419 228 3385.

3 Grammar Verb *be* ❓

A ▶1.20 Put the words in 1–7 in order to make questions. Then match them to the answers. Listen and check. In pairs, practice.

1 's / in / what / this / English / ?
   What's this in English?
2 you / married / are / ?
3 you / today / how / are / ?
4 name / your / what / 's / ?
5 from / where / you / are / ?
6 phone / 's / your / what / number / ?
7 cell / where / my / 's / phone / ?

➡ Grammar 1C p.72

⚠ **Common mistake**
~~Are you
You are married?~~

☐ No, I'm single.
☐ Paulo.
☐ It's an eraser.
☐ It's on the table.
☐ I'm from Córdoba.
☐ It's 631… er, sorry, I don't remember.
☐ I'm OK, thanks.

B ▶1.21 Listen and follow the model. Practice the sentences.

2274 3690 – Question. *What's your phone number?*

C 🎧 **Make it personal** In groups of three, ask questions to complete the table.

Name	Phone number	Hometown

What's your name?
What's your phone number?
Where are you from?

B Tell sts to read questions 1–6 from the conversation and match to the answers. Paircheck. Play ◐1.19 and tell sts to check their answers. Classcheck by dividing the class – one half is Angela, the other half is Daniel. Replay the track for sts to repeat their lines.

> **Extra activity** In pairs, sts take turns asking questions 1–6 and replying using their own, real answers. Then, tell sts to close their books and walk around the class asking and answering the questions from memory. You could give extra support by writing the questions on the board.

◐1.19 Turn to p. 168 for the complete audioscript.

1 At the New ID School of English? Yes, I am.
2 I'm fine, thanks.
3 It's 78190366.
4 It's Angela Ochoa.
5 O-C-H-O-A. It's a Mexican name.
6 Yes, I am. Message me.

C Read the information in the box with the class. Refer sts to the speech bubbles and demonstrate the activity with a stronger student. Then, sts do the same in pairs using the information in the Contact list on the phone. Monitor and correct errors.

> **Tip** To add challenge, tell sts to invent a name and phone number with double letters and numbers. Then, sts work in groups of four or walk around the class asking and answering, *What's your name? What's your phone number?* They write the names and numbers. Monitor and listen for errors and good pronunciation of letters, and go through this with the whole class at the end. Afterward, tell everyone to sit down and indicate another st and ask: *What's his / her name? What's his / her number?*

D **Make it personal** Ask: *What's the phone number for an emergency?* (They can give the number in their country, or they may know it is 911 in the U.S. from TV shows and movies). Ask: *What other telephone numbers are important?* Elicit some ideas and write them on the board. Tell sts to use mobile devices to look up at least three important numbers and write them down.

Put sts in pairs or groups of three and ask them to dictate their numbers to each other. Refer them to the speech bubble for an example. Then ask: *What numbers do you know?* Ask sts to dictate for you to write them on the board. Ask the class: *Is this correct?*

3 Grammar Verb *be*

A Write *What_____?* on the board and ask sts to say questions they know starting with *What*. Write them on the board, but don't correct them yet. Ask sts to look at example 1 in the grammar box and tell them to order the words in 2–7. Then, tell sts to match questions 1–7 to the answers below the box. Paircheck. Play ◐1.20 and class check answers. Check they understand *I don't remember*.

If there were any errors in the sts' questions you wrote on the board, refer back to them and invite sts to correct them.

Common mistakes Read with the class, and show how word order changes from statements to questions.

Tell sts to work in pairs and take turns asking and answering questions.

> **Language tip** Question word order can be difficult for L1 Spanish and Portuguese speakers, because in their L1 the word order doesn't change. Make sure sts understand this by having them transform a few more simple affirmative sentences into questions.

There is more information on questions with verb *be* in Grammar 1C on p. 72.

◐1.20 Turn to p. 168 for the complete audioscript.

1 It's an eraser.
2 Are you married? No, I'm single.
3 How are you today? I'm OK, thanks.
4 What's your name? Paulo.
5 Where are you from? I'm from Córdoba.
6 What's your phone number? It's 631 … er, sorry, I don't remember.
7 Where's my cell phone? It's on the table.

B Transformation drill. Say: *Listen and follow the model.* and refer sts to the model in the speech bubbles. Play ◐1.21 until you hear "Your turn" and the first beep and prompt. Elicit the correct question. Point again to the speech bubbles and clarify sts have to say the correct question for the answers they hear.

Resume ◐1.21 and pause after the next beep. Elicit the correct question from sts and resume playing the track to check. Play the rest of the track, pausing after each beep and picking a different student to say the correct question.

◐1.21 Turn to p. 169 for the complete audioscript.

C **Make it personal** Write the headings of the three columns in the chart on the board, and elicit the questions the sts need to ask. Invite different sts to ask you the questions, and have them write the answers on the board. Model *Sorry, can you spell that?* to encourage sts to use the alphabet. Have sts work in groups of three to ask and answer the questions and complete their table. Remind them to ask for spellings. Monitor and listen for good language in question forms and pronunciation of letters. Write these on the board and go over them at the end.

> **Tip** Try to end the class with positive reinforcement, not errors, so sts leave feeling motivated. Focus end-of-class feedback on examples of good language you heard.

1.5 What's your email address?

ID Skills Recognizing cognates

A What do these words have in common? Check your answer at the bottom of page 15.

alphabet   bar   dialogue   experience   interesting   restaurant
complete   dictionary   identity   plural   vocabulary

B Read the blogs. Who likes English more, wallyjoe or Roxanne? Underline the cognates in the blogs and guess the pronunciation.

Bloggers English

English is an incredible language. It's flexible and receptive. English is, in effect, a collection of languages. About 60% of its vocabulary is Latin-based!

(posted by wallyjoe on www.mylot.com)

English is an incredible language. I adore it! There's a perfect word or expression for anything a person can imagine. For example, 'adore'… It's a splendid word! It transcends 'love.' It contains respect, devotion, and a sense of eternity. Wow …

(posted by Roxanne on urthmthr.blogspot.com.br)

C ▶1.22 Reread and listen to the blogs to check. Circle the words you don't understand. In pairs, compare. Any surprises?

D In pairs, find 10 more cognates in Unit 1. What other English words or phrases do you know?

I love you.   Pop music.   Made in China.

E ▶1.23 Listen and complete the form.

Name:
City / country: _____, Brazil
Email: _____.ch@_____.com
Phone number:

F ▶1.24 Listen to, read, and repeat the words. Then say email addresses 1–3.

@ = at   . = dot   - = hyphen   _ = underscore   # = hashtag
Spell combinations of letters, for example, .ar, .mx.
Pronounce .com, .co, .org, .net as words.

1 email.account1234@portmail.com.mx
2 josy_turner@cpg.net
3 always-smiling@fishers.org.us

G 🔵 Make it personal What's your email address in English? Say it to the class and make a class email list.

1.5 What's your email address?

Lesson aims: Sts continue to practice verb *be* and letters and numbers by asking for personal information.

Function
Reading and listening to blog entries about the English language.
Recognizing cognates.
Filling in a form.
Understanding and saying email addresses.

Language
What's your email, please?

Vocabulary: Cognates (flexible, alphabet, incredible, respect). (.) dot, (@) at, com
Grammar: Review verb *be* ❓

Warm-up Before class, write some words from Unit 1 on small pieces of recycled paper.

Give out three pieces of paper to each student and review the question *How do you spell_____?* In pairs, sts test each other using their words. If their partner spells the word correctly, they get a point. Encourage peer correction if they make mistakes. Sts then work with a different partner and repeat the activity.

ID SKILLS Recognizing cognates

A Tell sts to work in pairs, look at the colored words, and guess what the words have in common. Elicit some ideas and then tell sts to check the answer at the bottom of p. 15. Review the pronunciation of the words. Ask: *Do you know any more cognates in English and your language?* Write their ideas on the board and confirm if they are cognates and what the correct spelling and pronunciation is in English. Leave these on the board so you can come back to them in **D**.

> **Language tip** Make sure sts realize there are many cognates in English and their L1, and that recognizing cognates can help them to learn faster. Tell sts to start a Cognates section in their notebooks. Remind them the pronunciation of cognates is often different to their language so it's important to make a note of how the words sound in English, along with a translation and example sentence.

B Ask: *Do you read blogs?* Elicit some responses, then tell sts to read the blog posts. Ask: *What are the blog posts about?* (English) *Who likes English more?* (Roxanne) Then, tell sts to underline the cognates. Paircheck, then classcheck.

🔑
English, incredible, language, flexible, receptive, effect, collection, vocabulary, Latin, adore, perfect, expression, person, imagine, example, splendid, transcends, contains, respect, devotion, eternity

C Play ▶1.22 and ask sts to read, listen, and circle words they don't understand. Paircheck and encourage peer teaching. Monitor and write words that sts don't know on the board and teach meaning afterwards. Ask sts to try to pronounce the words, and remind them that pink letters show word stress. Listen and correct any mistakes, then go over the words with the class.

> **Tip** Show sts how to mark word stress using bubbles Ooo, underlining the stressed syllable, or showing it (as in dictionaries) with an apostrophe. Tell them to mark stress as they record new vocabulary in their notebooks.

D Tell sts to look at the cognates you wrote on the board earlier. In pairs, tell them to try and find 10 more cognates in Unit 1. Set a four-minute time limit and make it a competition. The pair who can find the most cognates in four minutes is the winner. Then, ask sts to look at the speech bubbles. Ask sts if they know any other English words or phrases. Write them on the board and teach the pronunciation.

> **Tip** You could ask some sts to look in **1.1**, others in **1.2**, others in **1.3**, etc. to make this activity shorter.

🔑
Cognates: moment, circle, correct, student, repeat, practice, information, important, pronunciation, letter, introduce, extract, dictation, instruction, exercise, interactive, grammar, consonant, elephant, opera, model, familiar, doctor, acronym, contact, hospital, question

E Direct sts to the photo and explain they are going to listen to a student speaking to a receptionist. Ask sts to look at the form and tell them they have to listen and complete it. Play ▶1.23 and pause once or twice so sts can write answers. Paircheck, then classcheck.

🔑
Antonio Chaves, Rio de Janeiro, toni, gvr, 21 8977 4053

▶1.23 Turn to p. 169 for the complete audioscript.

F Play ▶1.24 and tell sts to listen and read. Check they are clear on the pronunciation of .com, .co, and .net. Play the track again for sts to repeat chorally. Then have them practice saying email addresses 1–3 with a partner.

G Give sts pieces of recycled paper and ask them to walk around the class asking: "What's your email address?" They have to write each other's names and email addresses. Remind them to ask: "How do you spell that?" if they don't know. Afterwards, ask some sts: *What's (student's name)'s email address?* They dictate it to you. Write it on the board and ask the class: *Is that correct?*

1.5 How are you today?

*Baby, we don't stand a chance,
It's sad but it's true
I'm way too good at goodbyes.*

ID in Action Greetings and personal information

A ▶1.25 Match photos 1 and 2 to groups A and B. Then listen to and repeat the phrases.

A
☐ Hi.
Hello.
Good morning.
Good afternoon.
Good evening.

B
☐ Bye!
Bye for now!
Goodbye.
See you.
Good night.

B ▶1.26 Listen to three conversations. Check the expressions in **A** that you hear.

C ▶1.26 Listen again and match pictures a–c to conversations 1–3.

> ⚠ **Common mistake**
> ~~Hello, good night!~~ *evening*
> Use *Good night* to say goodbye after 6 p.m.

D ▶1.27 Complete 1–7 with these words. Listen, check, and repeat.

| are (x2) email Good See What's (x2) you your |

1 How __are__ you?
2 _____ your name?
3 Bye! _____ you!
4 What's your _____ address?
5 Where _____ _____ from?
6 Hello! _____ evening!
7 _____ _____ phone number?

E 🗣 **Make it personal** In pairs, say hello and ask questions to complete the form.

Name: _____	Address: _____
Hometown: _____	Phone number: _____
Email: _____	Vehicle registration number: _____
ID card number: _____	

> *Good afternoon. How are you today?*
> *Hello, I'm fine, thanks. And you?*
> *I'm fine. What's your name?*
> *I'm …*

Answer: They are all cognates. A cognate is a word similar in origin to your language.

1.5 How are you today?

Lesson aims: Sts learn more greetings and review questions and phrases for exchanging personal information.

Function
Greeting people.
Asking for and giving personal information.

Language
Good morning / afternoon / evening / night.
Bye for now.
See you.
What's your ID card number?

Vocabulary: Greetings (Good morning / afternoon / evening. See you.)
Grammar: Verb *be*

ID in action Greetings and personal information

A Ask sts to look quickly at photos 1 and 2 and the groups of greetings A and B. Point to group A and the photos and ask: *Is it photo 1 or 2?* (photo 1) Ask: *What about group B?* (photo 2). Play ▶1.25 and ask sts to listen and repeat.

Common mistakes Read with the class. Ask: *Is this the same in your country?*

1 A   2 B

♪ **Song line:** Turn to p. 176 for notes about this song and an accompanying task.

B Read the instructions with sts and tell them to check the phrases in **A** as they hear them. Play ▶1.26 once or twice. Paircheck, then classcheck.

▶1.26 Turn to p. 169 for the complete audioscript.

Hello, Hi, Good evening, Good night, Bye!

C Tell sts to look at pictures a–c and ask: *Where are they?* (a party, a shopping mall, a restaurant). Play ▶1.26 again and tell sts to match pictures a–c to conversations 1–3. Paircheck, then classcheck.

a 3
b 1
c 2

Tip Play the audio for each picture again and ask sts to practice the conversation from memory. Play the audio two or three times if necessary.

D Direct sts to the example and then ask them to complete 2–7. Play ▶1.27 so they can check answers. Play it again and tell sts to listen and repeat.

▶1.27 Turn to p. 169 for the complete audioscript.

2 What's
3 See
4 email
5 are, you
6 Good
7 What's, your

Tip Sts can test each other in pairs. St **A** has the book open and says the start of a question, e.g. "How…?" St **B** finishes the question: "… are you?" Then they change roles, and continue with the other questions in the same way.

E Make it personal Tell sts to look at the form and ask you questions to get your personal information. Tell sts they are going to say hello to a partner and complete the form. Direct them to the speech bubbles for ideas. In pairs, sts greet each other and ask and answer questions to complete the form for each other.

Tip Set this up as a role-play at school or a local place where sts have to ask for and give information. Half the class are receptionists and the other half are students / visitors, etc. The students / visitors have to give their information two or three times to different receptionists. Then sts change roles. You could do this in a conveyer belt format where students sit in two circles or two lines facing each other: line one and line two. Line one stays in the same seat and line two moves one seat to the left each time they finish the conversation, so they speak to different students. Ask them to change three or four times.

➔ **Workbook** p. 89

➔ **Richmond Learning Platform**

➔ **Writing** p. 16

➔ **Café** p. 17

Writing 1 An online introduction

♪ *Beautiful people,*
Drop top, designer clothes,
Front row at fashion shows.

A ▶ 1.28 Read the posts in this social network group and complete the forms for the two new members.

Welcome new members!

To start: intro**duce** yourself and give us your o**pin**ion about a fa**vo**rite ce**leb**rity. Use one word to des**cribe** him or her!

Ana Belle

Aysel Evren

<mark>Nice to meet you all.</mark> My name's Aysel Evren. I'm Turkish, from Izmir. I'm 17 years old, I'm a student, and I'm single. Ed Sheeran's my favorite mu**si**cian. I think he's fan**tas**tic.

Ale Benítez

<mark>Hi, everyone.</mark> I'm Alejandro Benítez, but please call me Ale. I'm from Guadalajara, Mexico, I'm a chef, and I'm 24. I'm married. My favorite celebrity's Jennifer Lawrence. I think she's an ex**cell**ent ac**tor**.

Profile

1	Name	Aysel Evren	Alejandro _____	
2	Nickname			
3	City / Country (nationality)	Izmir, Turkey (Turkish)		
4	Age			
5	**Mar**ital status			
6	Favorite celebrity		Jennifer Lawrence	
7	Opinion word			

B Match 1–7 in **A** to these questions.
☐ Where are you from?
☐ What's your name?
☐ Are you married?
☐ What's your nickname?
☐ How old are you?
☐ Who's your favorite celebrity?
☐ What's your opinion of him / her?

C Reread the posts and write down the sentences that mean 1–4.
1 I'm from Turkey. = I'm _____
2 I'm not married. = _____
3 I'm Mexican, from Guadalajara. = _____
4 I'm 24 years old. = _____

D Read *Write it right!* and (circle) …
• 14 contractions
• six commas
• three uses of *and*
• one use of *but*

⊘ Write it right!
Use contractions ('m, 's, 're) in posts.
Use a comma (,), *and*, or *but* to connect two ideas.

E *Your turn!* Write a post to the group.

Before	Answer the questions in **B** and complete your profile.
While	Use a <mark>highlighted</mark> phrase to say hello to the group. Check your use of *and*, *but*, and commas.
After	"Post" your texts around the class. Any coincidences?

Writing 1 An online introduction

♪ **Song line:** Turn to p. 177 for notes about this song and an accompanying task.

A **Books closed.** Ask sts: *Are you on Facebook or other social media sites? Are you in any Facebook groups or other social network groups? What are these groups about?* Tell sts they're going to read a post on a social network group.

Books open. Read Ana Belle's welcoming post with the whole class. Ask: *What do new members do to start?* (introduce themselves and give their opinion about a favorite celebrity in one word). Point to Aysel's and Ale's posts and tell sts to complete the profile about them. Paircheck. Classcheck with answers on the board.

> Aysel Evren. Nickname: none; City / Country (nationality): Izmir, Turkey (Turkish); Age: 17; Marital status: single; Favorite celebrity: Ed Sheeran; Opinion word: fantastic
> Alejandro Benítez: Nickname: Ale; City / Country (nationality): Guadalajara, Mexico (Mexican); Age: 24; Marital status: married; Favorite celebrity: Jennifer Lawrence; Opinion word: excellent

B Read the first question with sts: *Where are you from?* Point to headings 1–7 in the profile in **A** and ask: *What number?* (3, City / Country). Tell sts to match 1–7 in **A** to the questions by writing the correct numbers next to the questions. Paircheck. Classcheck with answers on the board.

> 3, 1, 5, 4, 6, 7

C Read 1 and ask sts to find a similar sentence in Aysel's post in **A**. Sts copy sentences that mean the same as 1–4. Paircheck. Classcheck with answers on the board.

> 1 Turkish.
> 2 I'm single.
> 3 I'm from Guadalajara, Mexico.
> 4 I'm 24.

D Tell sts to read **Write it right!** and explain that contractions are more common in informal English, such as on social media. Ask sts to look at the texts in **A** again and circle the items in the four bullet points. Paircheck. Classcheck with answers on the board. If technology is available, use the **Digital Book for Teachers** and have sts circle answers on the board.

> - contractions: (Aysel) name's, I'm, I'm, I'm, I'm, Sheeran's, he's; (Ale) I'm, I'm, I'm, I'm, I'm, celebrity's, she's
> - commas after: Turkish, old, student, Benítez, Guadalajara, Mexico, chef
> - uses of *and*: introduce yourself and give us your opinion; I'm a student and I'm single. I'm a chef, and I'm 24.
> - *but*: but please call me Ale

E *Your turn!*

Before Tell sts they're going to write a post to the group. Sts answer the questions in **B** about themselves and fill in the third column in the form in **A**, 1–7.

While Draw sts' attention to the highlighted phrases in Aysel's and Ale's posts in **A**. Ask sts to choose one of those phrases to start their own posts. Sts write their own posts, saying hello to the online group and including all information from 1–7 in **A** about themselves.

After In pairs, sts exchange and read each other's posts to paircheck / spot mistakes. Monitor closely and give feedback. Then, ask sts to stick their posts onto the class mural or board. Invite all sts to stand up and read as many posts as they can. Encourage them to look for coincidences, e.g. two sts who wrote about the same celebrity. When they go back to their seats, test their memory by indicating all of the posts and asking, e.g.: *Are there any posts about Shakira? Are there any coincidences?*

1 First class

1 Before watching

A Match the opposites. Then test a partner.

1. beautiful
2. first
3. here
4. Hurry up!
5. an instructor
6. late
7. please
8. start
9. this
10. tired

☐ last
☐ Slow down!
☐ thanks
☐ energetic
☐ early
☐ finish
☐ there
☐ a student
☐ ugly
☐ that

What's the opposite of tired? — *Energetic. What's ...*

B Look at the picture. Where are they?

☐ in a gym
☐ in an apartment
☐ in a classroom
☐ in a theater

2 While watching

A Watch until 0:44 and complete extracts 1–3.

1. **Jim** Could you spell that for me, please?
   Andrea Sure. __ - A - I - N - __ - __ - I - G - H - T.
2. **Jim** What's your _____?
   Andrea Andrea.
   Jim Great. OK, __ __, please?
3. **Jim** Could you spell your last name, please?
   Lucy __ - E - __ - E - __ - __ - A   __ - A - R - __ - I - __.

B 🔴 **Make it personal** In pairs, spell your name. Then each invent another name and ask and answer.

What's your name, please? — *Salceda. That's S - A - L - C - E - D - A.*

C Watch the complete video. True (T) or false (F)?

1. The instructor's name is Jim Landry.
2. It's a beginner class.
3. The yoga class is in Room 2.
4. August isn't in the yoga class.
5. Daniel's in the capoeira class.
6. August is on the class list.
7. The class isn't very good.

D Complete the extract. Watch from 2:12 to 2:45 again to check.

Daniel: Uh, _____ this Room 2?
Instructor: No. Room 2 _____ next door.
August: Oh. Sorry. What _____ is this?
Andrea: August? _____ you in our _____ class?
August: Yoga? Yes. Actually, yes, I _____.
Daniel: Huh? August, we _____ in the capoeira _____.
August: No, no ... You'_____ in capoeira. I _____ in the _____ class!

3 After watching

A Complete 1–8 with August (Au), Andrea (An), the instructor (I), Daniel (D), or Lucy (Lu).

1. _____ is in line first.
2. _____ arrives late and brings coffee.
3. _____ says, "It's so early!"
4. _____ signs her name on _____'s list first.
5. _____ says, "The yoga class starts at 8:30."
6. _____ and _____ have the same last name.
7. _____ goes to the capoeira class.
8. _____ thinks the first class is great.

B Check the category for phrases 1–9: greeting or goodbye (GOG), introducing yourself (IY), or asking for information (AFI).

	GOG	IY	AFI
1 Hey, Lucy!			
2 Good morning.			
3 I'm Jim Landry!			
4 Could you spell your name?			
5 ID, please?			
6 You can call me Lucy.			
7 Hello, everyone!			
8 Is this room 2?			
9 See you later!			

C 🔴 **Make it personal** **Role-play!** In groups of three, **A**: You're the instructor. **B** and **C**: You're in the class. Use the phrases in **B**. Introduce yourself, give information and say goodbye to your partners. Change roles.

Hello, I'm Sam. Is this the yoga class? — *Hi, yes, it is. I'm the instructor. My name's Juan Carlos.*

ID Café 1 First class

1 Before watching

A Explain the ID Café feature of the Student Book. Tell sts they will follow the story of the people in the videos throughout the book. Point to words and phrases 1–10 and tell sts they will hear these in the video they're going to watch. Sts match 1–10 to the opposites, and then paircheck. Classcheck.

> 1 ugly 2 last 3 there 4 Slow down! 5 a student
> 6 early 7 thanks 8 finish 9 that 10 energetic

B Point to the men in the video still (on the left, August; on the right, Daniel), and say: *This is August and this is Daniel.* Ask the whole class: *How do you spell "August"?* and let sts have a guess as you write the name on the board. Ask: *How do you spell "Daniel"?* and write it on the board too. Then, point to the video still again and ask: *Where are they?* Sts check the right answer.

> in a gym

2 While watching

A Have sts read extracts 1–3 and predict the missing information. Play ▶1 without subtitles from start to 0:44 (pause after Lucy Pereira García spells her last name and then says "OK. Thank you so much.") Sts complete the extracts. Replay the video if necessary. Paircheck. Then play the video with subtitles to classcheck answers.

> 1 W-A-I-N-W-R-I-G-H-T
> 2 first name, ID
> 3 P-E-R-E-I-R-A G-A-R-C-I-A

B ◉ **Make it personal** Pair up with a st to model the activity. Say: *Spell your name, please.* As he / she says and spells it, write it letter by letter on the board. In pairs, sts take turns spelling their names. Ensure they write the names down as their partners spell them. Monitor closely for pronunciation. Sts then check their partner has spelled their name correctly. Then have sts invent new names. Point to the speech bubbles and model with a confident student. Sts take turns asking about, answering, and spelling the new names. Invite a few sts to ask and answer for the whole class.

C Read statements 1–7 with sts. Tell them you're going to play the complete video this time and they have to mark 1–7 T (true) or F (false). Play ▶1 in full. Paircheck. Classcheck with answers on the board.

> 1 T 2 T 3 F (Room 2 is next door.) 4 F (August is supposed to be in the capoeira class.) 5 T 6 F 7 F

D Tell sts to read the extracts and complete them. Play ▶1 from 2:12 to 2:45 for sts to check their answers. Paircheck. Replay the video to classcheck answers.

> is, is, class, Are, yoga, am, 're, 're, I'm, yoga

3 After watching

A Sts decide whether sentences 1–8 refer to August, Andrea, the instructor, Daniel, or Lucy. Do number 1 with the class (Andrea) and then tell sts to complete 2–8. Paircheck, then classcheck.

> 1 Andrea 2 Lucy 3 Andrea 4 Andrea, the instructor's
> 5 The instructor 6 Andrea, August 7 Daniel 8 August

B Make sure sts understand what the chart headings mean by reading out each abbreviated heading and the expanded version in the rubric. Read the first sentence, *Hey Lucy!*, and ask: *Greeting or goodbye, introducing yourself, or asking for information?* (greeting). Sts check the correct category in the chart, then continue checking the categories for the other sentences. Classcheck.

	Greeting or goodbye	Introducing yourself	Asking for information
1 Hey Lucy!	✓		
2 Good morning.	✓		
3 I'm Jim Landry!		✓	
4 Could you spell your name?			✓
5 ID, please?			✓
6 You can call me Lucy.		✓	
7 Hello, everyone!	✓		
8 Is this room 2?			✓
9 See you later!	✓		

C ◉ **Make it personal** In groups of three, sts role-play being an instructor and two students in a yoga or capoeira class. Assign roles or let sts choose their own. Refer sts to the sentences in B and the model dialogue in the speech bubbles. Give them time to plan what they're going to say or even to write down mini-dialogues. Monitor their preparation and offer help when necessary. In their groups, sts act out being at the class, introducing themselves, asking for and giving information, and saying goodbye to each other.

> **Weaker classes** You might find it helpful to give each student pre-set lines and have them organize / role-play the dialogue using those lines.

2

2.1 Are you a student?

1 Vocabulary Countries and nationalities

A ▶2.1 Follow the instructions.
1 Do the country quiz. Match photos a–g to countries 1–7.
2 Read the text about nationalities. Then complete the words in the quiz.
3 Use the pink stressed letters to guess the pronunciation. Then listen, check, and repeat.

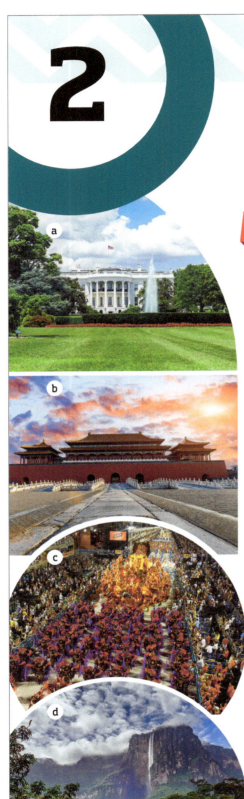

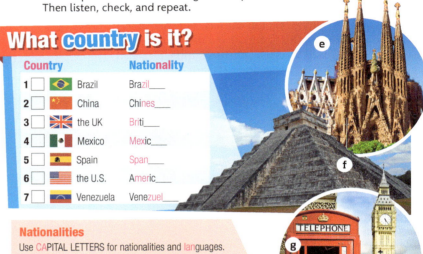

What country is it?

	Country	Nationality
1 ☐	Brazil	Brazil___
2 ☐	China	Chines___
3 ☐	the UK	Briti___
4 ☐	Mexico	Mexic___
5 ☐	Spain	Span___
6 ☐	the U.S.	Americ___
7 ☐	Venezuela	Venezuel___

Nationalities
Use CAPITAL LETTERS for nationalities and languages.
In the Americas, 35 nationalities end in *-an*, *-ian*, or *-ean*.
For example, Costa Rican, Peruvian, Chilean.
-ish and *-ese* are common endings too.
For example, Spanish, Portuguese, Japanese.

B ▶2.2 Listen and follow the model. Practice the sentences.

Where are you from? – Brazil.   I'm from Brazil. I'm Brazilian.

C 🎤 Make it personal   In pairs, ask and answer. Imagine new identities!

What's your name?   I'm Son Heung-min.

Where are you from?   I'm from Chuncheon. I'm South Korean.

2 Grammar *I am / you are* ➕ ➖

A ▶2.3 Read the *Guess who?* game. Who is it? Listen to check your answer.

Are you from Australia?
Yes, I am.

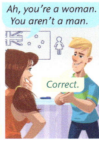

Ah, you're a woman. You aren't a man.
Correct.

Are you an actor?
No, I'm not.

OK, I'm a woman. I'm Australian. I'm not an actor. I'm a musician! Who am I?
I know! You're …

18

Unit overview: In the context of talking about countries and nationalities, sts review singular forms of verb *be* and learn and practice plural forms. They practice using opinion adjectives to talk about people and things, and learn and practice numbers 13–100+.

2.1 Are you a student?

Lesson aims: Sts learn and practice nouns and adjectives to describe countries and nationalities. They practice verb *be* – *I am* and *You are*, numbers 13–20, and plurals.

Function
Name countries and nationalities.
Ask and answer questions about nationalities and personal information.
Counting 13–20.

Language
I'm Brazilian. I'm from Brazil.
Are you from Australia? Are you an actor? Yes, I am. / No, I'm not.
Thirteen dollars.

Vocabulary: Numbers 13-20. Countries and nationalities (Brazil, Brazilian, China, Chinese, the UK, British, Mexico, Mexican, Spain, Spanish, the U.S., American, Venezuela, Venezuelan).
Grammar: Verb *be* – *I am* and *You are*. Suffixes *-ian*, *-ish*, *-ese*, *-an* for nationality adjectives.

Warm-up Briefly review verb *be* questions, spelling names, and saying phone numbers and email addresses. Write the question prompts below on the board. Elicit and drill all questions. Then have sts ask and answer them in pairs. Change roles. Monitor closely for accuracy.

Hello. How / you?
What / your last name?
Spell that, please?
Where / you from?
What / your phone number?
What / your email address?

1 Vocabulary Countries and nationalities

A Use the photos to pre-teach some vocabulary items: *a palace, a waterfall, a telephone box, a pyramid, a festival, a cathedral*. Point to each of photos a–g, or use the **Digital Book for Teachers** and ask: *What's this?* Prompt / Present the new items, saying, e.g.: *It's a cathedral / a palace*, etc. Have sts repeat the new words after you. For photo a, ask: *What's this?* Elicit "The White House", or tell sts what it is. Ask: *Who lives in The White House?* (The President of the U.S.).

Point to photo e and ask: *Where's this cathedral? Is it in China?* (It's in Spain.) Ask sts to write the letter *e* next to Spain in the Country column of the quiz. Sts then match the other photos to the countries. Paircheck. Do not correct sts at this stage.

Read the information on nationalities with the class and tell them to complete the nationalities in the quiz. Paircheck. Elicit their guesses about the pronunciation of each country but don't correct sts yet. Play ⏵2.1 and ask them to listen, check answers, and notice pronunciation. Play it again and say: *Listen and repeat*.

⏵2.1 Turn to p. 169 for the complete audioscript.

1 c Brazilian   2 b Chinese   3 g British   4 f Mexican
5 e Spanish   6 a American   7 d Venezuelan

B Point to the speech bubbles and say: *Listen and follow the model*. Play ⏵2.2 up to "Your turn" and the first beep and prompt. Elicit the correct response (I'm from the U.S. I'm American), and continue playing the track for sts to check. Play the rest of the track and after each prompt pick a different st to transform the model. Correct any errors in pronunciation of nationalities, then play the audio again so sts can practice.

⏵2.2 Turn to p. 169 for the complete audioscript.

C 🎙 **Make it personal**   Point to the speech bubbles. Read the instructions and demonstrate the activity with a student by inventing a new name and nationality. Sts do this in pairs. Tell them to change pairs and repeat the activity three or four times.

Tip Add challenge by telling sts to ask each other to spell their new names.

♪ **Song line:** Turn to p. 177 for notes about this song and an accompanying task.

2 Grammar *I am / you are* ➕ ➖

A Point to the cartoon strip and read it with the class. Ask: *Do you know this game?* (It exists in many languages and cultures.). Say: *So, she's Australian. She's a singer. Who is it?* Elicit some ideas, then play ⏵2.3 and tell sts to listen and check the answer. Ask: *Do you know Sia? Do you like her music?*

⏵2.3 Turn to p. 169 for the complete audioscript.

Sia

B Reread the game in **A** and complete the grammar box.

Positive +	Negative −
I _____ from Brazil.	I _____ a singer.
You _____ an actor.	You _____ a teacher.
Question ?	**Short answers**
Am I a student?	Yes, I _____. / No, I _____.
_____ you Chilean?	Yes, you are. / No, you aren't.

➔ Grammar 2A p. 74

♫ And I got my hands up,
They're playing my song,
I know I'm gonna be ok,
Yeah, it's a party in the USA.

Common mistakes

Are you ~~p~~araguayan? → P

I'm ~~politician~~. → a

C Circle the correct words.

1
A Your / You're Colombian.
B Correct!
A Am / Are you an actor?
B No, I'm not / I not.
A OK. You am not / aren't an actor.
   Am / Are you a musician?
B Yes, I am / I'm.
A Oh, you am / 're …!

2
A You're / Are you Puerto Rican?
B Yes, I am / am.
A Are / Are you a director?
B Yes, and I'm / I an actor too.
A Be / Are you …?

D 🎤 **Make it personal** In pairs, play **Guess who?**
A: Be a famous person. Draw or mime clues for your partner.
B: Ask questions and guess who **A** is. Then change roles.

Are you Latin American?

3 Vocabulary Numbers 13–20 and plurals

A ▶ 2.4 Match photos a–h to the numbers. Listen, check, and repeat.

☐ thirteen   ☐ fifteen   ☐ seventeen   ☐ nineteen
☐ fourteen   ☐ sixteen   ☐ eighteen   ☐ twenty

B ▶ 2.5 Listen and match the words to the photos in **A**. Then in pairs, cover the words and remember the phrase for each photo.

☐ apartment   ☐ channel   ☐ dollars   ☐ Happy birthday
☐ kilos   ☐ liters   ☐ miles per hour   ☐ kilometers

Twenty dollars.

C 🎤 **Make it personal** In pairs, play the game, then change roles.
A: Write a number with your finger on **B**'s back.
B: Say the number.

B Point to the grammar box and elicit the answer to the first gap (am). Tell sts to read the speech bubbles in **A** and complete the other gaps in the grammar box. Classcheck.

Common mistakes Read with the class. Explain we always put *a* or *an* before jobs. Sts often have problems with short answers, so spend time clarifying that we can't say *Yes, I'm.* or *Yes, you're.*

Language tip Portuguese and Spanish do not include an article before jobs: *Eu sou professor / Yo soy maestro*. Also, nationalities are not capitalized: *português, español,* etc

There is more information on *I am* and *You are* in Grammar 2A on p.74.

Tip Use this opportunity to review the rules for *a* and *an* and ask for examples of other jobs with *a* or *an*.

Positive: 'm, 're
Negative: 'm not, aren't
Question: Are
Short answers: am, 'm not

C Point to picture 1 and say: *Who is it? Hmm, I don't know.* Tell sts to look at the first sentence and ask: *Which is correct? "Your" or "You're"?* (You're). Then have sts circle the correct options in the two dialogues. Paircheck, then classcheck. Ask: *Who are they?*

Shakira and Benicio del Toro
1 You're, Are, I'm not, aren't, Are, I am, 're
2 Are you, I am, Are you, I'm, Are

D **Make it personal** Think of a famous person your sts will know and demonstrate the game with the class by giving clues for the sts to guess who you are. Put sts into pairs and have them play the game. Monitor and make a note of any errors you hear and write them on the board afterward, asking sts to correct the errors in their pairs. Then, check the corrections with the class.

Tip To help sts get used to correcting their errors, write some good sentences and errors on the board and tell sts to work in pairs to identify the sentences that have errors, and then correct the errors. At the end, go through the corrections with the class, leaving the corrected sentences on the board.

3 Vocabulary Numbers 13–20 and plurals

A **Books closed.** Review numbers 1–12. Use the board or show numbers with your hands and elicit their pronunciation. If time allows, ask: *How do you spell eight / eleven / twelve?* and write the words for these numbers only. Continue the sequence on the board and present numbers 13–20. Do not write the words. Drill pronunciation of all items before sts look at written forms in the book.

Books open. Point to photos a–h and have sts match them to the number words. Paircheck. Play 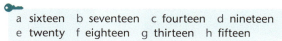 2.4 twice to check answers. Classcheck with answers on the board, and check word stress using the pink letters.

▶ 2.4 Turn to p. 169 for the complete audioscript.

a sixteen   b seventeen   c fourteen   d nineteen
e twenty   f eighteen   g thirteen   h fifteen

B Drill pronunciation of all words, again drawing attention to word stress. Point to the photos in **A** and ask: *Which photo is about "Happy birthday"?* (Photo f). Sts match the words to photos a–h in **A**. Paircheck. Play ▶ 2.5 and tell sts to listen and check answers. Classcheck with answers on the board.

Ask sts to cover the words in **A** and **B**. Point to photo c in **A** and ask: *Do you remember the phrase?* (apartment 14). In pairs, sts take turns saying the numbers and phrases for each photo. Monitor closely for pronunciation. Correct on the spot. At the end, ask the class: *Which phrase was the most difficult to remember?*

Tip Point out we add *-s* to make plurals in *kilo, dollar,* etc. Note that all these plurals are pronounced /z/. Drill these words with the class.

▶ 2.5 Turn to p. 169 for the complete audioscript.

apartment, c
kilos, d
channel, b
liters, g
dollars, e
miles per hour, h
Happy birthday, f
kilometers, a

C **Make it personal** Ask a student to stand up, facing the board and with her / his back to the class. With your finger, write *3* on her / his back. Make it visible to the rest of the class, and ask her / him: *What's the number?* Try again if she / he can't guess.

In pairs, have sts do the same. Tell them to write numbers between 1 and 20 only. Walk around the classroom and keep a note of any pronunciation mistakes. After three minutes, ask sts to change partners and play the game again. Round off the activity by drilling correct pronunciation of numbers.

2.2 Who's your favorite actor?

1 Grammar *he / she / it is* ⊕ ⊖ and personal pronouns

A Match headlines a–g to photos 1–7.

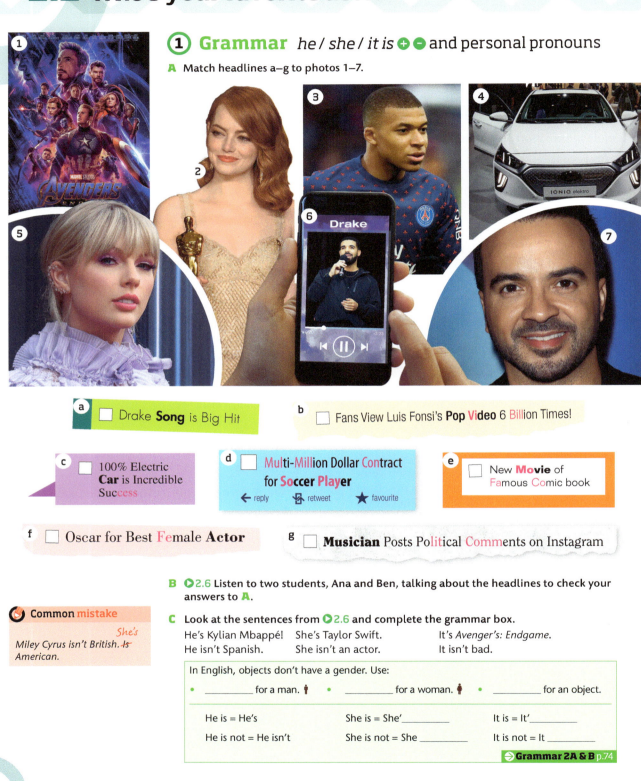

a ☐ Drake **S**ong is Big Hit

b ☐ Fans View Luis Fonsi's **P**op **V**ideo 6 **B**illion Times!

c ☐ 100% Electric **C**ar is Incredible Su**cc**ess

d ☐ Multi-**M**illion Dollar **C**ontract for **S**occer **P**layer
← reply ⇄ retweet ★ favourite

e ☐ New **M**ovie of **F**amous **C**omic book

f ☐ Oscar for Best **F**emale **A**ctor

g ☐ **M**usician Posts Po**l**itical **C**omments on Instagram

B ▶2.6 Listen to two students, Ana and Ben, talking about the headlines to check your answers to **A**.

C Look at the sentences from ▶2.6 and complete the grammar box.

He's Kylian Mbappé!   She's Taylor Swift.   It's *Avenger's: Endgame*.
He isn't Spanish.   She isn't an actor.   It isn't bad.

In English, objects don't have a gender. Use:
• _____ for a man. 👤 • _____ for a woman. 👤 • _____ for an object.
He is = He's   She is = She'_____   It is = It'_____
He is not = He isn't   She is not = She _____   It is not = It _____

➡ Grammar 2A & B p.74

⚠ Common mistake
Miley Cyrus isn't British. ~~Is~~ *She's* American.

2.2 Who's your favorite actor?

Lesson aims: Sts practice verb *be* for *he*, *she* and *it* in the context of famous people, and learn and use opinion adjectives.

Function
Reading newspaper headlines.
Describing and asking and answering questions about famous people, things, and places.
Reviewing nationalities.

Language
He's Drake. She's Taylor Swift. It's a movie.
She's American.
She's an actor. He isn't a musician.
Big Ben is in London.
It's a fantastic song. It's a terrible movie.

Vocabulary: Adjectives (fantastic, incredible, good, OK, not very good, bad, terrible, horrible). Jobs (actor, politician, director, musician, soccer player, dancer). Things (car, camera, video game, band, fast-food restaurant, city, pizza, song, sport, animal).
Grammar: Review verb *be*. Adjectives.

Warm-up Books closed. Play *Guess who?* from **D** on p. 19 with the class. Then tell them to play one round of the game in pairs.

1 Grammar *he / she / it is* ⊕ ⊖

A Books closed. Pre-teach *newspaper, online news*, and *headlines*. If possible, show the class a real newspaper and ask: *What's this in English?* Say: *It's a newspaper.* and have sts repeat *newspaper* after you. If technology is available, display an online news website in English and ask: *Do you read newspapers or online news?* Point to the headlines on the newspaper / the online news website or both, and tell sts they are *headlines*. Say: *Let's see the headlines in our books.*

Books open. Point to headlines a–g and photos 1–7 and elicit which photo headline a (Drake Song is Big Hit) relates to (photo 6). Sts read headlines and match them to photos 1–7. Paircheck.

a 6 b 7 c 4 d 3 e 1 f 2 g 5

B Say: *Listen to students Ana and Ben talking about the headlines, and check your answers.* Play ▶2.6. Replay the track if necessary. Classcheck.

▶2.6 Turn to p. 169 for the complete audioscript.

C Write *Taylor Swift is_____* on the board and ask: *Where is she from?* (America). Say: *So, she is …?* Elicit "American." Point to *is* and say: *We use this for 3rd person* (hold up three fingers). Read the six sentences with the class and complete the grammar box together.

There is more information on verb *be* and personal pronouns in Grammar 2A & 2B on p. 74.

Common mistakes Read with the class and remind sts that we always need a subject in English.

Language tip Compare English usage with their L1, where they may not need a subject pronoun when using the equivalent of the verb *be*. (*Es de Italia.* and *Él es de Italia.* are both correct in Spanish, for example.)

he, she, it; s, isn't, s, isn't

2.2

D In pairs, do the quiz. Circle the correct words. Then make sentences.

♪ *Bad things, It's a lot of bad things, That they wishin' and wishin', They wishin' on me, Bad things.*

1. Hollywood is in **New York** / **Los Angeles**.
2. Penelope Cruz is **Spanish** / **Mexican**.
3. Justin Trudeau is **a Canadian** / **an American** politician.
4. A Porsche is **an Italian** / **a German** car.
5. Big Ben is in **Paris** / **London**.
6. Cardi B is **Brazilian** / **American**.
7. Sushi is **Japanese** / **Chinese**.
8. Shaun Mendes is **a director** / **a musician**.
9. Mohammed Salah is a **soccer player** / **dancer**.
10. Samsung is a **Chinese** / **South Korean** company.

Hollywood isn't in New York. It's in Los Angeles.

E ▶ 2.7 Listen and follow the model. Practice the sentences.

Taylor Swift is a musician.   *She's a musician.*   *A Porsche is a car.*   *It's a car.*

F 🔵 **Make it personal** In pairs, write six quiz sentences about famous people, places, and things. Give your quiz to another pair. How many do you get right?

2 Vocabulary Adjectives (1)

A ▶ 2.8 Listen to Ana and Ben and check the four photos in **1A** they mention.

B ▶ 2.8 Listen again and circle the four adjectives from this chart that you hear. Then complete the speech bubbles. Remember to use *a* or *an*.

OPINION ADJECTIVES

👍 fantastic — incredible — good — OK — not very good — bad — terrible — horrible 👎

It's _____ song.
I think he's _____ musician.
I think she's _____ actor!
I think it's _____ movie!

C Study Common mistakes, then circle the correct rules in the grammar box.

Adjective order
Adjectives go **before** / **after** nouns and have **only one form** / **a singular and plural form**.
an American woman   two digital cameras   a fantastic car

➡ Grammar 2C p.74

🔴 **Common mistakes**
She's an actor ⟨excellent⟩.
I love restaurants ⟨Italian⟩.
They're singers ⟨fantastic⟩.

D Match sentences 1–4 to the responses.
1. Who's your favorite actor?
2. Ariana Grande is an incredible musician.
3. What's your favorite movie?
4. *Fortnite* is a terrible video game.

☐ I agree. She's fantastic!
☐ I disagree. I think it's good!
☐ Scarlett Johansson. I think she's incredible.
☐ *Bohemian Rhapsody*. I love the band Queen.

E ▶ 2.9 Listen and follow the model. Practice the sentences.

She's a very good politician. – Terrible.   *She's a terrible politician.*   *He*   *He's a terrible politician.*

F 🔵 **Make it personal** In groups, ask for and give opinions about your favorite people and things. Where possible, use the adjectives in **2B**. Any differences of opinion?

actor	animal	car	celebrity
city	fast food restaurant		
pizza	musician	song	sport

What's your favorite fast food restaurant?
I don't know. / Hmm, it's a difficult question.
It's ... I think it's incredible.

Who's your favorite celebrity?
It's Bradley Cooper. He's fantastic.
I agree. / I disagree. I think he's ...

D Point to the quiz and ask sts: *Do you like quizzes? Let's test what you know! What's number 1? New York or Los Angeles?* (Los Angeles). Then point to the speech bubbles and model for sts to repeat: *Hollywood isn't in New York. It's in Los Angeles.* Write the speech bubbles on the board and show how we can replace *Hollywood* with *It's*. Tell sts to circle the correct words in sentences 1–10. Paircheck. Then, in pairs, have sts make sentences using *he / she / it* for 1–10, using the speech bubbles as a model. Monitor and prompt self-correction if you hear errors. Ask sts: *Is Hollywood in New York?* and elicit a full response (No, it isn't. It's in Los Angeles.) Do the same for the other sentences, but don't do them in order and try to do it quickly to make it more fun.

1 Los Angeles
2 Spanish
3 a Canadian
4 a German
5 London
6 American
7 Japanese
8 a musician
9 soccer player
10 South Korean

E Point to the speech bubbles and say: *Listen and follow the model.* Play ▶2.7 up to "Your turn" and the first pair of beeps, before and after the st prompt. Pause the track and elicit the response from the whole class (He's a politician). Resume playing the track for sts to check their answer and listen for the next prompt. After each pair of beeps, pick a different st to respond. Correct any errors, then play the track again so sts can practice.

▶2.7 Turn to p. 169 for the complete audioscript.

F 🟢 **Make it personal** Tell sts to work in pairs. Say: *Now you write a quiz.* Point to exercise D and tell them: *You do the same. Write six quiz sentences for your classmates.* Make sure sts understand they have to include two options in their sentences, one correct and one incorrect. Set a time limit for writing the quiz. Monitor and help, and encourage sts to look for information online in their L1 if they are struggling with ideas for their sentences. Tell sts to exchange quizzes with another pair and do the quiz. When they've finished, have the two pairs correct the quizzes together. Ask: *Did you get all the sentences correct?*

2 Vocabulary Adjectives (1)

🎵 **Song line:** Turn to p. 177 for notes about this song and an accompanying task.

A Tell sts to listen to Ana and Ben and check the four photos in 1A they mention. Play ▶2.8 once or twice. Classcheck.

▶2.8 Turn to p. 169 for the complete audioscript.

1, 2, 5, 6

B Point to the cline diagram and show sts the thumbs up and thumbs down symbols to indicate very good and very bad. Read out the adjectives and then play ▶2.8 again so sts can listen and circle the adjectives they hear. Paircheck, then classcheck. Play the track again and tell sts to listen and complete the speech bubbles. Classcheck.

fantastic, incredible, good, terrible;
an incredible, a fantastic, a good, a terrible

Tip Ask sts to practice the pronunciation of the longer adjectives, using the letters in pink to help them. Listen and find a st who has good pronunciation and use them as a model for some quick drilling.

C Ask: *Do adjectives go before nouns in your language?* and elicit a couple of examples.

▶ **Common mistakes** Read with the class, and ask them to notice the position of the adjectives. Complete the grammar box with the class and clarify we don't make adjectives plural, e.g. we can't say *two reds cars*.

There is more information on adjectives in Grammar 2C on p. 74.

before, only one form

D Ask sts: *Who's your favorite singer?* Elicit some replies and then ask sts to match sentences 1–4 to the correct responses. Classcheck.

Tip Tell sts to work in pairs to practice the mini dialogues. Encourage them to try to say them from memory, with books closed.

1 Scarlett Johansson. I think she's incredible.
2 I agree. She's fantastic!
3 *Bohemian Rhapsody*. I love the band Queen.
4 I disagree. I think it's good!

E Point to the speech bubbles and say: *Listen and follow the model.* Play ▶2.9 up to "Your turn" and the first pair of beeps, before and after the prompt. Pause the track and elicit the response from the whole class (He's a fantastic actor.). Resume playing the track for sts to check the answer and listen for the next prompt. After each pair of beeps, pick a different student to respond. Correct any errors, then play the track again so sts can practice.

▶2.9 Turn to p. 169 for the complete audioscript.

F 🟢 **Make it personal** Point to the words in the box and the speech bubbles. Demonstrate the activity with two sts by asking the questions and having the sts respond. Put sts into groups of three and tell them to take turns asking and answering about their favorite people / things. Monitor and make a note of good language and errors. Write both on the board and ask sts to identify the errors and correct them. Then tell sts to make new groups of three and have them repeat the activity, but not making the same mistakes.

Extra writing Ask sts to research information about a famous person or thing (they can do this in L1) and write a short description (without writing the name of the person / thing). Then, they give their descriptions to another st who has to guess who or what it is about.

2.3 Is ceviche Mexican?

1 Grammar *Is he / she / it ...?*

A ▶ 2.10 Listen to Ana and Ben talking about *This Week* magazine. Which two photos do they talk about?

Images from around the world **this week**

B ▶ 2.10 Listen again, read, and complete the dialogue.

Ana Look at this ___photo___.
Ben What's her name? Oh, I don't remember. She's a fantastic _____.
Ana Yes, and she's a model too! Is she from _____?
Ben No, she isn't! She's from _____. Oh, what's her _____?!
Ana Sorry, I don't remember. Hey, what's _____?
Ben It's a berimbau, a musical instrument.
Ana Wow! Is it _____?
Ben No, it isn't! It's from _____.
Ana What's the name again?
Ben A berimbau. Oh, and she's Sofía Vergara.
Ana Yes, correct!

C Reread the dialogue and complete the grammar box with *is* or *isn't*.

Question ❓		Short answers					
	he a student?	Yes,	he		No,	he	
	she Mexican?		she			she	
	it a good pop video?		it			it	

→ Grammar 2A p.74

D ▶ 2.11 Listen and follow the model. Practice the sentences.

She's Brazilian. Question.   Is she Brazilian?   Negative.   She isn't Brazilian.

2.3 Is ceviche Mexican?

Lesson aims: Sts learn and practice question forms of verb *be* in the 3rd person singular, and learn and use numbers 20–100+ with more plural nouns.

Function
Listening to people talk about magazine photos.
Asking and answering questions about famous people and things.
Saying, writing, and understanding numbers 20–100+.

Language
Is he a student? Yes, he is. / No, he isn't.
What's her name? Who is he?
Eighty. Thirty-four.
1998. 2008.
How old are you? I'm 19 (years old).

Vocabulary: Numbers 20–100+. Years (2008, 1999).
Grammar: Verb *be* ? + − *he, she, it*

Warm-up Books closed. Review introductions and describing people. Play some cheerful background music and ask sts to stand up. Say: *We're at a party! You are famous people. Walk around and find out who you all are and where you are from.* Model the activity using the following dialogue. Walk up to a student and say: *Hello! What's your name?* Encourage them to say the name of a famous person. Say: *Nice to meet you.* and encourage them to respond. Ask: *Where are you from?* The student replies, e.g. "I'm from Mexico." Sts mingle, greeting classmates and asking and answering questions as if they were famous people. Monitor and offer help if necessary.

Then, tell sts to sit down and ask: *Who did you meet at the party?* Write *I met ...* on the board, and elicit a description of a person they met. Tell sts to tell their partner who they met, where they are from, and an opinion about them, e.g. *I met Rhianna and she's from Barbados! She's a musician, and she's great!*

Weaker classes Leave the model dialogue on the board.
1 Hi! What's your name?
2 Hi! I'm Rhianna. Nice to meet you.
1 Wow. Hi Rhianna. Nice to meet you too.
2 What's your name?
1 I'm Drake.
2 Cool. Where are you from Drake?
1 I'm from the U.S. ...

1 Grammar *Is he / she / it ...?*

A Books open. Point to the headline and teach the word *magazine*. Elicit what sts can see in the photos by pointing to them one at a time and asking: *What / Who's this? Where's she / he / it from?*

Ask sts to cover the dialogue. Tell them they're going to listen to Ana and Ben talking about the magazine. Ask: *Which photos do they mention?* Play ▶2.10. Paircheck. Replay the track. Classcheck.

▶2.10 Turn to p. 169 for the complete audioscript.

7, 5

B Sts uncover the dialogue. Replay ▶2.10 for sts to listen and fill in the blanks. Paircheck. Classcheck with answers on the board. Tell sts to practice the dialogue with a partner.

Tip Ask sts to tell each other what other things they know about the people and things in the photos, e.g. Photo 7: She's in *Modern Family*. She's Colombian. Photo 6: It's Mexican food. It's tortillas, meat, chiles, and tomatoes.

actor, Peru, Colombia, name, this, Chinese, Brazil

C Ask sts to reread the dialogue. Point to the grammar box and tell sts to complete it. Paircheck, then classcheck. Remind sts we can't contract *he / she / is* in short answers.

There is more information about *Is he / she / it ...?* in Grammar 2A on p. 74.

Question: Is
Short answers: is, isn't

D Point to the speech bubbles and say: *Listen and follow the model.* Play ▶2.11 up to "Your turn" and the first pair of beeps, before and after the student prompt. Pause the track and elicit the correct question from the whole class (Is it a fantastic song?). Resume playing the track for sts to check their answer and listen for the next prompt. Make sure they understand that the next prompt asks for a negative sentence. After each pair of beeps, pick a different student to respond. Correct any errors, then play the track again so sts can practice.

▶2.11 Turn to p. 170 for the complete audioscript.

2.3

E Put the words in order. Find the items in photos 1–7. Then write a similar dialogue for the other three photos.

1 A is / Who / he / ?
   B entrepreneur / He / an / 's
   A British / he / Is / ?
   B he / No, / isn't / 's / American / He

2 A this / 's / What / ?
   B game / It / video / 's / a
   A a / Is / game / it / good / ?
   B is / Yes, / it

♪ *You are the dancing queen, Young and sweet, only seventeen.*

F 🔊 Make it personal In groups, play *10 questions*. Give your opinion of a very famous place / person / thing. Your group has only 10 chances to guess.

I think he's fantastic. *No, he isn't.* *Yes, he is.*
OK, it's a man. Is he an actor? *Is he American?*

> **⏱ Common mistake**
> What's ~~the~~ name ~~of he~~? *his*
> Use *his* for a man, *her* for a woman.

2 Vocabulary Numbers 20-100+ and plurals (2)

A ▶ 2.12 Match the words to the numbers. Listen, check, and write the extra word you hear for each number.

eigh**ty**   fif**ty**   for**ty**   a hun**dred**   nine**ty**
sev**enty**   six**ty**   thir**ty**   twen**ty**

20 _____   30 _____   40 _____   50 _____   60 _____
70 _____   80 _____   90 _____   100 _____

B ▶ 2.13 Listen and (circle) the correct ages.

1 21 / 22 / 23
2 36 / 38 / 41
3 49 / 54 / 62
4 75 / 85 / 95

C ▶ 2.14 Listen and follow the model. Practice the numbers.

12 + 3   *fifteen*   24 + 10   *thirty-four*

D 🔊 Make it personal Read the information and answer 1–4.

Numbers
- Use a **hy**phen in numbers from 21 to 99: *twenty-one, thirty-two, forty-three.*
- Say years as two numbers: 1998 = *nineteen ninety-eight*; 2018 = *twenty eighteen*.
- To talk about age, use *be* + age + *years old* (**op**tional): *I'm seventeen (years old)*.

1 What year is it? And the next three years?
2 What's your year of birth?
3 What's your lucky number?
4 How old are you? Ask the whole class and form an age line.

> **⏱ Common mistakes**
> How ~~many years you have~~? *old are you?*
> I ~~have~~ 19 ~~years~~. *am* *old*

How old are you?
I'm ... years and ... months old.

E Put dialogue 1 in order with the class, and tell them to do the same for dialogue 2. Paircheck, then classcheck, and ask: *Which photo is dialogue one / two?* (photo 1: Mark Zuckerberg / photo 3: a video game). Tell sts to write similar dialogues for the other three photos (2, 4, 6) and make it clear they should not include the name of the person or thing. Sts can write the dialogue individually or in pairs. Monitor and help with ideas and language, and prompt self-correction of errors you see. Tell sts to give their dialogues to another pair to read and guess the photos they relate to.

Common mistakes Read with the class to clarify the use of *his* and *her*. Point to different sts and prompt the rest of the class to ask chorally: "What's his name? / What's her name?" Answer the class when they say it correctly.

Tip Encourage peer correction of any errors in the dialogues.

1 A: Who is he?
B: He's an entrepreneur.
A: Is he British?
B: No, he isn't. He's American. (Photo 1)
2 A: What's this?
B: It's a video game.
A: Is it a good game?
B: Yes, it is. (Photo 3)

F **Make it personal** In groups of three or four, sts play *10 Questions*. Use the model in the speech bubbles to demonstrate the activity. Think of a famous actor and read aloud the first speech bubble: *I think he's fantastic*. Get sts to ask you the next speech bubble, "OK, it's a man. Is he an actor?". Carry on until sts guess your actor. Explain sts can ask up to 10 questions. Elicit "Is he / she ...?" questions if necessary, with prompts, e.g. musician / actor / Colombian, etc.

In their groups, each student chooses a famous place, person, or thing. Other group members ask up to 10 questions and try to guess who / what the mystery thing is. Walk around the classroom and keep a record of sts' mistakes for delayed correction. At the end, ask which place / person / thing was the most difficult to guess in each group.

2 Vocabulary Numbers 20-100+ and plurals (2)

🎵 **Song line:** Turn to p. 177 for notes about this song and an accompanying task.

A Books closed. Write *20* on the board and ask: *What's this in English? How do you spell it?* Write *twenty* as sts spell it for you. Write / Teach *30 / thirty* and underline the suffix *-ty* in both words.

Books open. Have sts complete the chart with the number words 30–100. Tell sts to listen and check their answers, and write the extra word they hear after each number. Play ▶2.12. Paircheck, then play the track again to classcheck answers and drill pronunciation of all numbers, referring to the pink letters to show word stress.

Language tip Sts tend to confuse the pronunciation of *-teen* and *-ty* numbers. Write *19* and *90* on the board and ask: *What number?* Say: *Ninety*, and elicit the correct answer. Draw Oo and oO on the board and ask: *Which is 90?* (Oo). Clarify the difference in word stress between *-teen* and *-ty* suffixes.

▶2.12 Turn to p. 170 for the complete audioscript.

20 twenty tablets
30 thirty things
40 forty photos
50 fifty phones
60 sixty students
70 seventy seconds
80 eighty trains
90 ninety notebooks
100 a hundred hamburgers

B Show sts an old object (or a photo of it) and say, e.g.: *This pen is very old ... It's 30 years old!* Point to the photo of the car and ask: *How old is it? Listen and circle.* Play dialogue 1, ▶2.13 and pause for sts to circle the answer (23). Classcheck. Play the rest of the recording. Paircheck. Replay the track if necessary. Classcheck with answers on the board.

▶2.13 Turn to p. 170 for the complete audioscript.

1 23   2 38   3 49   4 95

C Write on the board $15 + 2 =$ _____ and elicit the sum from sts (17). Point to the speech bubbles and say: *Listen and follow the model.* Play ▶2.14 up to "Your turn" and the first pair of beeps, before and after the student prompt. Pause the track and elicit the correct answer (twenty-seven) from the whole class. Resume playing the track for sts to check their answer and listen for the next prompt.

Make it a game and set a time limit, e.g. five seconds, to say the correct sum. After each pair of beeps, pick a different student to respond. Ask for choral repetition now and then, e.g. after a student gets a number right, the whole class repeats.

▶2.14 Turn to p. 170 for the complete audioscript.

D **Make it personal** Ask some sts: *How old are you?* to see if they can answer correctly. Don't correct mistakes yet.

Common mistakes Read with the class. Point out that we use verb *be* to talk about age.

Language tip Portuguese and Spanish use the equivalent of *have* to talk about age: *Tenho 18 anos. Tengo 18 años.* (not *be* as in English: *I am 18 years old.*) For this reason, the question to ask about age is also different. Tell sts that the errors in Common mistakes are a direct result of translating incorrectly from their L1.

Read the information box about numbers with the class. Then have them work in pairs to ask and answer the questions.

If appropriate, have sts form an age line. Point to the speech bubbles and ask: *How old are you?* Sts reply with their age in years and months. Have all sts stand up and mingle, asking and answering "How old are you?" to form an age line, from youngest to eldest. When they've finished forming the line, briefly have each student say how old he / she is to check line order.

2.4 Where are your two favorite places?

1 Vocabulary Adjectives (2)

A ▶2.15 Match photos 1–14 to these adjectives. Listen, check, and repeat.

beautiful ☐ / ugly ☐   hot ☐ / cold ☐   big ☐ / small ☐
expensive ☐ / cheap ☐   friendly ☐ / unfriendly ☐
old ☐ / new ☐   happy ☐ / unhappy ☐

B ▶2.16 Listen and follow the model. Practice the opposite adjectives.

What's the opposite of hot?   cold

C 🎤 Make it personal In pairs, write a sentence (true or false) for each adjective. Exchange your sentences with another pair and guess true or false.

The students in this school are friendly. My tablet is very old!

It's true. The students are very friendly.

2 Reading

A ▶2.17 Read and listen to the online chat and circle the correct answers.
1 Roberto and Maria are on vacation in **Bogotá / Lima / Mexico City**.
2 They are having **a terrible / a great** time.

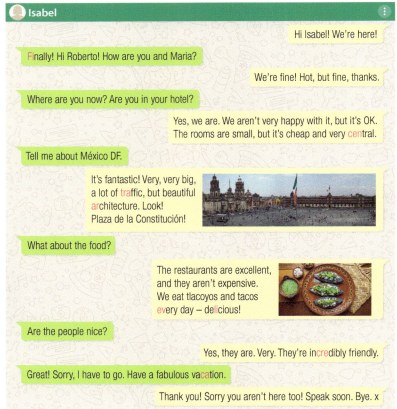

Isabel

Hi Isabel! We're here!

Finally! Hi Roberto! How are you and Maria?

We're fine! Hot, but fine, thanks.

Where are you now? Are you in your hotel?

Yes, we are. We aren't very happy with it, but it's OK. The rooms are small, but it's cheap and very central.

Tell me about México DF.

It's fantastic! Very, very big, a lot of traffic, but beautiful architecture. Look! Plaza de la Constitución!

What about the food?

The restaurants are excellent, and they aren't expensive. We eat tlacoyos and tacos every day – delicious!

Are the people nice?

Yes, they are. Very. They're incredibly friendly.

Great! Sorry, I have to go. Have a fabulous vacation.

Thank you! Sorry you aren't here too! Speak soon. Bye. x

2.4 Where are your two favorite places?

Lesson aims: Sts learn adjectives to describe places, people, and food, and write an online chat about a vacation.

Function
Describing people, places, and things.
Reading an online chat.
Describing a vacation.

Language
It's hot.
The people are friendly.
Hi Ana! We're here!
Is the hotel nice? Yes, it's fantastic!
Are the restaurants expensive? Yes, they are. / No, they're not.

Vocabulary: Adjectives (beautiful / ugly, hot / cold, big / small, expensive / cheap, friendly /unfriendly, old / new, happy / unhappy)
Grammar: Plural forms of verb *be* ➕ ➖ ❓ with contractions

Warm-up Do a dictation of commonly confused numbers. Make sure sts have paper and a pen / pencil and then dictate these numbers:

19 30 50 16 90 60 80 18 15

Ask a volunteer to come to the board and write the numbers. Ask sts: *Is this correct?* Correct errors with the class and ask sts to practice the pronunciation of the numbers in pairs, focusing on word stress.

Sts can then do their own dictations in pairs if they need more practice.

1 Vocabulary Adjectives (2)

A Point to photo 1 and ask: *Where is it?* (the desert). Teach the correct pronunciation, then point to *hot / cold* in the word box and ask: *Is it hot or cold there?* (hot). Tell sts to complete the matching activity. Play ▶ 2.15 so sts can check answers. Play ▶ 2.15 again and tell sts to listen and repeat.

> **Language tip** Focus on the pronunciation of *friendly* and *beautiful* as sts sometimes mispronounce the vowels and stress the wrong syllables. Write the transcriptions on the board to help them see how the vowels are pronounced /ˈfrendlɪ/ /ˈbjʊtɪfəl/.

Extra activity Ask sts to think of one more thing or person for each adjective and tell them to share ideas in pairs or small groups. Afterwards, ask: *What's big? What's beautiful?* and encourage sts to use full sentences in their replies.

▶ 2.15 Turn to p. 170 for the complete audioscript.

> beautiful 11 / ugly 12
> hot 1 / cold 2
> big 5 / small 6
> expensive 3 / cheap 4
> friendly 9 / unfriendly 10
> old 7 / new 8
> happy 13 / unhappy 14

B Tell sts to cover the adjectives in **A**. Point to the speech bubbles and say: *Listen and follow the model*. Play ▶ 2.16 up to "Your turn" and the first pair of beeps, before and after the student prompt. Pause the track and elicit the opposite from the whole class (expensive). Resume playing the track for sts to check their answer and listen for the next prompt. After each pair of beeps, pick a different student to say the opposite. Correct any errors, then play the track again for sts to practice.

▶ 2.16 Turn to p. 170 for the complete audioscript.

C **Make it personal** Tell sts they are going to write true or false sentences about the adjectives in **A**. Tell them to read the speech bubbles, then elicit example sentences for a couple of the adjectives and write them on the board. Have sts do the activity in pairs, then exchange their sentences with another pair and guess whether they're true or false. Tell sts that some people might disagree on what is, e.g. beautiful or ugly, so tell sts these are just opinions.

> **Tip** Tell sts they can write eight to twelve sentences. Giving a minimum and maximum number of sentences can help to differentiate for levels and abilities in your class.

2 Reading

A Tell sts to look at the text and say: *This is an online chat between Roberto and a friend. Roberto is on vacation with Maria. Read the text quickly.* After they have read, have them circle the correct answers in 1 and 2. Play ▶ 2.17 and tell sts to reread, listen, and check their answers. Paircheck, then classcheck.

▶ 2.17 Turn to p. 170 for the complete audioscript.

> 1 Mexico City
> 2 a great

B Test your memory. Cover the online chat in **2A**. Which adjectives in **1A** describe …

1 the hotel?
2 the city?
3 the food?
4 the people?

🎵 *Are we human, or are we dancer? My sign is vital, my hands are cold, And I'm on my knees looking for the answer.*

3 Grammar *you / we / they are* ➕ ➖ ❓

A Reread the chat in **2A** and complete the plural forms in the grammar box.

Positive ➕		Negative ➖	
You're fine.		You _____ unhappy.	
We _____ finally here.		We _____ in an expensive hotel.	
They _____ very friendly.		They _____ difficult.	
Question ❓		**Short answers**	
_____ you in your hotel?	Yes,	we	No,	we	aren't.
_____ we good friends?		you		you	
_____ the restaurants expensive?		they		they	
Contractions: _____ = you are we're = we are _____ = they are			

> **Common mistakes**
> ~~Are the tacos~~
> The tacos are delicious?
> ~~they are.~~ Very.
> Yes, ~~are very.~~

➡️ **Grammar 2A** p.74

B ▶ 2.18 Listen and follow the model. Practice the sentences.

They're friendly. – Negative.   *They aren't friendly.*   *Question.*   *Are they friendly?*

C ▶ 2.19 Read the message and add *is / isn't* and *are / aren't*. Use contractions where possible. Listen to check.

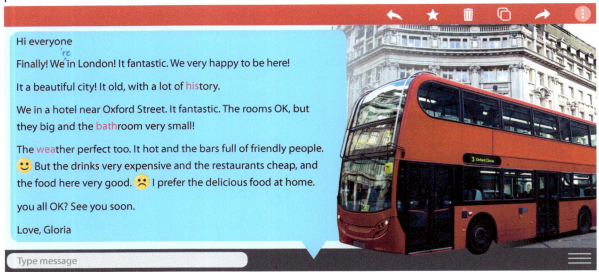

Hi everyone
Finally! We're in London! It _____ fantastic. We _____ very happy to be here!

It _____ a beautiful city! It _____ old, with a lot of history.

We _____ in a hotel near Oxford Street. It _____ fantastic. The rooms _____ OK, but they _____ big and the bathroom _____ very small!

The weather _____ perfect too. It _____ hot and the bars _____ full of friendly people. 🙂 But the drinks _____ very expensive and the restaurants _____ cheap, and the food here _____ very good. 😟 I prefer the delicious food at home.

_____ you all OK? See you soon.

Love, Gloria

D 🟢 **Make it personal** *Fantasy vacation!* In pairs, imagine you're on a special vacation. Imagine the place, the hotel, the food, the people, what's good and what's bad. Write an online chat with a friend at home.

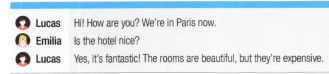

Lucas: Hi! How are you? We're in Paris now.
Emilia: Is the hotel nice?
Lucas: Yes, it's fantastic! The rooms are beautiful, but they're expensive.

2.4

B Tell sts to cover the text in **A**. Ask: *How do Roberto and Maria feel? How are they?* (They are fine, but hot.). Tell sts to work in pairs and remember the adjectives for 1–4. Set a time limit of three minutes, then tell sts to look at the text and see if they were correct. Classcheck. Correct any errors in pronunciation you heard while they were doing the activity.

> 1 small, cheap
> 2 fantastic, big, beautiful
> 3 delicious (restaurants: excellent, not expensive)
> 4 nice, friendly

3 Grammar *you / we / they are* ➕ ➖ ❓

Common mistakes Write *The tacos are delicious?* on the board and ask: *Is this correct?* Elicit the correct form and point to Common mistakes. Ask sts to think of other foods they could ask about and elicit some examples.

Look at the second incorrect sentence and ask sts to identify the error (the subject is missing).

Language tip Keep reminding sts that word order for questions in English is different from their L1 (where word order does not change).

A Write *Robert and Maria _____ friends.* on the board and elicit what word goes in the gap (are). Ask: *When do we use "are"?* (with plural *you*, *we*, and *they*) to see if sts know the grammar. Direct them to the grammar box and tell them to complete it. Paircheck, then classcheck to teach the pronunciation of the contracted forms.

There is more information on questions using *you / we / they are* in Grammar 2A on p. 74.

> Positive: are, are
> Negative: aren't, aren't, aren't
> Question: Are
> Short answers: are
> Contractions: you're, they're

B Point to the speech bubbles and say: *Listen and follow the model*. Play ▶2.18 up to "Your turn" and the first pair of beeps, before and after the student prompt. Pause the track and elicit the response from the whole class (Are the restaurants expensive?). Resume playing the track for sts to check their answer and listen for the next prompt. After each pair of beeps, pick a different student to respond. Correct any errors, then play the track again so sts can practice.

▶2.18 Turn to p. 170 for the complete audioscript.

♪ **Song line**: Turn to p. 177 for notes about this song and an accompanying task.

C Point to the photo of the bus and ask: *Where is it?* (London). Tell sts to read the message quickly. Ask: *What's good and bad about Gloria's vacation?* Elicit some answers to check sts understand the text. Point out the example in the text and write *We're in London!* on the board. Tell sts to read the text again and add the missing verbs, using contractions where possible. Paircheck, then play ▶2.19 so sts can listen and check their answers. Classcheck on the board.

Tip Display the text on the board or IWB, and mark the corrections.

> Hi everyone
> Finally! We**'re** in London! It**'s** fantastic. We**'re** very happy to be here!
> It**'s** a beautiful city! It**'s** old, with a lot of history.
> We**'re** in a hotel near Oxford Street. It**'s** fantastic. The rooms **are** OK, but they **aren't** big and the bathroom **is** very small! The weather **is** perfect too. It**'s** hot and the bars **are** full of friendly people. But the drinks **are** very expensive and the restaurants **aren't** cheap, and the food here **isn't** very good. I prefer the delicious food at home.
> **Are** you all OK? See you soon.
> Love, Gloria

Tip It is a good idea to ask sts to read texts in language exercises like this before focusing on grammar, so the practice is clearer and more meaningful. Tell sts to read the texts quickly and ask a couple of comprehension questions to engage them with the text, then do the grammar work.

Extra activity Point to the *Type message* box below the text, and ask sts to write a short reply to Gloria. Ask sts to compare their replies in pairs. Ask: *Are your replies similar?* Then, tell them to check their grammar together and encourage peer correction. Monitor and help sts.

D 🎤 **Make it personal** Write *Fantasy vacation* on the board and ask: *Where is your fantasy vacation?* Write their locations on the board. Ask: *Is the hotel big or small on your fantasy vacation? And the rooms?* Elicit adjectives. Explain the task by showing them the example, and tell sts to write their own online chat in pairs. They could also do this for homework.

Alternative activity You could do this in a more interactive way. After the same lead-in above, give each student a piece of recycled paper and tell them to write an opening message, similar to Lucas at the top of their page. Then, they exchange papers with a partner and write a reply and question. They exchange again and carry on writing the conversation as if they were texting on a phone. Then they read the texts with their partner, say what they like about the dialogue, and correct any errors in grammar or spelling.

2.5 Is English essential for your future?

Skills Reading for general comprehension

A Read the text. Choose the best ending for the title. Which other languages are international?

1. essential for Latin America   2. a global language   3. the language of business

English – ...

English is an essential language in the modern world. In over 100 countries, it is part of the school curriculum and the most important international language for government, education, business, media, and art. Chinese politicians use English to communicate with American politicians, Brazilian artists with Nigerian artists, Russian scientists with Japanese scientists. Globally, over two billion people speak or study English.

It's THE international language of this planet.

B ▶ 2.20 Listen and reread. Underline all the cognates. Then circle the words you don't understand. In pairs, can you guess the meaning?

Common mistake

~~I need the English for the~~ *my* job.

C Why do you need English? Check your top three reasons. Can you find a classmate with exactly the same reasons?

- [ ] to travel
- [ ] to meet and communicate with new people
- [ ] to get a good job
- [ ] to study in the future
- [ ] to get a certificate
- [ ] to understand music and movies
- [ ] for pleasure

D ▶ 2.21 Listen and number the questions in the order you hear them, 1–9.

- [ ] Who are the girls?
- [ ] Where are they from?
- [ ] Where's he from?
- [ ] How old are they?
- [ ] Who's she?
- [ ] How old is he?
- [ ] Is he married?
- [ ] Where's she from?
- [ ] What city is he from?

E ▶ 2.21 Listen again and complete profiles 1–3. Are they famous in your country?

1
Name: Ryan Gosling / actor
Nationality: _____ (London, Ontario)
Age: _____
Marital status: _____

2
Name: Girls Generation / musicians
Nationality: _____ (Seoul)
Age: _____
Marital status: _____

3
Name: Simona Halep / tennis player
Nationality: _____ (Constanta)
Age: _____
Marital status: _____

F ▶ 2.22 Listen and follow the model. Practice the questions.

How old – she   How old is she?

G **Make it personal** In pairs, ask questions and complete the form. Change partners, and ask and answer about your old partners.

What city are you from?

Where's your old partner from?

Name: _____   City: _____
Nationality: _____   Marital status: _____
Age: _____

2.5 Is English essential for your future?

Lesson aims: Sts continue to practice verb *be* and ask and answer questions about people. Sts use cognates and context to develop reading comprehension skills.

Function
Reading a text about English as a global language.
Listening to people talk about celebrities.
Asking and answering questions about other people.

Language
English is an international language.
Who's he? I have no idea.
How old is she?

Vocabulary: Cognates (official, government, communicate, scientists, artists, etc.). Phrases (You're right! I don't know. No idea).
Grammar: Review verb *be*

Warm-up Tell the class you're thinking of a number. Write 20–50 on the board and say: *My secret number is between 20 and 50*. Write it on a piece of paper but don't let the class see it. Sts try to guess the secret number. Ask each student to write down one guess only, between 20 and 50. Sts say their guesses. The student whose guess is closest to your number is the winner. If there's time, play the game again with a number between 50 and 100.

ID SKILLS Reading for general comprehension

A Point to the title of the lesson and ask sts the question. Then ask: *Do you agree?* Elicit some ideas. Tell sts to read the text and choose the best ending 1–3 for the title (2). Paircheck. Classcheck.

B Play ▶2.20 and tell sts to listen and reread the text in **A**. Ask them to underline words they think are similar in their language (remind them of the meaning of *cognates*).

Sts then circle any words they don't know, and work in pairs to guess the meaning of these new words. Classcheck.

Language tip Tell sts that while cognates look similar to words in their L1, the stress and pronunciation are often very different. This may mean that, if sts only hear the words, they do not recognize them as cognates because they sound so different to their L1. Emphasize the importance of keeping a record of pronunciation. Remind sts to use the pink letters to help with the pronunciation of the English words.

essential, language, modern, curriculum, important, international, government, education, media, art, politicians, communicate, artists, scientists, globally, billion, study, planet

Common mistakes Tell sts these are common mistakes due to translation from their L1. Remind them we do not use *the* before the names of languages in English, and we say *my job* (not *the job*).

C Ask sts: *Why do we need English?* Elicit ideas and then tell sts to read the eight reasons in the book. Pre-teach the meaning of *certificate* and *for pleasure*, then tell sts to check their top three reasons. Put sts into groups of four and ask them to compare their choices. Ask: *Who has exactly the same reasons?*

D Tell sts to listen to a conversation and ask: *What are they talking about?* Play ▶2.21 and tell sts to compare their ideas in pairs. Then ask one or two sts to tell the class what the conversation is about. Tell sts to read the questions quickly, then replay ▶2.21 and ask sts to write the order of the questions, 1–9. Paircheck, then classcheck.

▶2.21 Turn to p. 170 for the complete audioscript.

1 Where's he from?
2 What city is he from?
3 How old is he?
4 Is he married?
5 Who are the girls?
6 Where are they from?
7 How old are they?
8 Who's she?
9 Where's she from?

E Direct sts to the ID badges and ask them to complete the information. Play ▶2.21 again and tell sts to listen and check their answers. Paircheck, then classcheck.

Tip If sts found the listening difficult, ask them to look at the transcript and play the track one more time.

1 Canadian, around 38, married
2 South Korean, –, single
3 Romanian, around 30, married (the woman says "I think she's married.")

F Point to the speech bubbles and say: *Listen and follow the model*. Play ▶2.22 up to "Your turn" and the first pair of beeps, before and after the student prompt. Pause the track and elicit the question from the whole class (How old is he?). Resume playing the track for sts to check their answer and listen for the next prompt. After each pair of beeps, pick a different student to respond.

▶2.22 Turn to p. 170 for the complete audioscript.

G Make it personal Point to the yellow form and elicit the correct question for each item, e.g. *What's your name?* Write the questions on the board. Then invite sts to ask you the questions. Refer sts to the speech bubbles, and have them complete the form in pairs. Then, in new pairs, they ask and answer about their old partners. Model this with a student, asking: *What's her name?*, etc.

How old is Ariana Grande?

*We're up all night to the sun.
We're up all night to get some.
We're up all night for good fun.
We're up all night to get lucky.*

ID in Action Sharing information about other people

A ▶ 2.23 Match 1–6 to the responses. Listen, check, and repeat.

1. Where's he from?
2. Are you sure?
3. How old is he?
4. Is he married?
5. How old are they?
6. She's a tennis player.

- [ ] You're right. Number one in the world.
- [ ] I don't know. No idea.
- [ ] Yes, he is.
- [1] I think he's from the U.S.
- [ ] Hmm. No, he's Canadian!
- [ ] He's around 38.

B Respond to 1–6. Use the expressions in **A** to help you. In pairs, practice.

1. Justin Bieber is a fantastic singer.
2. Ariana Grande is British.
3. How old is Adam Levine?
4. Is Adele married?
5. Coldplay are American tennis players.
6. Are Kim Kardashian and Kanye West married?

C **Make it personal** In groups, share information about these celebrities. Do you know them all?

the JB · Married? · DL · From? · Who? · VD · ND · LS · ZE · BE · MM & CA · Your opinion? · How old?

Who's Dua Lipa? — I have no idea. — I think she's an American singer. — No, she's from the UK.

2.5 How old is Ariana Grande?

Lesson aims: Sts review verb *be* questions to share information about celebrities.

Function
Asking for and giving information about other people.

Language
Where's he from? He's from the U.S.
How old is she? She's around 22.

Vocabulary: Review adjectives (fantastic, good, bad). Marital status (single, married, divorced, separated).
Grammar: Verb *be* ❓

ID in action Sharing information about other people

🎵 **Song line:** Turn to p. 178 for notes about this song and an accompanying task.

A Have sts read both columns and play ▶2.23 so they can match 1–6 to the correct responses. Paircheck. Replay the track and have sts listen, check their answers, and repeat.

Ask sts to read the lesson title and ask sts to guess the answer. Tell the class that Ariana Grande was born on June 26, 1993, so ask sts to calculate her age now.

Tell sts they are going to share information about other famous people in this lesson.

▶2.23 Turn to p. 170 for the complete audioscript.

> 1 I think he's from the U.S.
> 2 Hmm. No, he's Canadian!
> 3 He's around 38.
> 4 Yes, he is.
> 5 I don't know. No idea.
> 6 You're right. Number one in the world.

B In pairs, sts take turns starting mini-dialogues with sentences 1–6 and responding with phrases from **A**. Monitor and help with pronunciation.

C **Make it personal** Model the activity. Point to the questions and responses in **A** and have sts ask you / other sts in the class about famous people, for example Billie Eilish. Encourage the use of phrases *I don't know.*, *I have no idea.*, etc. In groups of three or four, sts ask and share information about the celebrities in the photos. Direct sts to the question prompts and the speech bubbles. Tell sts they can also use the initials to help them identify the celebrities. Afterwards, elicit the names of all the celebrities, then ask: *Who's your favorite celebrity here? Why do you like him / her?*

Extra activity Ask sts to research one of the people / groups in this lesson and write a short profile using language from Unit 2. If they did the Extra writing activity in lesson **2.2**, they can compare their profiles now to the descriptions they wrote then to see how their English has improved.

➡ **Workbook** p. 94

➡ Ⓓ **Richmond Learning Platform**

➡ **Writing** p. 28

➡ Ⓓ **Café** p. 29

Writing 2 A blog post

♪ *Maybe I'm crazy,
Maybe you're crazy,
Maybe we're crazy,
Probably ooh hmm.*

A ▶ 2.24 Look at the photos on Victor's blog post. Where is he? Read the first sentence and check.

B Read the blog post and put sentences 1–4 in the correct place.
1 It's small, but the breakfast in the morning is very big!
2 Where are you at the moment?
3 Mission Dolores was founded in 1776.
4 It's not very hot, but not too cold.

Victor's Adventures

It's fantastic here in San Francisco, California! We're very happy. It's a beautiful city with a lot of history. Parts of the city are very old. ☐ And the cable cars are from 1873! We're in a new hotel near Lombard Street. ☐ That's good because restaurants are expensive here. The people are very friendly in this city, and the weather is perfect. ☐ What about you? ☐ Tell me in the comments below.

C Read *Write it right!* Find the 11 adjectives Victor uses to describe 1–7.
1 the city (2) *fantastic* _____
2 parts of San Francisco (1) _____
3 the people (1) _____
4 the weather (3) _____ _____ _____
5 the restaurants (1) _____
6 the hotel (2) _____ _____
7 the breakfast (1) _____

✓ **Write it right!**

Use a variety of adjectives to make your writing interesting. Adjectives do NOT have plural forms.
The hotels are cheap. NOT ~~cheaps~~
Use a plural verb after *people*.
The people are very nice. NOT ~~The people is ...~~

D Singular or plural? (Circle) the correct form of *be*.
1 The food here in Peru **is / are** delicious.
2 My city **is / are** famous for chocolate cakes.
3 The famous places there **isn't / aren't** very interesting.
4 Costa Rican bananas **is / are** incredible, and cheap.
5 The taxis in Switzerland **is / are** very, very expensive.
6 The big hotel in my street **isn't / aren't** very good.

E Think of a place you know or want to visit. Write one or two different adjectives to describe the following:
- the city
- parts of the city
- the people
- the weather
- the food
- the restaurants
- other famous or important things

F   **Make it personal** Imagine you are visiting your place from **E**. Write a blog post about it.

Before	Read Victor's blog and plan what you want to say.
While	Use your adjectives in **E** to describe your place. Check the forms of the verb *be*.
After	Share your blog post with a partner. Check it for mistakes. Send it to your teacher.

28

Writing 2 A blog post

♪ **Song line:** Turn to p. 178 for notes about this song and an accompanying task.

A If you can, display the blog image using the **Digital Book for Teachers**. Point to Victor and explain he writes a travel blog. Point to the photos and ask: *Where is Victor?* Elicit some ideas and then tell sts to read the first sentence of the text to check. Ask sts: *What do you know about San Francisco?*

> He's in San Francisco.

B Ask sts to read sentences 1–4, then read the text. Tell them to put the sentences in the correct places in the text. Do sentence 1 as an example with weaker classes. Paircheck, then classcheck.

> 3 1 4 2

C Ask sts to read **Write it right!** and explain that adjectives help to make texts more interesting for the reader. Point out the example answer in 1, then ask sts to find the second adjective used to describe the city (beautiful). Ask sts to find the other adjectives and complete 2–7. Paircheck, then classcheck. Go over the pronunciation of the adjectives, paying attention to word stress in longer words.

> 1 beautiful
> 2 old
> 3 friendly
> 4 hot, cold, perfect
> 5 expensive
> 6 small, new
> 7 big

D Ask sts: *Do we say "The food is good." or "The food are good."?* to check grammar rules for plural nouns with verb *be*. (The food is good.) Ask them to complete 1–6, then paircheck and classcheck.

> 1 is
> 2 is
> 3 aren't
> 4 are
> 5 are
> 6 isn't

E Ask sts: *What cities would you like to visit?* Write their ideas on the board. Correct pronunciation of the cities. Point to the bullet points and ask sts to suggest adjectives to describe one of the cities on the board, e.g. Barcelona (beautiful city, old parts, friendly people, warm weather, delicious food, small restaurants, fantastic buildings, interesting monuments). Tell sts to choose a city they want to visit and write one or two adjectives to describe each item in the list.

F **Make it personal**

Before Tell sts they're going to write their own travel blog post about the city they chose in **E**. Ask them to reread Victor's blog and think about their own blog. What do they want to say?

During Sts write their blog posts using their adjectives from **E**. Monitor and check their writing is accurate. Help sts self-correct any errors in adjectives and forms of verb *be*.

After Put sts into pairs and ask them to read each other's blog posts. Ask them to find three good sentences and one or two errors. Tell them to work together to correct the errors. If they wrote their posts electronically, they could email them to you. Alternatively, they could display them around the room, and do a gallery reading task where they read each other's posts and add comments, as in Victor's blog.

2 People, places, passports!

 Café

1 Before watching

A Look at the flags and characters. Then, in pairs, ask and answer about their nationalities.

Where's she from? What's her nationality?

She's from Argentina and the U.S. She's Argentinian and American.

2 While watching

A Watch until 0:57. Circle the correct word.
1. Daniel's friend is a computer **programmer** / **technician**.
2. The computer server is **up** / **down**.
3. Their yoga class is on **Monday** / **Tuesday**.
4. Lucy, August and Andrea go to the **Argentinian** / **International** school.
5. Lucy's **American** / **Argentinian** now.
6. Daniel's from the **Midwest** / **South**.

B Watch from 0:57 to 1:36 and check Daniel (D), Rory (R), Lucy (L), or Genevieve (G). Where's Andrea now?

D	R	L	G	
				goes to computer class.
				is American.
				is Canadian.
				is originally Irish.
				has a new passport.
				is from two countries.

C Watch from 1:36 to the end. Who's …
1. Lucy's favourite actor?
2. almost 19?
3. 20 in July?
4. giving a party on Friday?
5. invited to the party?
6. going to a class now?

D Watch the last part and write the girls' phone numbers.

3 After watching

A Order the words in 1–5 to make questions. In pairs, ask and answer. Use contractions.
1. you / where / from / are / originally / ?
2. birthday / your / when / 's / ?
3. your / cell / what / 's / number / ?
4. favorite / who / 's / your / actor / ?
5. he / from / she / or / where / 's / ?

Where are you from originally from?

I'm from Montevideo, Uruguay.

B What do we say? Check the situation for expressions 1–10: introductions (I), asking for information (AFI) or giving personal information (GPI).

Expressions	I	AFI	GPI
1 You're the computer technician here, right?			
2 You're from that yoga class, right?			
3 Lucy, meet Rory.			
4 I'm originally from Dublin, Ireland.			
5 Daniel, this is Genevieve.			
6 Good to meet you.			
7 My birthday's in July.			
8 Nice meeting you too.			
9 Oh. It's 847-555-1976.			
10 I'm almost 17.			

C ⬤ **Make it personal** In pairs, ask and answer using expressions from **B**.

Are you almost 21?

No, I'm only 18!

I'm sorry. When's your birthday?

It's October 4th.

ID Café 2 People, places, passports!

1 Before watching

A Point to the photos and check if sts can recognize the four characters from ID Café 1: Lucy, Daniel, Andrea, and August. The two new characters are Rory and Genevieve.

Ask: *Where's Lucy from? What's her nationality?* Point to both flags on her photo and elicit the answer, "She's from Argentina and the U.S. She's Argentinian and American." In pairs, sts ask and answer about the characters' nationalities, referring to the flags on the photos and the model dialogue in the speech bubbles. Classcheck. At the end, check if any of your sts have dual nationality like Lucy.

2 While watching

A Have sts read questions 1–6. Play ▶ 2 without subtitles until 0:57. Sts circle the correct words, then paircheck. Replay the video if necessary. Classcheck.

> 1 technician
> 2 down
> 3 Tuesday
> 4 International
> 5 American
> 6 Midwest

B Have sts look at the chart and explain D is for Daniel, R is for Rory, L is for Lucy, and G is for Genevieve. Tell sts they're going to watch more of the video. They check the correct columns in the table. Play ▶ 2 from 0:57 to 1:36. Paircheck, then classcheck. Ask: *Where's Andrea now?* (in class)

> goes to computer class: D, R
> is American: D, R, L
> is Canadian: G
> is originally Irish: R
> has a new passport: L
> is from two countries: R, L, G

C Ask the class: *Who's Lucy's favorite actor?* Elicit the answer (Rachel McAdams), and then tell sts to read questions 1–6. Play ▶ 2 from 1:36 to the end. Sts answer the questions, then paircheck. Classcheck.

> 1 Rachel McAdams
> 2 Lucy
> 3 Genevieve
> 4 Lucy
> 5 Genevieve, Daniel, Rory
> 6 Daniel, Rory

D Tell sts to listen carefully and try to write down Lucy's and Genevieve's phone numbers. Play ▶ 2 from 2:14 and pause after each set of numbers so sts have time to write. Paircheck (playing the video again if necessary), then classcheck.

> G: 847 555 1976 L: 312 555 2468

3 After watching

A Tell sts to look at 1, and put the words in the correct order to make a question. Elicit the question and write it on the board: *Where are you from originally?* Sts reorder 2–5. Classcheck with answers on the board.

In pairs, sts take turns asking and answering 1–5. Refer them to the speech bubbles for help, and remind them to use contractions. Monitor closely for accuracy and correct errors on the spot.

> 1 Where are you from originally?
> 2 When's your birthday?
> 3 What's your cell number?
> 4 Who's your favorite actor?
> 5 Where's he or she from?

B Point to the chart headings and explain that I is introductions, AFI is asking for information, and GPI is giving personal information. Read expression 1 and have sts check the correct situation (AFI). Classcheck. Sts do the same for expressions 2–10 and paircheck. Classcheck with answers on the board.

> 1 AFI 2 AFI 3 I 4 GPI 5 I 6 I 7 GPI 8 I
> 9 GPI 10 GPI

C **Make it personal** Get sts to sit next to a partner they haven't worked with recently. Provide them with some prompts on the board such as *phone number*, *birthday*, *age*, *name*, *nationality*. Elicit questions for each topic on the board. In pairs, sts take turns asking and answering questions. Refer them to the speech bubbles for help, and encourage them to use the questions on the board and expressions from **B**.

R1 Grammar and vocabulary

A *Picture dictionary.* Cover the words on these pages and remember.

page	
7	numbers 1–12
	12 items similar in your language
8	6 classroom language expressions
10	12 classroom objects
12	26 letters of the alphabet
14	pronunciation of 11 cognates
15	5 ways to say *Hi*, and 5 ways to say *Bye*
18	7 countries and nationalities
19	numbers 13–20 and 7 plural nouns
21	8 opinion adjectives
23	numbers 20–100
24	14 more opinion adjectives

B 🔴 **Make it personal** Choose a verb and write a list of instructions with that verb. Compare your lists—score 1 point for each correct sentence. Who's the winner?

listen (to)   look (at)   read   repeat
say   write

Say your name.
Don't say…

C Add the verb *be* in the correct place. Use contractions where possible.
1 What your name?
2 How old you?
3 you married?
4 What your phone number?
5 Who Greta Thunberg?
6 Robert Pattinson from the UK?
7 Where the Backstreet Boys from?
8 this a pen or a pencil?

D ⊙ R1.1 Now complete the answers and match them to questions 1–8 in **C**. Listen to check.
☐ Yes, he _____. He's from London.
☐ Yes, I _____. But I don't have children.
☐ She _____ a young activist from Sweden.
☐ It _____ a mechanical pencil!
☐ They _____ from Orlando. _____ American.
☐ I _____ 23 years old. And you?
☐ My name _____ Carmen.
☐ My cell? It _____ 41-8777-4883.

E 🔴 **Make it personal** In pairs, ask and answer 1–4 in **C** and adapt 5–8 with locally relevant examples.

F Work in pairs. **A:** Spell the name of a country. **B:** Say what the nationality is. Then change roles.

A country: C-H-I-N-A. The nationality?   Chinese.

G Write four addition problems. Don't show them to your partner. Say them for your partner to answer.

What's four plus seven plus eighteen?   Twenty-nine.

H In groups of three, play **Mime!** Choose three items from photos in units 1 and 2. Mime them for your partners to name. Then change roles.

What's this?   I think it's a tablet.

I Correct the mistakes. Check your answers in units 1 and 2.

▶ **Common mistakes**
1 Please look the text and listen the dialogue. (2 mistakes)
2 I from Brazil. Where you from? (2 mistakes)
3 Hello, good night! Good meet you! (2 mistakes)
4 Mariah Carey's musician. (1 mistake)
5 Who's she? Is British actor. (2 mistakes)
6 This's car. (2 mistakes)
7 What's this? Is my new tablet. (1 mistake)
8 You are a doctor? (1 mistake)
9 She's singer fantastic! (2 mistakes)
10 I have 35 years. (2 mistakes)

Review 1 Units 1-2

Grammar and vocabulary

A **Picture dictionary.** Pairwork. Sts work together to review the main vocabulary items learned in units 1 and 2. Tell them to look at the pages in the list, cover the words on those pages, and, using the pictures, remember as many of the vocabulary items as they can. Remind sts to use the pink syllables to help with pronunciation. Monitor as sts work and correct pronunciation where necessary.

> **Tip** In order to provide sts with as much fluency practice as possible, expand the activity into mini-dialogues based on the key language on the pages listed in the chart. For example, on p. 7 sts can take turns saying numbers 1–12, and pointing to pictures of cognates for their partner to remember.

B **Make it personal** Split the class into six groups. Assign each group a different verb from the box. Individually, sts write their own lists of possible classroom instructions using the group's verb. Within their groups, sts compare lists and score one point for each correct sentence. Ask sts to refer to p. 8 when checking answers. Classcheck and ask: *Who's the winner in your group?*

C Point to question 1 and elicit the full sentence from sts (What's your name?). Sts add the verb *be* in the correct place in the other sentences. Ask sts to use contractions where possible. Paircheck, then classcheck with answers on the board.

1. What**'s** your name?
2. How old **are** you?
3. **Are** you married?
4. What**'s** your phone number?
5. Who**'s** Greta Thunberg?
6. **Is** Robert Pattinson from the UK?
7. Where **are** the Backstreet Boys from?
8. **Is** this a pen or a pencil?

D Sts complete the answers with verb *be*. Paircheck. Then have the pairs match the answers to questions 1–8 in **C**. Play ▶R1.1 for sts to check answers. Classcheck by inviting individual sts to ask a question, then nominate another st to say the answer.

▶R1.1 Turn to p. 170 for the complete audioscript.

1. My name**'s** Carmen.
2. I**'m** 23 years old. And you?
3. Yes, I **am**. But I don't have children.
4. My cell? It**'s** 41-8777-4833.
5. She**'s** a young activist from Sweden.
6. Yes, he **is**. He's from London.
7. They**'re** from Orlando. **They're** American.
8. It**'s** a mechanical pencil!

E **Make it personal** In pairs, sts ask and answer questions 1–4 in **C**. Classcheck by asking sts about their partners, e.g. *What's his name? How old is he?*. Point to question 5 and demonstrate how to adapt it with local examples, ask: *Who's (name of a local president / actor / musician)?* Explain that sts have to change questions 5–8 to make them relevant to their country, culture, or an item in the classroom (for question 8). Then have sts take turns asking and answering their new questions in pairs. Monitor closely for accuracy. Have some sts ask their questions to the whole class.

F Model the activity. Point to the Chinese flag in the photos and spell China: *C-H-I-N-A*. Ask the class: *What's the nationality?* (Chinese). In pairs, sts take turns spelling the name of a country and saying the nationality. Refer them to the speech bubbles if they need help. Monitor closely for accuracy.

G Model the activity. Write *4 + 7 + 18* on the board. Say: *Four plus seven plus eighteen* and elicit the result from the whole class. Ask sts to write four addition problems on a piece of paper. Tell them to use only numbers 1–20. In new pairs, sts test each other. Ensure sts do not show their written sums to each other but say them, using the word "plus." Refer them to the model in the speech bubbles for guidance. Monitor closely for accuracy and, at the end, have some sts test the whole class.

H Model the activity. Choose an object from the photos / pictures in units 1 and 2 that is easy to mime and guess, e.g. the car on p. 23. Mime driving a car and elicit the answer. Point to the photo to confirm. Then ask sts to look at the photos / pictures in units 1 and 2, and choose three of them to mime. In groups of three, sts take turns miming their objects for their partners to guess.

> **Tip** Fast-finishers can carry on testing each other by asking "How do you spell …?" about some of the objects they've guessed.

I Point to Common mistakes and tell sts that there are two mistakes in number 1. Write the sentence on the board and elicit the corrections from the whole class. Tell sts it's now their turn to correct the sentences. Point out that the number of mistakes is in parentheses. In pairs, sts correct sentences 2–10. Whenever sts are uncertain, encourage them to look back through units 1 and 2 to check their answers. Classcheck with answers on the board.

1. Please look **at** the text and listen **to** the dialogue.
2. I**'m** from Brazil. Where **are** you from?
3. Hello, good **evening**! Good **to** meet you!
4. Mariah Carey**'s a** musician.
5. Who's she? She**'s a** British actor.
6. This **is a** car.
7. What's this? **It's** my new tablet.
8. **Are you** a doctor?
9. She's **a fantastic singer**!
10. I'm 35 (**years old**).

73

Skills practice

I am a giant. Stand up on my shoulders, tell me what you see.
I am a giant. (We'll be breaking boulders underneath our feet.)

R1

A ▶R1.2 Read the website bio and guess the missing words 1–12. Listen to check.

First name: Camila Carraro
Last ¹_____ : Mendes
Date of birth: June 29, 1994

Camila Mendes is ²_____ American actor. She's ³_____ Virginia, USA, but her family ⁴_____ from Brazil. Camila is a ⁵_____ beautiful woman, ⁶_____ she's ⁷_____ a number of movies. But she's internationally ⁸_____ for her part in the teen drama series *Riverdale* as Veronica Lodge. In the series, Veronica ⁹_____ the daughter of Hiram Lodge, the richest ¹⁰_____ in Riverdale. Camila ¹¹_____ also a graduate of the New York University Tisch School of the Arts. She speaks English and fluent ¹²_____.

B Reread and answer.
1. How old is Camila Mendes now?
2. True (T) or false (F)?
   a Camila's Brazilian.
   b She's a movie and television actor.
   c She's famous in many countries.
   d Her father is Hiram Lodge.

C 🔵 Make it personal Write your opinion of 1–4. Use adjectives from p. 18. Compare opinions with a partner. Do you agree?

| actor | car | movie | musician |

1. The BMW: *I think it's a fantastic car.*
2. Miley Cyrus: _____
3. Maggie Gylennhaal: _____
4. *Avengers: Endgame*: _____

D Choose a celebrity or place from the photos in unit 2 or your imagination. Work in pairs. **A**: Give information for **B** to guess who she, he, or it is. Then change roles.

She's an excellent American actor. She's about 30 years old, and I don't think she's married.

Is she Emma Stone?

E ▶R1.3 Listen. Where's Alessandra from?

F ▶R1.3 Complete the dialogue with these words. Listen to check. Practice in groups of three.

agree	are	call	city	evening	from
Italian	meet	nice	right	see	
thanks	this	too	where	you	

Eddy   Good _____, Paul. Good to _____ you.
Paul   Hello, Eddy. How are _____?
Eddy   I'm fine, _____. Paul, _____ is my friend Alessandra.
Paul   Nice to _____ you, Alessandra.
Sandra _____ to meet you _____. Please, _____ me Sandra.
Paul   _____ are you from, Sandra? Italy?
Eddy   Yes, you're _____. She's _____.
Paul   _____ you from Rome?
Sandra No, I'm _____ Siena.
Paul   Wow! Siena's a beautiful _____!
Sandra Yes, I _____!

G Mini role-play.
A: You and **B** are friends. Say hello. But you don't know **C**.
B: You're friends with **A** and **C**. Introduce **A** to **C**.
C: You don't know **A**. Respond to the introduction. Look at the dialogue in **F** for help.

H ▶R1.4 Listen to an interview with a student and complete column A in the form.

	A	B
Name		
Nationality		
Marital status	☐ single ☐ married ☐ divorced ☐ other	☐ single ☐ married ☐ divorced ☐ other
Age		
Phone number		
Email		

I 🔵 Make it personal In pairs, interview your partner and complete column B in the form.

J 🔵 Make it personal **Question time.**
In pairs, practice asking and answering the 12 lesson titles in units 1 and 2. Use the book map on p. 2–3. Where possible, ask follow-up questions, too. Can you comfortably ask and answer all the questions?

What's your name?   *My name's / I'm Ricardo, but call me Rick.*

Skills practice

🎵 **Song line:** Turn to p. 178 for notes about this song and an accompanying task.

A Ask sts to read the website bio and guess the missing words. Paircheck. Then play ▶R1.2 to classcheck the answers. Ask if any pairs guessed all the missing words correctly.

1 name	5 very	9 is
2 an	6 and	10 man
3 from	7 in	11 is
4 is	8 famous	12 Portuguese

▶R1.2 Turn to p. 170 for the complete audioscript.

B Ask sts to reread the text and answer the questions. Paircheck, then classcheck.

1 Sts calculate her age from her date of birth and the current date 2a F (Camila's American) 2b T 2c T 2d F (Hiram Lodge is the father of Camila's character Veronica in *Riverdale*.)

C 🔵 **Make it personal** Elicit / quickly drill pronunciation of the four words in the box. Point to *car* in the box and ask sts what number sentence it refers to (1). As a class, quickly match the other words in the box to sentences 2–4 (Miley Cyrus = musician, Maggie Gyllenhaal = actor, *Avengers: Endgame* = movie). Point out the example opinion (I think it's a fantastic car.) and tell sts to write their own opinions for 1–4. Tell them to use the opinion adjectives on p. 21. Monitor for accuracy.

Ask a st to read out their opinion for 1. Say: *I agree!* or *I don't know.* or *I disagree.* followed by a similar sentence to the sts, but using a different opinion adjective, e.g. *I think the BMW's an OK car.* In pairs, sts compare their opinions. Make sure they are speaking to each other and not just reading each other's sentences. Refer them to the speech bubbles in **E** on p. 21 if necessary. Classcheck by asking some pairs to compare their opinions for the class.

D **Books closed.** Model the activity. Give clues about a famous person or place for sts to guess.

Books open. Have sts read the model dialogue in the speech bubbles. Tell them to choose a famous person or place from Unit 2 or their own choice, and write three sentences about him / her / it. In pairs, sts take turns giving the information and guessing the answer. Encourage sts to come up with more information if their partners can't guess the answer after three sentences. Monitor closely for accuracy and offer help when necessary. Classcheck by having a few sts test the whole class.

E Tell sts they're going to hear three people talking. Ask sts to listen and answer the question. Play ▶R1.3 and elicit the answer.

▶R1.3 Turn to p. 170 for the complete audioscript.

Italy

F Elicit pronunciation of all the words in the box. Then have sts complete the conversation with the words. Paircheck. Play ▶R1.3 for sts to check answers. Classcheck with answers on the board.

Tip In groups of three, sts role-play the conversation. Monitor closely for intonation. At the end, ask one group to act out their dialogue to the whole class.

Eddy	Good **evening**, Paul. Good to **see** you.
Paul	Hello, Eddy. How **are** you?
Eddy	I'm fine, **thanks**. Paul, **this** is my friend Alessandra.
Paul	Nice to meet you, Alessandra.
Sandra	Nice to **meet** you **too**. Please, **call** me Sandra.
Paul	**Where** are you from, Sandra? Italy?
Eddy	Yes, you're **right**. She's **Italian**.
Paul	**Are** you from Rome?
Sandra	No, I'm **from** Siena.
Paul	Wow! Siena's a beautiful **city**!
Sandra	Yes, I **agree**!

G Read the instructions with the class. In groups of three, sts act out the situation, using the conversation in **F** as a model. Tell them to use their real names but pretend they don't know one of the group members. If necessary, demonstrate by role-playing the dialogue with two sts. Then have sts change partners to form new groups. They act out the dialogue once more. Monitor closely for accuracy and intonation. Ask a group to act out their conversation for the whole class.

H Tell sts they're going to listen to an interview with a student. Point to column A in the form and tell sts to complete it with the information they hear. Play ▶R1.4. Paircheck. Replay the track if necessary. Classcheck with answers on the board.

▶R1.4 Turn to p. 170 for the complete audioscript.

Column A
Name: Pablo Castillo
Nationality: Chilean
Marital status: married
Age: 36
Phone number: 312-8977-0346
Email: pabloc@qhy.net

I 🔵 **Make it personal** Pair sts with classmates they don't usually sit next to. Elicit the questions sts will need to interview their partner. Sts ask questions to complete column B about their partner. Ask some sts to tell the class about their partner.

J 🔵 **Make it personal** **Question time.** Sts look at the Language map on p. 2–3 and take turns asking and answering the lesson question titles from units 1 and 2. Monitor closely for accuracy and encourage sts to ask follow-up questions when appropriate. At the end, ask them how they felt performing the task: *Do you feel comfortable with all questions? Which ones are easy? Which ones are difficult?*

3

3.1 What do you do?

1 Vocabulary Jobs

A ▶3.1 How do you pronounce jobs a–e? Listen to an ad for a TV show to check. Then match photos 1–5 to jobs f–j.

a ___ bank ca**shier**
b ___ **doc**tor
c ___ engin**eer**
d ___ po**lice o**fficer
e ___ uni**ver**sity pro**fe**ssor

f ___ **law**yer /lɔjər/
g ___ **ser**ver
h ___ **hair**dresser
i ___ **sales** clerk /seɪlsklɜrk/
j ___ IT pro**fe**ssional

B Read the information and Common mistakes, then complete the jobs in **A** with *a* or *an*.

> The usual question for jobs is:
> *What do you do? What does he / she do?*
> To answer, use verb *be* + *a / an*:
> *I'm a student. / He's a den*tist.
> Be careful with adjectives: *He's re*tired.

Common mistakes

What ~~/~~ you do? → *do*
I'm ~~/~~ doctor and she's ~~/~~ architect. → *a* ... *an*
I'm ~~an~~ unemployed.
They're ~~a~~ doctors.

C ▶3.2 Listen to the TV show and match eight jobs from **A** to the participants. Which two jobs are not mentioned?

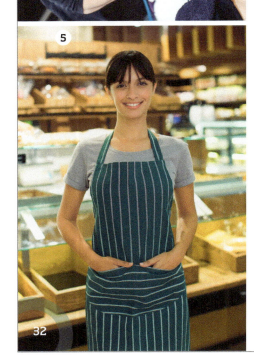

Unit overview: In the context of talking about jobs, family, and places of work, sts learn and practice simple present verbs. They also review indefinite articles *a* and *an,* and learn to use possessive adjectives and pronouns.

3.1 What do you do?

Lesson aims: Sts learn jobs vocabulary and language to talk about work. They also listen to an ad for a TV show and talk about TV series characters' jobs.

Function
Listening to an ad.
Understanding descriptions of jobs.
Asking and answering questions about jobs.
Talking about TV characters and their jobs.

Language
My name's Tessa and I'm a hairdresser.
What do you do? I'm an engineer. I want to be an actor.
Ross Geller's a university professor.

Vocabulary: Jobs (cognates: bank cashier, doctor, engineer, police officer, university professor; non-cognates: lawyer, server, hairdresser, salesclerk, IT professional). What do you do?
Grammar: Review indefinite articles *a / an*

Warm-up To set the context of famous TV series' characters and their jobs, start the class with an informal chat about the topic. Ask sts: *Do you like TV series? What's your favorite?* Elicit some shows and write them on the board, e.g. *House M.D., Friends, The Big Bang Theory*. If technology is available, show photos of episodes / characters and ask sts: *Who's your favorite TV character? What does he / she do? / What's his / her job?* Use this opportunity to pre-teach some jobs vocabulary sts will see in the lesson.

1 Vocabulary Jobs

A Point to the first column of jobs a–e and tell sts these words are cognates with their L1. Ask: *How do you pronounce the words?* Have sts guess pronunciation of a–e in pairs and ensure they notice the pink letters. Elicit guesses but don't correct them just yet. Tell sts they are going to listen to an ad for a TV show, and ask them to notice / check pronunciation of a–e. Play ▶3.1. Replay for choral repetition of each item.

Focus on photos 1–5. Point to the server in photo 2 and ask: *What does he do?* Prompt the answer and have sts repeat after you, "He's a server." Repeat with the rest of the photos. Then, get sts to quickly match jobs f–j to photos 1–5. Paircheck. Classcheck and drill pronunciation of the jobs.

▶3.1 Turn to p. 171 for the complete audioscript.

1 j   2 g   3 f   4 h   5 i

B **Common mistakes** Read with the class and remind sts about the rules for the indefinite article. Tell sts to complete the jobs in **A** with *a / an*. Paircheck, then classcheck with answers on the board.

Language tip L1 speakers of Portuguese and Spanish may find it difficult to remember the auxiliary verb when forming questions in English, because it is not used in their L1. Briefly explain that *do* in the question *What do you do?* is an auxiliary verb, which they will learn more about in the next lessons. Tell sts that the auxiliary is needed to form questions and negative sentences in English.

a a   b a   c an   d a   e a   f a   g a   h a   i a   j an

C Point to the picture and ask: *Do you know any TV shows like this?* Make sure sts understand that it is a game show with two families competing against each other. Tell sts to look at the names in the two families. Explain they have to listen for the jobs each person does. Play ▶3.2 and tell sts to match the participants to eight of the jobs in **A**. Paircheck. Replay the track, this time asking sts to listen for the two jobs in **A** that are not mentioned. Classcheck, correcting any errors with the pronunciation of jobs.

▶3.2 Turn to p. 171 for the complete audioscript.

Tessa: hairdresser
Paul: salesclerk
Gloria: lawyer
Fred: server
Maria: engineer
Roger: police officer
Sophia: bank cashier
James: IT professional
Not mentioned: doctor, university professor

D ▶ 3.3 Listen to extracts 1–9 and say *He / She* and the correct job in **A** after the beep.

🎵 *I want to be the one to walk in the sun, Oh girls they want to have fun, Oh girls just want to have fun.*

E In pairs, try to remember the people's jobs in **C**.

> *Tessa's a hairdresser.*

F 🎧 **Make it personal**

1 What do you do or what do you want to do? Ask your teacher for the name of your job in English if necessary. Complete the sentences.

| I'm _____. | I want to be _____. |

2 Ask your classmates about their jobs. Are you a student? What do you want to be? How many different jobs are there in the class?

> *What do you do?* *What do you want to be?*
> *I'm unemployed.* *I want to be a lawyer.*

2 Listening and Vocabulary Job suffixes

A ▶ 3.4 Listen to part two of *Fantastic Families*. Check the characters you hear and match them to their jobs.

1 Amy Farrah Fowler — *The Big Bang Theory* ☐
2 Ross Geller — *Friends* ☐
3 Jessica Pearson — *Suits* ☐
4 Conrad Hawkins — *The Resident* ☐

☐ doctor ☐ lawyer ☐ scientist ☐ university professor

B ▶ 3.5 Listen and follow the model. Practice the sentences.

> *Ross Geller – university professor* *He's a university professor.*

C Look at the characters and jobs in **A** again. What do the others do? Guess if you don't know.

> *I think Amy Farrah Fowler is a …* *You're right. / I'm not sure. / I don't know. / You're wrong.*

D ▶ 3.6 The most common suffixes for jobs are *-er* and *-or*. Complete these jobs, then use an online dictionary to check. Listen to the pronunciation.

an act___	a manag___	a profess___	a teach___
a bank___	a movie direct___	a programm___	a writ___
a doct___	an office work___	a serv___	
a hairdress___	a paint___	a soccer play___	
a lawy___	a police offic___	a taxi driv___	

E 🎧 **Make it personal** In groups, mime a job for the others to guess.

> *You're a writer.*

3.1

D Tell sts they are going to listen to clues about jobs and they have to guess the jobs after the beeps. Play ▶ 3.3 up to the first beep and ask: *What does she do?* Elicit "She's a lawyer." Play the rest of the track, pausing after each beep so sts can say the correct job.

▶ 3.3 Turn to p. 171 for the complete audioscript.

Tip Play the track again and ask sts to listen to the pronunciation of the different jobs. Pause after each job and tell sts to repeat.

E Point to Tessa in the picture in **1C** and say: *Tessa's a hairdresser*. Point to Paul and elicit the full sentence, "Paul's a salesclerk." In pairs, sts take turns remembering and saying what each family member does. Classcheck by having different sts say a sentence each.

F 🎧 **Make it personal**

1 Write on the board *I'm a teacher.* and ask a student: *What about you? What do you do?* Write their answer on the board. Then write on the board: *I want to be an opera singer.* (or choose any other job you would like to do). Ask sts what they want to be, and write a few answers on the board. Help with vocabulary as needed. Have sts complete the note about themselves, then compare with a partner. Remind them to use *a / an*. Monitor and help with names of jobs and spelling.

2 Use the speech bubbles to model the activity with a student. In pairs, sts ask and answer about what they do and what they want to be. Then have them change partners and repeat the activity. After they have finished, ask sts about their partners: *What does he / she do?* Finally, ask the class to say the names of all the jobs from this lesson. Make a list on the board and together count how many different jobs there are.

🎵 **Song line:** Turn to p. 178 for notes about this song and an accompanying task.

2 Listening and Vocabulary Job suffixes

A Point to photos 1–4 and check if sts know the shows / characters. Elicit what sts know, e.g. ask: *Where do they live in Friends?* (New York) *How many main characters are there in Friends?* (six). Point to the four jobs and tell sts to listen, check the characters they hear, and match them to their jobs. Play ▶ 3.4 once or twice. Paircheck, then classcheck.

▶ 3.4 Turn to p. 171 for the complete audioscript.

> Ross Geller = university professor
> Jessica Pearson = lawyer

B Transformation drill. Point to the speech bubbles and say: *Listen and follow the model.* Play ▶ 3.5 up to "Your turn" and the first pair of beeps, before and after the student prompt. Pause the track and elicit the response from the whole class (They're soccer players.). Resume playing the track for students to check their answer and listen for the next prompt. Vary the task by picking one student at a time, pairs, or the whole class to say the correct response. Correct any errors, then play the track again for sts to practice.

▶ 3.5 Turn to p. 171 for the complete audioscript.

C Ask sts to look at the photos in **A** again. In pairs, sts take turns saying what these characters do. Tell sts to guess if they don't know, and encourage them to use the language chunks in the speech bubbles. Then invite pairs to talk about the characters / jobs for the whole class.

D Write *act* _____ and *bank* _____ on the board and elicit the suffixes *-or* and *-er*. Tell sts to complete the other jobs. Paircheck, using an online dictionary if available. Play ▶ 3.6 so sts can listen and check answers. Then play the track again for sts to listen to the pronunciation and repeat.

> an actor, a banker, a doctor, a hairdresser, a lawyer, a manager, a movie director, an office worker, a painter, a police officer, a professor, a programmer, a server, a soccer player, a taxi driver, a teacher, a writer

Tip Tell sts that the suffixes are never stressed. Introduce the schwa /ə/ and show the mouth position and how it is relaxed and neutral. Then drill the words and tell sts to practice them in pairs. **A** points to a word for **B** to pronounce and vice versa.

E 🎧 **Make it personal** Demonstrate the miming game by acting out a job for the class to guess. Put sts into pairs, then two pairs into groups of four. The two teams take turns acting out jobs to their partner. Tell them they have 30 seconds to guess their partner's job. They get a point for each correct guess. The team with the most points is the winner.

Alernative activity You could also play this as "pictionary". Instead of miming jobs, sts have to draw the jobs for their team to guess.

3.2 Do you have brothers and sisters?

The next king

The royal family is the most famous family in the UK. Queen Elizabeth and her husband Philip are very old, and their son Charles is next in line to be king, and after him, his first son William. (William's brother Harry is not in line.) William has three children: two sons (George and Louis) and a daughter (Charlotte). Kate is their mother. George is third in line to be king after his father and his grandfather.

1 Reading

A ▶ 3.7 Listen to and read the text about the British royal family. Who are the next kings? Order the names, 1–3. One name is not used.

☐ Charles   ☐ George   ☐ Harry   ☐ William

Common mistakes

My family is big. I have a lot of ~~parents~~.
    relatives
    parents
My ~~fathers~~ live in Madrid.
    siblings
I have two ~~brothers~~: Lucy and Jack.

2 Vocabulary Family and possessive adjectives

A ▶ 3.8 Reread the text in **1A** and complete the table with the highlighted words. Listen, check, and repeat.

Female	Male	Both
mother		parents
wife		couple
	son	
sister		siblings
grandmother		grandparents

B Find George in the photo in **1A** then complete his family tree.

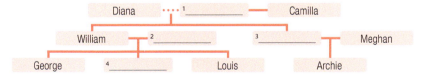

C In groups of three, follow the instructions. Then change roles.

A: Say a female form.   B: Say the male form.   C: Say the word for both.

3.2

3.2 Do you have brothers and sisters?

Lesson aims: Sts learn and use the simple present and possessive adjectives to talk about families.

Function
Reading and listening to a text about the British royal family.
Giving information about a family member.
Asking and answering questions about family.

Language
William has three children.
This is my sister. Her name's Teresa.
I have two brothers.
Do you have children?
Are you married? Yes, I am. Her name is Susana.

Vocabulary: Family members (mother, father, parents, wife, husband, couple, daughter, son, sister, brother, siblings, grandmother, grandfather, grandparents).
Grammar: Simple present: *I, you, we, they* ➕ ➖ ❓. Possessive adjectives and pronouns. Review verb *be* questions.

Warm-up Books closed. Write *What _____? I'm a teacher.* on the board and elicit the question (What do you do?). Drill it a few times, focusing on the weak forms in *do you*. Tell sts they have to find out everyone's job as quickly as possible and try to remember them. If sts don't have a job, tell them to invent one. Sts mingle and ask as many classmates as possible about what they do. When the time is up, ask sts to sit down. Tell sts to write sentences about what their classmates do. Elicit an example and write it on the board, e.g. *Julia is a server*. Sts paircheck to see what sentences they have in common and correct / help each other. At the end, ask sts to read some of their sentences. Check with the whole class if the information is correct, e.g. *Is Julia a lawyer? Is Patricia an engineer?*

1 Reading

A Tell sts to look at the photo and ask: *Where is this family from?* (the UK / Britain) *Do you know any of their names?* Tell them to cover the text and tell each other in pairs what they know about the British royal family (names, relationships, etc). Get a few ideas from the class and write relevant vocabulary on the board. Then, read the instructions and play ▶3.7 twice so sts can listen, read, and order the names of the next kings 1–3. Remind sts one name is not used. Paircheck, then classcheck.

Tip The key royal family members in the photo are (front row, l–r): William, his wife Kate, their children George, Charlotte, and Louis; Charles (his wife Camilla is on his left); Queen Elizabeth; Andrew. Harry and his wife Meghan are in the top right corner.

Queen Elizabeth is married to Philip. They have four children: Charles, Anne, Andrew, and Edward. Charles is next in line to be king, and he has two children, William and Harry. William is next to be king after Charles. Harry is William's younger brother. In 2020 it was announced that he and his wife Meghan no longer have an official role in the royal family.

Common mistakes Read with the class. Explain that these mistakes happen because of translation from their L1.

Language tip Spanish and Portuguese speakers often confuse English words for family members with false cognates in their language. *Parientes / parentes* means *relatives* in L1, whereas English *parents* means *father and mother*. We cannot make *father* plural to mean *parents* in English. Also explain to sts that we cannot talk about *brothers and sisters* in English by making the word *brother* plural. Note that *siblings* is quite formal and many people simply say, e.g. *I have a brother and two sisters.*

🔑 1 Charles 2 William 3 George

2 Vocabulary Family and possessive adjectives

A Point to the text in **1A** and the words highlighted in yellow. Tell sts to complete the chart with the words, and then play ▶3.8 so sts can check their answers. Classcheck and pre-teach *siblings*. Replay the track and tell sts to listen and repeat.

Tip Pay attention to the *-er* suffix in *mother, brother*, etc., and remind sts of the rule about stress and this suffix (it isn't stressed and uses the schwa). Tell sts to practice the pronunciation of family words with a partner. Monitor and correct pronunciation.

▶3.8 Turn to p. 171 for the complete audioscript.

🔑
Female: daughter
Male: father, husband, brother, grandfather
Both: children

B Tell sts George is one of William's children. Ask them to find and point to him in the photo. Ask: *Who is George's mother?* (Kate). Point to the family tree and ask sts to complete it using the photos and text. Paircheck, then classcheck.

🔑 1 Charles 2 Kate 3 Harry 4 Charlotte

C Put sts into groups of three and read the instructions. Tell sts to say the family words as quickly as possible. They can look at the chart in **A** but then encourage them to say the words with their books closed.

81

3.2

D Read *Mystery Man* and guess who he is. Notice the bold words, then circle the correct word in 1–3.

1. My husband is a doctor. **His** / **Your** name's Bruce.
2. This is my sister. **Our** / **Her** name's Teresa.
3. These are my parents. **They** / **Their** names are Joy and Felix.

➡ **Grammar 3A** p.76

🎵 *Whether you're a brother or whether you're a mother, You're stayin' alive, stayin' alive.*

E 🎧 **Make it personal** 📶 Play *Mystery person*. Write a text about a famous person (dead or alive). Go online for information if necessary. In pairs, take turns reading your text. Can your partner guess who it is?

> I'm from Mexico and I'm an artist. My husband's Mexican. His name's Diego. He's an artist, too.

> Are you Frida Kahlo?

MYSTERY MAN

Our mystery man today is from Rosario, Argentina. He's married. **His** wife is a model. **Her** name is Antonella. They have three sons. **Their** names are Thiago, Mateo, and Ciro. He has tattoos of all **his** children. In my opinion, he's the best soccer player of **his** generation.

3 Grammar Simple present: *I / you / we / they* ➕ ➖ ❓

A ▶ 3.9 Listen and match conversations 1–3 to pictures a–c.

⚠ **Common mistakes**

~~Her~~ → *She* name's Jessica.

Meghan is married ~~with~~ *to* Harry.

~~His~~ → *Their* last name is Windsor.

B ▶ 3.10 Complete extracts 1–3 with these words. Listen, check, and repeat.

don't   family   ~~have~~   live   son   with

1. **A** Do you ___have___ children?
   B Yes, I do. I have a _____.
2. **A** Do you _____ alone?
   B No, I don't. I live _____ my grandmother.
3. **A** Do you have a big _____?
   B No, I _____ have siblings. I'm an only child.

C Complete the grammar box with *do* or *don't*. Notice *don't* = *do not*.

Positive ➕	Negative ➖	Questions ❓	Short answers
I have two brothers. I live with my parents.	I don't have a big family. I _____ live alone.	Do you have siblings? _____ you live alone?	Yes, I _____. No, I _____.

➡ **Grammar 3B** p.76

D ▶ 3.11 Listen and follow the model. Practice the questions and answers.

> children – question   Do you have children?   children – negative   I don't have children.

E Match 1–6 to the responses. Who is the "mystery woman"?

1. Do you have brothers and sisters?
2. What is his name?
3. Do you have children?
4. Do you live alone?
5. Are you married?
6. What's your husband's name?

☐ His name's Barack.
☐ Yes, I am.
☐ Yes, I do. I have a brother.
☐ Yes, I have two daughters. Their names are Malia and Sasha.
☐ My brother's name is Craig.
☐ No, I don't. I live with my family.

⚠ **Common mistakes**

~~Do you~~ You live alone?

I ~~not~~ *don't* have a car.

F 🎧 **Make it personal** In pairs, ask and answer questions like those in **E**. Who has more brothers or sisters? Who lives with the most people? Who has the most animals?

3.2

D Ask sts: *What's the British queen's name?* Elicit the answer *Her name is Elizabeth.* and write it on the board, underlining the possessive adjective. Tell sts to read about the Mystery Man, then ask: *Who is it?* Sts guess who it is. Point to the bold words in the text and tell sts these are possessive adjectives. Ask: *What are these words in your language?*

🔑 **Common mistakes** Read with the class so they are clear on the differences between L2 and L1. Tell sts to circle the correct words in sentences 1–3. Paircheck and classcheck.

> Lionel Messi
> 1 His   2 Her   3 Their

Tip Tell sts to make sentences about the British royal family using the adjectives *his, her, their*.

E 🔊 **Make it personal** Direct sts to the first speech bubble and tell them to write a similar description of a famous person they know about. Encourage them to search for details online. They can search in their L1 if they wish and then write in English. When they have finished, tell them to read their text to a partner, who guesses the famous person. Put sts into new pairs and ask them to repeat the activity.

Extra activity Play **Back to the board**. Display the photo of the British royal family (or another famous family) and ask one student to sit with his / her back to the board. The class take turns describing one of the family members, e.g. "He's the queen's son. He's married to …" The student with her / his back to the board guesses the correct family member. Then, another student sits with her / his back to the board. Continue the game until all the family members have been named.

🎵 **Song line:** Turn to p. 178 for notes about this song and an accompanying task.

3 Grammar *Simple present: I / you / we / they* ➕ ➖ ❓

A Before sts listen, tell them to look at pictures a–c and encourage them to say what they think the people are talking about in the pictures. Elicit the questions.

Tell the sts they're going to listen to three conversations. Say: *Listen to conversation 1 and tell me, is this picture a, b, or c?* Play ▶ 3.9 and pause after the first conversation. Ask: *What's the picture?* Replay if necessary. Play the rest of the track for sts to listen and match the other two conversations to the pictures. Paircheck, then classcheck.

▶ 3.9 Turn to p. 171 for the complete audioscript.

> 1 b   2 a   3 c

B Sts complete extracts 1–3 with the words in the box. Paircheck. Play ▶ 3.10 to check answers. Replay and pause after each sentence for choral repetition.

▶ 3.10 Turn to p. 171 for the complete audioscript.

> 1 son   2 live, with   2 family, don't

C Write these questions and answers from **B** on the board:
Do you have children? Yes, I do. Do you live alone? No, I don't.

Elicit / Circle the main verbs in each question and underline *Do*. Tell sts we use *do* as an auxiliary verb to make questions. Then point to the answers to the questions on the board and underline *do* and *don't*. Explain that *don't* is the contraction of *do not*.

Tell sts to complete the grammar box with *do* or *don't*. Paircheck. Classcheck and drill all sentences.

There is more information on the simple present in Grammar 3B on p. 76.

> Negative: don't
> Questions: Do
> Short answers: do, don't

D Transformation drill. Point to the speech bubbles and say: *Listen and follow the model.* Play ▶ 3.11 up to "Your turn" and the first pair of beeps, before and after the student prompt. Pause the track and elicit the question from the whole class (Do you have a daughter?). Resume playing the track for students to check the answer and listen for the next prompt. After each pair of beeps, pick a different student to respond. Replay the track for sts to say the responses chorally.

▶ 3.11 Turn to p. 171 for the complete audioscript.

E Tell sts to look at questions 1–6 and the responses. Ask sts to find the correct response to question 1, and elicit the answer (Yes, I do. I have a brother.). Then tell sts to match questions 2–6 to the responses. Paircheck, then classcheck. Then ask: *Who is the mystery woman?*

🔑 **Common mistakes** Read with the class and remind sts to use auxiliary verbs with questions and negatives.

> 1 Yes, I do. I have a brother.
> 2 My brother's name is Craig.
> 3 Yes, I have two daughters. Their names are Malia and Sasha.
> 4 No, I don't. I live with my family.
> 5 Yes, I am.
> 6 His name's Barack.
> The mystery woman is Michelle Obama.

Extra activity Sts work in pairs or small groups to practice asking and answering the questions. Tell them to try and remember the questions and do the activity without looking at the book. Monitor and drill pronunciation of the question forms and correct grammar errors at the end.

F 🔊 **Make it personal** Point to the lesson title and ask the whole class: *Do you have brothers and sisters?* Put sts into new pairs, and have them take turns asking and answering about their own families, using questions from **E**. At the end, ask sts to report their partners' answers. Ask questions to help, e.g. *Who has lots of brothers or sisters? Who has a small family? Who lives alone?*, etc.

3.3 Do you have a job?

1 Vocabulary Places of work

A Guess the pronunciation of the places in group 1. Then match photos a–e to the places in group 2. In pairs, check your answers.

> **Common mistakes**
>
> ~~Where you work?~~ *do*
> ~~I work in the downtown.~~
> ~~I work in the factory.~~ *a*
> ~~I work in home.~~ *at*
> ~~She's not here. She's in school.~~ *at*

1
- in a bank ___
- in a hospital ___
- in a restaurant ___
- in a school _1_

2
- [ ] downtown ___
- [ ] in a drugstore ___
- [ ] at home ___
- [ ] in an office ___
- [ ] in a travel agency ___

B ▶3.12 Listen to the start of a podcast and number the places in **A** in the order you hear them, 1–9. What's the podcast about?

C Cover the words in **A**. In pairs, remember the nine places.

2 Listening

A ▶3.13 Listen to the podcast and complete the sentences with their second job. Check their favorite job.

PEOPLE WITH TWO JOBS
- Who are they?
- What do they do?
- Where do they work?

▶ Listen to this week's podcast and meet Hanna and Victor.

Hanna Randal is a personal assistant [ ] and a _____ [ ].

Victor Bell is a freelance web designer [ ] and a _____ [ ].

B ▶3.13 Listen again. Where do they work? Write Hanna (H) or Victor (V) next to the four places in **1A**.

C ▶3.14 Listen to and repeat the four sentences. Connect the *k* in *work* to the prepositions.

> I work in a drugstore.

36

3.3 Do you have a job?

Lesson aims: Sts learn and practice simple present *Yes / No* and *Wh-* questions in the context of places of work and jobs.

Function
Identifying cognates related to jobs.
Listening to a podcast about people's jobs.
Asking and answering questions about jobs.

Language
He works in a hospital.
Do you work at home? No, I don't.
Where do you work?

Vocabulary: Prepositions and places of work. Review jobs.
Grammar: Simple present *Yes / No* and *Wh-* ❓.

Warm-up Start a mind map on the board. Write *JOBS* in the center and circle the word. Then, draw a line from it and write *a lawyer*. Elicit more occupations from sts, then elicit / drill pronunciation of all jobs and add any vocabulary from lesson **3.1A** on p. 32 that sts do not mention. Then, in pairs, have sts ask and answer the questions *What do you do?* and *What does your sister / brother / father / mother do?*

1 Vocabulary Places of work

A Books closed. Say: *I'm a teacher. I work in a school.* Point to one of the jobs on the board and ask: *Where does a doctor work?* Elicit "In a hospital."

Books open. Point to the places of work in group 1 and encourage sts to guess the pronunciation. Then point to photo a and the places in group 2. Ask: *Where's this?* (downtown). Sts match photos a–e to group 2. Paircheck. Classcheck with answers on the board.

🔑 **Common mistakes** Read with the class. Encourage sts to learn the prepositions the different places.

Language tip Use the sentences in Common mistakes to remind sts about differences with their L1. Remind them to use the auxiliary verb when forming questions, and to learn as a chunk *at home* and *at school* because the preposition is different in their L1. Point out that *downtown* is used on its own (with no article or preposition, unlike their L1).

🔑
a downtown   b in an office   c at home
d in a travel agency   e in a drugstore

B Tell sts they're going to listen to the start of a podcast. Tell sts to listen and number the places in **A** in the order they hear them, 1–9. Point out the example answer (in a school, 1). Play ▶ 3.12, pausing occasionally for sts to write. Paircheck. Replay the track to classcheck answers. Ask: *What's the podcast about?* (people who have two jobs and where they work) *Do you work in one or two places?* Then drill pronunciation of the places. Draw attention to the pink letters.

▶ 3.12 Turn to p. 171 for the complete audioscript.

🔑
2 in a restaurant   6 in a bank
3 in a hospital   7 in an office
4 in a drugstore   8 downtown
5 in a travel agency 9 at home
The podcast is about people who have two jobs.

C Focus on Common mistakes to review some typical errors from lessons **3.1** and **3.2**. Then ask sts to cover the words in **A** and, in pairs, try to remember all the places of work. Ensure sts say prepositions / complete phrases. Monitor closely and correct on the spot.

2 Listening

A Point to the photos and the questions "Who are they?" and "What do they do?". Tell sts they're going to listen to the podcast about Hanna and Victor's jobs. Ask: *What's Hanna's second job?* Elicit some ideas and then play ▶ 3.13. Pause after Hanna says *salesclerk* and ask sts to complete the sentence on the webpage. Ask: *What's her favorite job?* Play the rest of her interview and have sts check Hanna's preference.

Say: *Now listen to Victor and complete.* Play the interview without pausing. Paircheck, then classcheck.

▶ 3.13 Turn to p. 171 for the complete audioscript.

🔑
Hanna: salesclerk; personal assistant ✓
Victor: server; freelance web designer ✓

B Say: *Hanna works at two different places. Victor also works at two places.* Point to the places in **1A** and ask: *Where do Hanna and Victor work?* Replay ▶ 3.13. Sts write H or V next to the four places of work mentioned. Paircheck, then classcheck.

🔑
Hanna: in an office, in a drugstore
Victor: at home, in a restaurant

C Write *I work in a bank.* on the board, and show sts how *work* and *in* connect to sound like one word when we pronounce them. Point to the example in the speech bubble and play ▶ 3.14 for sts to listen and repeat chorally. Replay the track for sts to practice pronunciation with a partner.

▶ 3.14 Turn to p. 172 for the complete audioscript.

3 Grammar Simple present

♪ Do you really want to hurt me?
Do you really want to make me cry?

A ▶ 3.15 Complete 1–6 in the grammar box. Listen to check.

Yes / No questions A S I		
Auxiliary	Subject	Infinitive
1 _____	you	work at home?
2 _____	you	want to be a doctor?
3 _____	you	live here?

Wh- questions Q A S I			
Question word	Auxiliary	Subject	Infinitive
4 _____	do	you	do?
5 Where	_____	you	work?
6 Where	_____	you	want to work?

→ Grammar 3B p. 76

B Match these answers to questions 1–6 in **A**. In pairs, practice asking and answering.
- ☐ No, I don't. I want to be a lawyer. It's an interesting job.
- ☐ I'm a bank cashier. I like it very much.
- ☐ I want to work at home. No traffic!
- ☐ Yes, apartment 61. It's a beautiful apartment.
- ☐ Yes, I do. I work freelance. It's great.
- ☐ I work in an office in Ventura.

C ▶ 3.16 Listen and follow the model. Practice the questions and answers. Copy the sentence stress.

work – question **Where** do you **work**? an office I **work** in an **office**.

D 🎧 Make it personal *Work, work, work!*
1 Do the questionnaire. Answer question 1. Then put a ✓ or ✗ in the first box for each place in question 2.
2 In pairs, ask and answer. Complete the second box with your partner's answers.
3 Do you and your partner have anything in common?
4 What are the most popular answers in your class? What are the least popular?

DO YOU KNOW WHAT'S BEST FOR YOU?

1 What do you (want to) do?   I'm (I want to be) _____ .
2 Do you (want to) work:
- at home? ☐ ☐
- in an office? ☐ ☐
- in a store? ☐ ☐
- in a bank? ☐ ☐
- downtown? ☐ ☐
- freelance? ☐ ☐
- online? ☐ ☐
- in a factory? ☐ ☐

We (want to) work in an office.
I (want to) work in a bank.

We don't (want to) work freelance.

♪ **Song line:** Turn to p. 179 for notes about this song and an accompanying task.

3 Grammar Simple present ❓

A Write these gapped questions on the board: _____ you have children? _____ do you live? _____ you live alone? Ask the whole class to complete them. Point to the grammar box and tell sts to complete 1–6. Paircheck. Play ▶3.15 to classcheck with answers on the board. Point out the ASI and QASI acronyms and the words they stand for. Explain these acronyms can help them remember the structure of questions. Replay ▶3.15 and pause after each question for choral repetition.

There is more information on simple present question forms in Grammar 3B on p. 76.

▶3.15 Turn to p. 172 for the complete audioscript.

1 Do
2 Do
3 Do
4 What
5 do
6 do

B Tell sts to complete the matching exercise. Paircheck, then classcheck. Put sts in pairs and tell them to practice asking and answering the questions. First they can look at the book, but then ask them to close their books and try to remember the questions and answers.

2 No, I don't. I want to be a lawyer. It's an interesting job.
4 I'm a bank cashier. I like it very much.
6 I want to work at home. No traffic!
3 Yes, apartment 61. It's a beautiful apartment.
1 Yes, I do. I work freelance. It's great.
5 I work in an office in Ventura.

C Transformation drill. Point to the speech bubbles and draw attention to the stressed words in bold. Say: *Listen and follow the model*. Play ▶3.16 up to "Your turn" and the first pair of beeps, before and after the st prompt. Pause the track and elicit the question from the whole class (Where do you work?). Make sure sts stress *Where* and *work*. Resume playing the track for sts to check the answer and listen for the next prompt. After each pair of beeps, pick a different st to respond. Then play the track again for sts to respond chorally.

Write the question and answer prompts on the board. In pairs, sts practice asking and answering questions. Monitor, and correct any pronunciation errors you hear with the class at the end.

▶3.16 Turn to p. 172 for the complete audioscript.

D **Make it personal** Point to the questionnaire and ask: *What's this?* (a questionnaire). Ask sts if they like doing questionnaires in magazines or online. Read the instructions with the class, if possible displaying the questionnaire on an IWB, or projected onto the board. Do an example. Complete 1 with your job and 2 by checking one of the places where you work, or want to work. Then ask a student the questions, and complete the questionnaire with their answers, using the second box. In pairs, sts do steps 1 and 2. Then ask: *Do you and your partner have anything in common?* Refer sts to the speech bubbles and have pairs say what they do and don't have in common. Invite some pairs to tell the class. Finally, do a survey on the board to find out the most and least popular answers in the class. Ask the class: *What are the most popular jobs?* Ask sts to say the job they wrote in 1, and write a list of the jobs on the board. Keep a tally of the number of sts who wrote each job to find out the most popular. Then write the eight places of work on the board, and keep a tally of the number of sts who checked or crossed them to find out the most and least popular places of work.

Extra writing Ask sts to write a brief description of themselves, saying what they do and where they work. If possible, display their sentences on the school / class mural. Provide them with models, e.g.

"I'm Juan and I'm married. I'm 34 years old. I live with my wife and two sons in Buenos Aires. I'm an engineer and I work in an office downtown."

"I'm Renata and I'm single. I'm 21 years old. I live with my parents in Bogotá. I want to be a doctor or a nurse. I want to work in a hospital."

3.4 Where does your mother work?

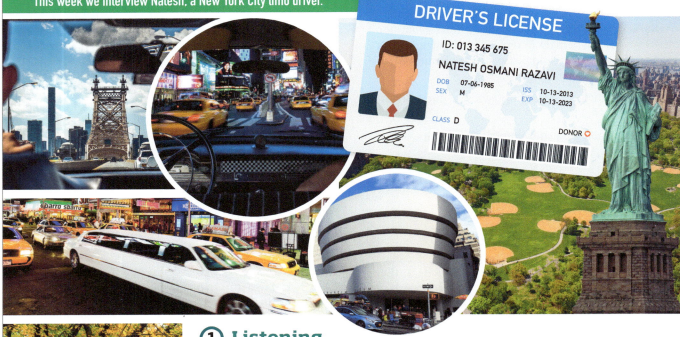

PEOPLE WITH UNUSUAL JOBS
This week we interview Natesh, a New York City limo driver.

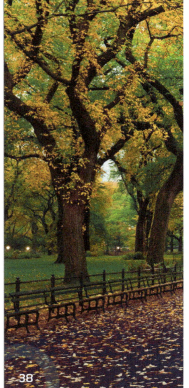

1 Listening

A ▶ 3.17 Listen to the interview. True (T) or False (F)? Correct the false sentences.
1. Natesh is from Pakistan.
2. He lives in New York City.
3. He lives with his sister and his brother.
4. His parents are retired.
5. His brother works in a factory.
6. He isn't married.
7. He works 14 hours a day.
8. He loves his car!

B ▶ 3.18 Put the words in order to make questions about Natesh. Match them to the answers. Listen, check, and repeat.

❶ he / from / where / 's / ? *Where's he from?*	☐ No, he doesn't. He has a brother.
❷ does / he / where / live / ?	☐ He's a limo driver.
❸ alone / live / he / does / ?	☐ Yes, he does. Very much.
❹ a sister / does / have / he / ?	[1] He's from Pakistan.
❺ he / is / married / ?	☐ No, but he has a girlfriend.
❻ what / do / he / does / ?	☐ No, he lives with his family.
❼ he / work / where / does / ?	☐ He works in Manhattan.
❽ his / he / does / job / like / ?	☐ He lives in New York City.

C  **Make it personal** Cover the answers in **B**. In pairs, ask and answer the questions to test your partner's memory. Do you like to drive? Do you know anyone with an unusual job?

Yes, I do. My cousin, Nico. He's a bed tester.

My brother works part-time at night in a grocery store.

3.4 Where does your mother work?

Lesson aims: Sts listen to an interview with a limo driver in New York and talk about unusual jobs. They practice using the simple present in the 3rd person singular in the context of asking and answering about a family member.

Function
Listening to an interview.
Asking and answering questions about other people.
Describing a family member.

Language
I live in Queens.
Where's he from? He's from Pakistan.
Who's this person? She's my mother.
She works in a hospital.

Vocabulary: Review family words and jobs
Grammar: Simple present 3rd person ❓ and short answers

Warm-up Review *Yes / No* questions in the 3rd person. Before class, write on the board 5-7 verb *be* sentences about your family and friends, mixing true and false facts, e.g.
My brother is from Guadalajara. My father is a lawyer.
My sister is a fantastic actor. My best friend is German.
My boss is 85 years old.

Ask sts: *Are these sentences about me true? Let's check. You ask me Yes / No questions. I answer yes for true or no for false.* Model / Prompt the question if necessary. Say: *Is your brother from …?* and elicit the complete question from sts (Is your brother from Guadalajara?). Ensure each question is asked by a different st. Encourage sts to guess the true information when you answer *no*. After they have discovered the true and false sentences about you, ask them to write their own sentences and repeat the activity in pairs or small groups of three.

① Listening

A Point to the photos and ask: *Where is it?* (New York) *Do you know New York city?* Explore the photos and check if sts recognize any of the places. Point to the limo and ask the class: *What type of car is this?* Pre-teach *limousine* and *limo*. Focus on the title "People With Unusual Jobs" and ask: *Is it common to be a limo driver?* Say: *It's an unusual job. It isn't common.*

Say: *Natesh is a limo driver in New York.* Tell the class they're going to listen to an interview with Natesh. Read sentences 1–8 with sts and tell them to mark the sentences true or false as they listen. Play ▶3.17. Paircheck and correct the false sentences. Replay ▶3.17 and classcheck with answers on the board.

▶3.17 Turn to p. 172 for the complete audioscript.

1 T
2 T
3 F He lives with his parents and his brother.
4 T
5 F His brother is unemployed.
6 T
7 F He works thirteen hours a day.
8 T

B Point to question 1 and the example answer, then point to number 1 next to "He's from Pakistan." in the second column. Sts order questions 2-8 and match them to answers. Paircheck. Play ▶3.18 to check answers. Then replay the track and pause after each question / answer for choral repetition.

▶3.18 Turn to p. 172 for the complete audioscript.

2 Where does he live? He lives in New York City.
3 Does he live alone? No, he lives with his family.
4 Does he have a sister? No, he doesn't. He has a brother.
5 Is he married? No, but he has a girlfriend.
6 What does he do? He's a limo driver.
7 Where does he work? He works in Manhattan.
8 Does he like his job? Yes, he does. Very much.

C 🎤 **Make it personal** Tell sts to change partners. Sts cover the answers in **B** and take turns asking questions 1–8 and answering them from memory. Monitor and help, and go through any common errors with the class at the end. Then ask: *Do you like to drive? Do you want to be a limo driver?* and elicit a few responses. Finish the lesson by asking sts if they know anyone with an unusual job. Refer them to the example answers in the speech bubbles, then ask sts to tell the class about people they know with unusual jobs.

2 Grammar Simple present: he / she / it ➕ ➖ ❓

🎵 *Oh, whatever it takes,*
'Cause I love the adrenaline in my veins,
I do whatever it takes,
'Cause I love how it feels when I break the chains.

A Look at the sentences and questions in **1A** and **1B** and study Common mistakes. Complete the grammar box with these verbs.

does (x2) doesn't (x3) has have like live (x2) lives work works

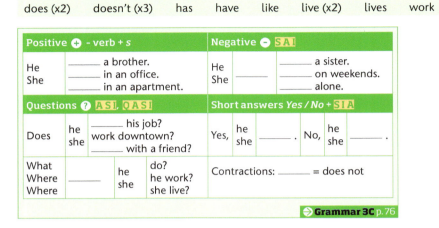

⚠️ **Common mistakes**

Suri ~~have~~ *has* a daughter.
She doesn't ~~works~~ *work* at home.
She ~~don't~~ *doesn't* live with her mother.

➡️ Grammar 3C p. 76

B ▶️ 3.19 Listen and follow the model. Practice the sentences.

💬 I live alone. – He   He lives alone.   I have a brother. – She   She has a brother.

C Read and complete the text with these verbs.

drives   have   live   lives

> Apart from the verb *be*, English verbs have only two simple present forms.
> **I, you, we, they + verb.**
> We _____ here. I _____ a bike.
> **He, she, it + verb + s.**
> He _____ there. She _____ a car.
> Make your teacher happy! Don't forget the *s*!

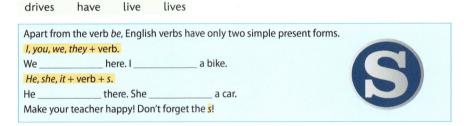

D 🔒 **Make it personal**

1 Complete the 🆔 form for a member of your family.

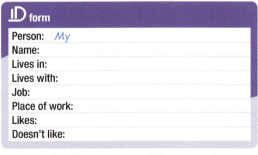

🆔 form	
Person:	My
Name:	
Lives in:	
Lives with:	
Job:	
Place of work:	
Likes:	
Doesn't like:	

2 In pairs, ask and answer to get information about your partner's person. Show a photo if you can.

💬 Who's this person?   What does she do?   Does she work in a restaurant?
   She's my mother.   She's a chef.   No, she works in a hotel.

♫ **Song line:** Turn to p. 179 for notes about this song and an accompanying task.

2 Grammar Simple present: *he / she / it* ⊕ ⊖ ❓

A Write *Where do you live?* on the board and ask: *What about Natesh?* Refer sts to the questions in **1B** and ask: *What's the question about Natesh?* (Where does he live?). Write the question on the board. Do the same transformation for *Do you live alone?* (Does he live alone?)

🕐 **Common mistakes** Read with the class. Write *I have a brother.* on the board and invite sts to transform / complete the same sentence with "He ..." (has a brother). Repeat this procedure with *I don't / He doesn't have a sister*. Make sure sts notice the *-s* for 3rd person singular is used only in affirmative sentences.

Focus on the grammar box and ask sts to complete it with the verbs in the box. Paircheck, then drill pronunciation of all sentences as you classcheck.

Language tip Use Common mistakes to explain that *have* is an irregular verb, and so doesn't follow the regular rule of adding *-s, -es,* or *-ies* in the third person (*he, she, it*). In questions or negative sentences, they need to use the auxiliary *does* in the third person, and change the main verb back to the infinitive form (*have*).

There is more information on the simple present in Grammar 3C on p. 76.

> Positive: has, works, lives
> Negative: doesn't have, doesn't work, doesn't live
> Questions: like, live; does
> Short answers: does, doesn't
> Contractions: doesn't

B Transformation drill. Point to the speech bubbles and say: *Listen and follow the model*. Play ▶3.19 up to "Your turn" and the first pair of beeps, before and after the student prompt. Pause the track and elicit the response from the whole class (She works at home.). Resume playing the track for students to check the answer and listen for the next prompt. After each pair of beeps, pick a different student to respond. Correct any errors, then play the track again for sts to repeat chorally.

▶3.19 Turn to p. 172 for the complete audioscript.

C Tell sts to read the text and complete the sentences with the verbs in the box. Paircheck. Write the completed sentences on the board and elicit what the two simple present verb forms are for regular verbs (verb + *s* for *he, she, it*; verb for all other persons).

> live, have, lives, drives

D ● **Make it personal**

1 Model the activity. Display the ID form using the **Digital Book for Teachers** or the board and complete it about a member of your family. Tell sts to do the same by completing the form about a member of their family.

2 Put sts into pairs. Tell them they're going to learn about their partner's family member. Refer sts to the lesson question title on top of p. 38 and the speech bubbles, and have them practice the model dialogue in their pairs. Elicit questions sts will need to ask to complete each row of the form. The sts interview each other about their chosen relatives. If possible, ask sts to show a photo of their family member on their smartphone.

Classcheck by asking some sts to tell the class about their partner's family member.

3.5 Do you live near here?

Skills Listening for specific information

A ▶ 3.20 Listen to and read the information. Then look at the photo of Laura and Charlie and try to predict the answers to questions 1–3.

Maybe they're friends on vacation.

> **Listening for specific information**
> Listening isn't easy — in any language!
> Here are three listening tips:
> 1 Before you listen, imagine the context, and the words or phrases people use in that situation.
> 2 Know your objective: What exactly do I need to understand?
> 3 Don't expect to understand or mentally translate every word. It isn't necessary.

1 What four questions do they ask?
 a Do you like this music?
 b Do you like this food?
 c Do you like this class?
 d Do you live near here?
 e How are you?
 f Is that good?
 g What about you?
 h What do you do?
 i What do you study?
 j What do you want to eat?

2 Where are they?
 a at a party
 b at work
 c at school

3 What is their relationship?
 a brother and sister
 b husband and wife
 c just friends
 d strangers

B ▶ 3.21 Listen to part one of their conversation to check.

C ▶ 3.21 Check the 10 words Laura and Charlie use. Listen again to check.

- beautiful
- computer
- fantastic
- hello
- hi
- incredible
- interesting
- live
- music
- nice
- office
- student
- teacher
- unemployed
- university
- work

D ▶ 3.22 Listen to the complete conversation and write Charlie (C) or Laura (L) in 1–9.
 1 ___ lives downtown.
 2 ___ lives near here.
 3 ___ is unemployed.
 4 ___ studies IT.
 5 ___ is an IT professional.
 6 ___ works for a bank.
 7 ___ isn't married.
 8 ___ doesn't live alone.
 9 ___ ends the conversation.

E ▶ 3.22 Listen again. How much can you understand: 50% / 60% / 80% / 100%? Go to AS 3.22 on p. 86 to check. In pairs, read the dialogue out loud. Change some of the information.

What do you do? *I'm a nurse.*

F 🔊 **Make it personal** In pairs. What do / don't you have in common with Charlie and Laura?

Charlie lives with his partner, and I live with my partner.

Laura is unemployed. I'm not unemployed. I have a job.

3.5 Do you live near here?

Lesson aims: Sts listen for specific information in a conversation between two people at a party.

Function
Reading and listening to tips about listening.
Listening to a conversation at a party.
Speaking about what you have in common with people.

Language
Do you like this music?
What do you do?
I have something in common with Laura.

Vocabulary: Review places of work and jobs.
Grammar: Review verb *be* 3rd person singular ➕ ➖ ❓

Warm-up Books open. Tell sts to look at **Sounds and Usual Spellings** on p. 82. Focus on Vowels. Ask sts to cover the words and look at the pictures only. Point to the *tree / three* picture and elicit vocabulary from the whole class. In pairs, sts take turns pointing and naming pictures for all eleven vowel sounds. Monitor closely for accuracy. Classcheck briefly.

> **Tip** Encourage sts to visit the pronunciation section on the Richmond Learning Platform.

ID SKILLS Listening for specific information

A Tell sts they are going to work on listening skills. Play ▶ 3.20 and tell them to listen and read the information in the box. Encourage sts to react to the tips. Is there anything they don't understand? Do they think the tips are useful? It may be useful to discuss this in L1 if you speak the sts' language.

Explore the photo. Say: *This is Laura and this is Charlie.* Ask: *Are they married? Or boyfriend and girlfriend? Are they friends? Do they work together?* Go over 1–3 with sts and tell them to predict 1) four questions from Laura and Charlie's conversation, 2) where they are, and 3) the relationship between them. Tell them to choose their predictions from the options given. Paircheck, but don't go through answers yet.

B Play ▶ 3.21 and tell sts to listen to the first part of the conversation to check their ideas. Classcheck.

▶ 3.21 Turn to p. 172 for the complete audioscript.

> 1 d, g, h, i
> 2 a
> 3 d

C Tell sts to read the words and try to remember if Laura or Charlie used them. Play ▶ 3.21 again and tell them to listen and check the 10 words. Paircheck and replay the track to classcheck.

> Check: fantiastic, hello, hi, interesting, live, nice, student, unemployed, university, work

D Tell sts they're going to listen to the complete conversation. Have them read 1–9, and tell them to listen and decide who each sentence relates to, Charlie (C) or Laura (L). Play ▶ 3.22 for sts to do the activity. Replay the track and classcheck.

▶ 3.22 Turn to p. 172 for the complete audioscript.

> 1 C 2 L 3 L 4 L 5 C 6 C 7 C 8 C 9 L

E Play ▶ 3.22 again and ask sts how much they understand now. Ask if they used any of the tips in **A** during the lesson.

Put sts into new pairs, direct them to the audioscript, and tell them to read aloud the dialogue with their partner, changing at least two pieces of information about Charlie and Laura. Point to the speech bubbles to clarify the task. When they've finished, go over any good language you heard and ask sts what information their partner changed.

> **Tip** Encourage sts to follow the tips in the box in **A** if they listen to something outside class. They should listen to it a few times if possible to try and understand more detail each time.

F 🗣 **Make it personal** Ask sts: *Are you similar to Laura or Charlie? Do you have anything in common? Jobs? Family?* Elicit a few comments and point to the speech bubbles. Invite two sts to make the speech bubbles true for them, helping if necessary. Put sts into new pairs to tell each other what they do / don't have in common with Charlie and Laura.

Where do you study?

*We are young we run free,
Stay up late, we don't sleep,
Got our friends, got the night
We'll be all right.*

ID in Action Exchanging personal information

A ▶ 3.23 Match questions 1–10 to the answers. Listen, check, and repeat. In pairs, ask the questions and give your own answers.

10 QUESTIONS TO ASK AT A PARTY

1. Do you live near here?
2. Do you live alone?
3. Do you have brothers and sisters?
4. Do you have children?
5. Do you have a boyfriend?
6. What do you do?
7. Where do you study?
8. Where does your father work?
9. What does your wife do?
10. How old are your children?

- Yes, I do. Two daughters.
- I'm an engineer.
- No, I live with my parents.
- He's retired.
- She's a university professor.
- Yes, I have one brother.
- No, I live downtown.
- Yes, I do. His name's Simon.
- They're 7 and 10.
- At UCLA.

B Imagine you're at a party. Think of six other questions to ask a person you don't know.

What do you study?   *Where do you work?*

C ▶ 3.24 In conversation, be positive to show you are interested. Listen and repeat these expressions.

Great talking to you. Bye!   Cool!   Wow!   Oh, I see.   Really?

Here's my number.   Another soda?   All right.   Nice!

D 🎤 **Make it personal** *Let's party!* Role-play meeting new people at a party. Create a new identity if you want to.

1. Move around the class and ask a lot of questions.

   Hi, I'm … . Nice to meet you.   *What do you do?*   *Do you live near here?*

   Hello. My name's Richard VeryRich. Nice to meet you too.   *I'm a banker and I work in the Bahamas.*   *Yes, I do. / No, I live on a yacht.*

2. In pairs, remember all the people you met. Who has an unusual new identity?

3.5 Where do you study?

Lesson aims: Sts ask and answer questions to practice exchanging personal information in the context of a party.

Function
Asking for and giving information about yourself.

Language
Do you live near here? Yes, I do.
What do you do? I'm a teacher.

Vocabulary: Phrases for responding in a conversation (Cool! Oh, I see. Really?)
Grammar: Review questions in the simple present and with verb *be*.

ID in action Exchanging personal information

♫ **Song line:** Turn to p. 179 for notes about this song and an accompanying task.

A Books closed. Write *10 questions to ask at a party* on the board and ask sts: *What questions can you ask someone at a party?* Elicit some ideas and write them on the board. Don't correct them at this point.

Books open. Tell sts to look at questions 1–10 and compare with their suggestions. Correct any errors in the questions on the board. Tell sts to match questions 1–10 to the answers, then play ▶ 3.23 and tell them to listen and check their answers. Classcheck, then replay ▶ 3.23 for sts to listen and repeat. Put sts into pairs and tell them to practice asking the questions and giving their own answers.

Tip Tell sts to ask the questions in a different order, so there is an element of surprise. Then, tell them to close their books and try to remember the questions.

⚷
4 Yes, I do. Two daughters.
6 I'm an engineer.
2 No, I live with my parents.
8 He's retired.
9 She's a university professor.
3 Yes, I have one brother.
1 No, I live downtown.
5 Yes, I do. His name's Simon.
10 They're 7 and 10.
7 At UCLA.

B Tell sts to imagine they're at a party. Ask them to think of six other questions they could ask someone they don't know. You could refer back to the questions they suggested in **A** and as a class build on this, writing more questions on the board. Alternatively, ask sts to work in pairs to think of more questions. Classcheck and write their suggestions on the board.

⚷
Suggested answers: Do you have a big family? Do you work in an office? What do you study? Do you live with your family? Do you like music? Do you have a pet?

C Point to the expressions and play ▶ 3.23 for sts to listen and repeat chorally. Then replay the track and ask individual sts to repeat. Listen to their intonation, and tell sts they can exaggerate their intonation to sound more interested. Tell them to practice saying the phrases with a partner, sounding as interested as possible.

Tip Ask sts to translate these phrases. This will help to clarify their function and meaning, especially *Really?* and *Oh, I see.*

D 🎧 **Make it personal** Point to the instructions and speech bubbles and explain sts are going to a party. They can be themselves or invent a new identity for the party.

1 Put on some music and tell sts they are at the party. Tell them to stand up and walk around, meeting as many people as possible and asking them lots of questions.

2 Stop the music and say: *It's the next day. Tell your friend about the party. Tell them about all the people you met and what they do, where they live, their families*, etc. Model the activity by saying, e.g.: *I met George Genius at the party. He's a famous scientist and he lives in New York ...* Write *I met ...* on the board so sts know how to start their description. Have sts share information in pairs. Then, ask the class: *Who has an unusual or interesting identity?* Encourage sts to talk about classmates' interesting new identites.

➡ **Workbook** p. 99

➡ **Richmond Learning Platform**

➡ **Writing** p. 42

➡ **Café** p. 43

Writing 3 A personal profile

You don't know you're beautiful,
Oh, oh
That's what makes you beautiful.

A ▶ 3.25 Read and complete Beth's profile with the words.

| a | Brazilian | daughters | has | in |
| lives | ~~old~~ | two | they're | works |

REGULAR PEOPLE, UNUSUAL FACTS

by Vicente Lucas, Brasília, Brazil

My sister Beth is a regular person in many ways. She's 48 years ___old___. She's divorced and she has two _____. Their names are Carol and Camila, and _____ 16 and 14. We're _____, from Rio de Janeiro, but Beth _____ in Argentina. She's _____ psychologist and she _____ in a school _____ Palermo, Buenos Aires. She's a happy person – very friendly and really popular. But _____ unusual facts about Beth: she doesn't have a car, but she _____ nine cats and four dogs in her apartment! She adores animals.

B Reread and answer questions 1–9.
1 How old is Beth?
2 Is she married?
3 How many children does she have?
4 How old are they?
5 Where's she from?
6 Where does she live?
7 What does she do?
8 Where does she work?
9 What's unusual about her?

C Read *Write it right!* Then, in the profile, circle:
- three examples of *but*
- 11 third person singular verbs
- an adjective intensified by *really*.

> **Write it right!**
>
> Use *but* to contrast two ideas.
> Remember the verb forms with *-s* for *he* or *she*.
> Use *very* or *really* to intensify adjectives.
> *My brother is **really** intelligent.*

D Think of a person you know. Complete 1–5 about him / her. What's unusual about him / her?
1 He / She has _____ in his / her house.
2 He / She lives with _____.
3 He / She is a(n) _____.
4 He / She works / studies in _____.
5 Other: _____.

E *Your turn!* Write a profile of the person in **D** for *Regular People, Unusual Facts*.

Before	Plan your answers to 1–9 in **B**. Compare with your sentences 1–5 in **D**.
While	Introduce your person and write the profile. Use *but* to contrast ideas, and *very* or *really* to intensify adjectives. Check the form of all your verbs.
After	Share your profile with the class. Who's the most unusual person?

42

Writing 3 A personal profile

🎵 **Song line:** Turn to p. 179 for notes about this song and an accompanying task.

A Point to the woman in the photo and ask the class: *Where's she from? What's her name? How old is she?* Allow sts to guess or briefly look for information in the text. Read the title with them, "Regular People, Unusual Facts," and elicit the meaning of *unusual*. Say: *It's the opposite of usual or regular.*

Tip Before sts perform the task, read the title of the personal profile with them and ask: *What are the two unusual facts about Beth?* Tell sts to read the text to find out. Ensure they do not try to fill in the blanks now. Classcheck (she doesn't have a car, but she has nine cats and four dogs in her house).

Point to the example answer (old) and the words in the box. Sts complete the profile with the other words. Paircheck. Classcheck with answers on the board.

🔑 old, daughters, they're, Brazilian, lives, a, works, in, two, has

B If technology is available, display the page in the **Digital Book for Teachers**. Read question 1 with the whole class and elicit the answer (She's 48 years old.). Tell sts to reread the profile and write the answers to questions 1–9. Paircheck, then classcheck.

🔑
1 She's 48 years old.
2 No. (She's divorced.)
3 She has two children / daughters.
4 They're 16 and 14.
5 She's from Brazil / Rio de Janeiro.
6 She lives in Argentina / Buenos Aires.
7 She's a psychologist.
8 She works in a school.
9 She doesn't have a car / she has nine cats and four dogs.

C Read **Write it Right!** with the class. Clarify what sts are looking for by eliciting an example for each bullet point. Tell sts to reread the profile and circle three examples of *but*, 11 examples of 3rd person singular verbs, and one adjective with *really*. Paircheck. Classcheck with answers on the board.

🔑
- *but*: but Beth lives in Argentina, But two unusual facts …, but she has nine cats and four dogs
- 3rd person singular verbs (choose from the following): is, s, 's, has, are, 're, lives, 's, works, 's, doesn't have, has, adores
- *really*: really popular

D Tell sts about a person you know (or invent someone) and something unusual about them, e.g. *My cousin Barbara lives in Australia. She's a chef in a fish restaurant, but she doesn't eat fish!* Then, ask sts to think of a person they know and complete 1–5 about him / her. Ask: *What's unusual about this person?* Sts write something unusual or interesting about their person. Walk around the class to monitor and help with vocabulary.

E **Your turn!** Tell sts they're going to write a profile of their person in **D**.

Before Tell sts to answer questions 1–9 in **B** about the person they chose in **D**. They can add brief notes to their answers in **B** and **D** to create a rough draft, before writing.

While Tell sts to start and finish their profiles with similar sentences to the ones in Beth's profile in **A**. Remind them to use *but* and *very* or *really*, and to check the form of the verbs. Make sure they include the unusual fact at the end of the profile. While sts write, monitor and check they include all information from **B** and **D**.

After In pairs, sts exchange and read each other's profiles. As they read, encourage them to peer correct the uses of *but*, 3rd person verbs, and *really* / *very* + adjective. Then, split the class into groups of three or four. Have sts read each other's profiles. Ask the class: *Who's the most interesting person? What's the most unusual fact?* Ask sts to tell the class about the most interesting person in their group, then have the class decide on the most unusual person overall.

3 Job interviews

 Café

1 Before watching

A Match photos 1–6 to these words. Which is not a job?
- ba**ri**sta
- **fil**mmaker
- **sci**entist
- **cu**stomer
- ma**na**ger
- **song**writer

B Guess two jobs for August, Rory, Andrea, and Lucy.

I think August works with computers—he's an IT professional!

2 While watching

A Watch and check Andrea (An), August (Au), Genevieve (G), Lucy (L), or Rory (R).

	An	Au	G	L	R	
1						fixes Internet settings.
2						works with design.
3						works with robot programs.
4						directs movies.
5						fixes problems on computers.
6						works at ID Café.
7						is a filmmaker.
8						writes and sings songs.
9						serves coffee.

B Listen to Genevieve. Complete what she says.

I work here in this c_____. It's a big p_____. There are a _____ _____ tables. I'm a s_____ and a b_____. Baristas serve or make c_____, and serve it to the c_____. I work a lot, but this is not my p_____. I'm also a m_____ student at the university. And I'm a m_____, and s_____, and a s_____.

C Watch from 2:50 to 3:40. Number the words 1–9 in the order Rory says them.
- ☐ assistant manager
- ☐ expert
- ☐ fix
- ☐ problem
- ☐ se**tt**ings
- ☐ **sig**nal
- ☐ strong
- ☐ 1 technician
- ☐ university

D Watch the complete video. True (T) or False (F)?
1. It's Andrea's office.
2. She works there with busy directors.
3. They work as **in**terns or assistants to university professors.
4. Andrea works in design and fashion.
5. She doesn't work with clothes or **fur**niture.
6. Her job is to com**bi**ne ma**te**rials and colors.
7. Lucy has two jobs.

3 After watching

A Complete 1–7 with *do*, *does*, *work* or *works*.
1. This is August. What _____ he do?
2. Where _____ you _____, and what _____ you do?
3. I _____ at home a lot and I _____ on robots.
4. Our computer signal _____.
5. We _____ with a lot of material for clothes.
6. _____ they work? Yeah, they _____.
7. That's what they _____.

B Complete the adjectives they use. Who says them?
1. Robots are s*pecial* and f_____!
2. Your work is really in_____.
3. Our computer signal is s_____.
4. That was g_____!
5. It's a very i_____ job.
6. The designers are very b_____.
7. Design is about e_____ taste and b_____ colors.

C What do the characters do? In pairs, ask and answer.

What does Andrea do? — *She works with colors and clothes.*

D 🔴 **Make it personal** Role-play! In pairs, **A:** Imagine you have one of the jobs in **1A**. **B:** Interview A. Use adjectives from **3B**. Change roles.

What do you do? — *I'm a songwriter.*

Really? That's great! What type of songs do you write?

43

ID Café 3 Job interviews

1 Before watching

A Ask sts: *What do you remember about August?* Elicit what sts remember from the last ID Café lesson. Tell sts to look at the photos and the words, and go through the pronunciation. Sts match photos 1–6 to the words. Paircheck, then classcheck, and ask: *Which is not a job?* (customer).

1 songwriter 2 barista 3 customer 4 filmmaker
5 manager 6 scientist

B Point to the video stills and tell sts to guess two work roles for each character. In pairs, sts take turns making guesses. Refer them to the speech bubble as an example. Don't classcheck until after **2A** below.

2 While watching

A Tell sts: *Lucy is making a video about jobs. Lucy interviews her friends about what they do.* Have sts look at phrases 1–9 in the chart, and tell them to watch and check the correct person or people for each expression. Play ▶3 right through. Paircheck. Replay the video to classcheck answers.

	An	Au	G	L	R	
1					✓	fixes Internet settings.
2	✓					works with design.
3		✓				works with robot programs.
4				✓		directs movies.
5	✓				✓	fixes problems on computers.
6		✓		✓		works at ID Café.
7				✓		is a filmmaker.
8		✓				writes and sings songs.
9				✓		serves coffee.

B Ask sts to read the text before they watch the video again. In pairs, they predict words which could go in the gaps. Play ▶3 from 1:56 to 2:50. Sts watch and complete the text. Paircheck, then classcheck.

café, place, about 20, server, barista, coffee, customer, profession, music, musician, songwriter, singer

C Read through the words with sts, then play ▶3 from 2:50 to 3:40. Tell sts to watch and number the words in the order Rory says them. Paircheck, then classcheck.

2 assistant manager 8 signal
3 expert 9 strong
6 fix 1 technician
5 problem 4 university
7 settings

D Tell sts to read sentences 1–7. Check they understand the meaning of *busy* and *interns*. Have sts guess if the sentences are true or false. Play ▶3 in full and ask sts to check their guesses. Have them mark the sentences T or F. Classcheck.

1 F (It's the supervisor's office.)
2 F (She works with busy designers.)
3 F (They work as interns or assistants to designers.)
4 T
5 F (She works with clothes or furniture.)
6 T
7 F

3 After watching

A Point to number 1 and elicit the correct answer (does). Sts complete the sentences using *do, does, work,* and *works*. Paircheck. Classcheck with answers on the board.

1 does
2 do, work, do
3 work, work
4 works
5 work
6 Do, do
7 do

B Elicit any adjectives sts can remember from the video. Tell them to work in pairs and complete 1–7. Classcheck by playing ▶3 again, and ask sts to make a note of the pronunciation of the adjectives, paying special attention to word stress. Then, in open class, ask sts which character says the sentences.

1 special, fascinating (Au)
2 interesting (L)
3 strong (R)
4 great (L)
5 interesting (An)
6 busy (An)
7 excellent, beautiful (An)

C Drill the question *What does (character's name) do?* for August, Rory, Andrea, Genevieve, and Lucy. Refer to the speech bubbles and model the dialogue with a confident st. In pairs, sts ask and answer about the characters' jobs. Monitor closely for use of the simple present 3rd person -s.

D **Make it personal** Have sts work in new pairs. Write on the board: *What's your name?* and *What do you do?* and leave the questions there while sts are role-playing. Give out cards with jobs from the video written on them. Sts take turns picking a card and pretending they are a barista, a computer technician, a designer, etc. The other st interviews them. Refer sts to the speech bubbles for help, and remind them to use adjectives from **B**. Go through good language and errors with the class at the end.

4

4.1 Is there an ATM near here?

① Vocabulary Personal items

A ▶4.1 Match these items to photos 1–10. Then listen to Vero talking about the contents of her purse, and say which item is not in the photos.

- [ ] pills
- [ ] a comb /koʊm/
- [ ] an ID card
- [ ] a lipstick
- [ ] a charger
- [ ] coins
- [1] an umbrella
- [ ] keys
- [ ] mints
- [ ] a wallet

B ▶4.2 Listen to, point to, and repeat items 1–10.

4

Unit overview: In the context of talking about personal items, sts continue to review the simple present, and learn and practice using *there + be* and demonstrative pronouns to identify and describe items. They also learn names of colors and telling the time.

4.1 Is there an ATM near here?

Lesson aims: Sts learn vocabulary to talk about personal items, practice the pronunciation of /ɪ/, /iː/, and /ð/, and use *there + be* to describe items and where they are.

Function
Understanding descriptions of personal items.
Understanding and pronouncing /ɪ/, /iː/, and /ð/.
Describing items.

Language
There are always mints in my purse, and my pills.
This is a lipstick. It's pink.
These are keys.
How many students are there in this class?
There's a bag on the seat.

Vocabulary: Personal items (pills, a comb, an ID card, a lipstick, a charger, coins, an umbrella, keys, mints, a wallet)
Grammar: *there + be*

Warm-up Books closed. To find out what vocabulary sts already know for personal items, show them your purse and ask: *What is in my purse?* Tell sts to guess and write their ideas on the board. Don't correct any grammar errors but help them with vocabulary and teach the correct pronunciation. Don't spend too long on this activity. Leave the words on the board.

Extra activity Ask sts to tell each other what is in their bags / purses. Have them work in pairs and take turns asking: "What's in your bag / purse?" They answer: "a lipstick, a wallet, a charger," etc. Listen and help with vocabulary and correct any errors in pronunciation.

1 Vocabulary Personal items

A Books open. Point to the words in **A** and have sts match them to photos 1–10. Paircheck. Classcheck with answers on the board. Tell sts they're going to listen to Vero looking inside her purse. Ask: *Which object is not in the photos?* Play ▶ 4.1. Classcheck.

▶ 4.1 Turn to p. 172 for the complete audioscript.

1 an umbrella
2 a wallet
3 an ID card
4 a lipstick
5 a comb
6 pills
7 mints
8 keys
9 a charger
10 coins
Not in the photos: a cell phone

B Ask sts to listen to and point to the objects they hear. Play ▶ 4.2. Then replay the track pausing after each item for sts to repeat.

> **Tip** Point out different pronunciations of the letter *s*: /s/ in *mints*, and /z/ in *coins*, *pills* and *keys*.

101

2 Pronunciation /ɪ/, /iː/ and /ð/

> ♪ This the part when I say I don't want it,
> I'm stronger than I've been before,
> This is the part when I break free.

A ▶ 4.3 Read and listen to the information. Then practice the examples.

> Be careful with /ɪ/ and /iː/.
> /ɪ/ This is a lipstick. It's pink.
> /iː/ These are keys. Three green keys.
> The *s* in *this* is pronounced /s/. The *s* in *these* is pronounced /z/.
> The *th* in *this*, *these*, and *there* is pronounced /ð/.

 ɪ iː   ð

B ▶ 4.4 Listen to 1–5 and check /ɪ/ or /iː/. Listen again and repeat.

		/ɪ/	/iː/
1	Nick's sister has six children.	✓	
2	Repeat, please.		
3	Big pills and little mints.		
4	Think of six big things.		
5	Read and complete these forms.		

⚠ **Common mistakes**
~~What's it?~~ *this (or What is it?)*
~~This are pens.~~ *These*

C ▶ 4.5 Play **Race the beep!** Look again at the photos in **1A**. Listen and say *This is a / These are* and the correct word before the beep.

1 This is an umbrella.   2 This is a wallet.

3 Grammar There + be

A Complete the grammar box with *There's* or *There are*.

Singular		Plural	
_____	a charger on the table. an ATM near my house.	_____	four candies in the box. a lot of coins in my wallet.
_____ is the contraction of *There is*.			

➡ Grammar 4A p.78

⚠ **Common mistakes**
~~There's~~ *are* 10 students in my class.
There are
~~Have~~ keys on the table.
are there
How many chairs ~~there are~~ in the office?

B ▶ 4.6 Listen and follow the model. Practice the sentences.

> There's a book on the table. – pens   There are pens on the table.

C Complete with *there's*, *there are*, or *are there*.
1 How many students _____ in this class?
2 _____ pills in my backpack.
3 Look, _____ a purse on the seat!
4 _____ an umbrella in my car.
5 How many objects _____ on the table?
6 _____ eight candies in the box.

D 🔘 **Make it personal** Play **Memory test!** Close your books. In pairs, in two columns, remember all the items in the photos on p. 44. Which pair can remember the most?

> There's ...   There are ...
> a hand   a lot of coins

4.1

♪ **Song line:** Turn to p. 180 for notes about this song and an accompanying task.

2 Pronunciation /ɪ/, /iː/, and /ð/

A Point to the photo of lipstick in **1A** and ask: *How do you pronounce this word?* Do the same for *keys*. Write /ɪ/ and /iː/ on the board and drill the two sounds.

> **Tip** To help sts pronounce the /ɪ/ and /iː/ sounds, show them the correct mouth position. We make /iː/ by spreading our lips into a smile position and pushing our tongue forward in our mouth. For /ɪ/, our lips are relaxed and our tongue moves slightly back in the mouth to a mid position.

Play ▶ 4.3 for sts to listen and read the information. Drill pronunciation of *this* and *these* and have sts repeat the example sentences for /ɪ/ and /iː/ sounds in the box. Point to the images for each symbol and ask sts to say the words.

Refer sts to **Sounds and usual spellings** on p. 82 and have them practice the sound /iː/ as in *three*, *tree*, *key*, and /ɪ/ as in *six*, *mix*, *it*.

B Refer sts to the chart and say: *Let's listen for /ɪ/ or /iː/.* Play ▶ 4.4. Pause after sentence 2 and ask: *Is it /ɪ/ or /iː/?* (/iː/) Play the rest of the track and tell sts to check the correct sound in the chart. Paircheck. Classcheck with answers on the board. Play the track again, pausing after each sentence, for sts to repeat.

⚬ 2 /iː/   3 /ɪ/   4 /ɪ/   5 /iː/

C Write *This is a / an ...* and *These are ...* on the board. Point to photo 2 in **1A** and elicit the correct sentence (This is a wallet.). Do the same for a couple of the other photos. Say: *Now play Race the beep!* Play ▶ 4.5 and, after each number, point to the relevant photo and elicit the correct sentence before the beep. Make sure sts understand they have to try to say the sentence before the beep each time. Pause the track only if necessary.

▶ 4.5 Turn to p. 172 for the complete audioscript.

✓ Common mistakes Read with the class. Sts often have problems with *this* and *these* because the words sound similar. Elicit the correct pronunciation.

Then, tell sts you cannot use *it* after the contraction *What's*. Also explain we use *these* for plural nouns, before you move on to the grammar section.

> **Language tip** In Portuguese, one of the verbs used as equivalent to *there is / there are* does not change to a plural form, even when it refers to plural people / things (*Tem um banco nessa rua? Tem muitos livros nessa bibliotcea.*). Explain this difference to L1 Portuguese speakers and remind sts to use *there is* for singular things, and *there are* for plural things.

3 Grammar *There + be*

A Ask sts: *How many students are there in this class?* Start counting and let sts finish and tell you the number. Prompt them to say a complete sentence: "There are X students in this class." Ask: *How many boards are there?* (one). Again, prompt "There's one board." Refer sts to the grammar box and tell them to complete it with *There's* or *There are*. Paircheck, then classcheck.

There is more information on *There + be* in Grammar 4A on p. 78.

✓ Common mistakes Read with the class. Explain we do not contract *there are* in written English. Point out the difference between *have* and *there are*. Sts may use *have* because of their L1. For example, *there are* in Spanish is *hay*, from *haber*, which translates as *have*, and in Portuguese the verb *ter* translates as both *have* and *there is / are*. Remind sts of the correct word order in questions.

⚬ Singular: There's   Plural: There are   There's

B Transformation drill. Point to the speech bubbles and say: *Listen and follow the model.* Play ▶ 4.6 up to "Your turn" and the first pair of beeps, before and after the student prompt. Pause the track and elicit the response from the whole class (There's an umbrella in my purse.). Resume playing the track for students to check the answer and listen for the next prompt. After each pair of beeps, pick a different student to respond. Correct any errors, then play the track again for sts to practice chorally.

▶ 4.6 Turn to p. 172 for the complete audioscript.

C Elicit question 1 (How many students are there in this class?). Sts complete questions 1–6 with *there's*, *there are*, or *are there*. Paircheck, then classcheck.

⚬
1 are there	4 There's
2 There are	5 are there
3 there's	6 There are

D 🔵 **Make it personal** Make this a competition. Put sts into pairs and tell them to close their books. Write *There's* and *There are* at the top of two columns on the board. Tell sts they have to remember all the items in the photos on p. 44. Refer them to the examples to clarify the task. Give them a time limit of two minutes, and tell them that the pair with most correct words is the winner. Say: *Go!* Ask the team with the most words to read them out for the class to check together, and add any missing words.

Extra activity Play a memory game to review classroom and personal items. Put 10 to 15 items on a table and tell sts to come and look at the table. Say: *You have 30 seconds to remember all the items*. After 30 seconds, cover the objects (e.g. with a cloth). Tell them to write down all the items they can remember. Then they compare their lists with a partner. Ask: *What items are there?* and ask a student to say the items. Sts can then do the same in small groups.

4.2 Are those your books?

1 Listening

A ▶ 4.7 Look at the picture. Listen to Marty and Amy and answer 1–3.
1. What do they find?
2. Who opens it?
3. Guess six items they find in it.

> I think there's a wallet in it.

| book | candies | cell phone | comb | flash drive | glasses |
| headphones | ID card | keys | pen | pills | wallet |

B ▶ 4.8 Listen to the rest of the conversation. What items do they find? How many correct guesses?

2 Grammar *this / that / these / those*

A ▶ 4.9 Match questions and pictures 1–4 to the answers. Listen, check, and repeat.

What's **that**?   What's **this**?   What are **these**?   What are **those**?

☐ They're candies. ☐ They're headphones. ☐ It's an ID card. ☐ It's a bag.

B Singular or plural? Write S or P next to the questions in **A**. Then complete the grammar box with *that*, *these* and *those*.

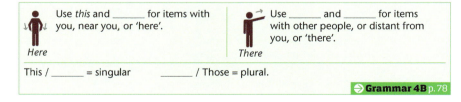

Use *this* and _____ for items with you, near you, or 'here'.
Here

Use _____ and _____ for items with other people, or distant from you, or 'there'.
There

This / _____ = singular   _____ / Those = plural.

➡ **Grammar 4B** p. 78

Common mistakes

~~that~~
What's *this*?

4.2 Are those your books?

Lesson aims: Sts learn colors and demonstrative pronouns *this, that, these, those* to describe everyday items.

Function
Listening to a conversation about a lost item.
Describing objects in the classroom.
Asking and answering questions about items.

Language
Over there.
What's that? It's a pencil.
What color are those chairs? They're pink.

Vocabulary: Review everyday objects
Grammar: Demonstrative pronouns *this, that, these, those*

Warm-up Books closed. Before class, prepare enough sets of word cards for groups of four sts, with two pairs in each group. Include vocabulary from 4.1 on the cards. In their groups, sts play pictionary (a drawing and guessing game). They draw the words on the cards for their partner to guess. Alternatively, prepare just one set of cards and ask some sts to draw items on the board for the whole class to guess. After they have finished, ask sts: *What words did you guess?* and write the words on the board, leaving them there for the lesson.

1 Listening

A Point to the picture and say: *This is Marty and Amy. They are on the subway. They see something.* Tell sts to listen to their conversation and play ▶4.7. Answer questions 1 and 2 with the class. Point to the words in the box and ask: *Guess six items they find in the bag?* Elicit ideas from the class.

▶4.7 Turn to p. 172 for the complete audioscript.

1 a bag
2 Marty

B Play ▶4.8 and tell sts to listen to the rest of the conversation and check their ideas about what is in the bag. Paircheck and then replay ▶4.8. Classcheck with the items on the board.

glasses, keys, cell phone, candies, headphones, ID card

▶4.8 Turn to p. 172 for the complete audioscript.

2 Grammar *this / that / these / those*

A Point to pictures 1–4 and the questions and tell sts to match them with the correct answers. Play ▶4.9 twice for sts to listen and check, and then repeat.

▶4.9 Turn to p. 173 for the complete audioscript.

1 It's a bag.
2 It's an ID card.
3 They're candies.
4 They're headphones.

B Write t_ _ _ _ *pens* and t_ _ _ *pen* on the board. Point to *pen* and ask sts: *Do we say this pen or these pen?* (this pen). Then point to *pens* and ask: *Do we say this pens or these pens?* (these pens). Elicit *this* is used with singular nouns and *these* is used with plural nouns. Point to something near you in the class and ask sts: *What's this?* Then point to something far away in the class and ask: *What's that?* Do the same with plural items that are near you in the classroom and further away from you: *What are these? What are those?* Elicit that we use *that / those* for far away things and *this / these* for nearer things. Tell sts to complete the grammar box. Classcheck.

There is more information on *this, that, these, those* in Grammar 4B on p. 78.

1 S 2 S 3 P 4 P
Here: these
There: that, those
This / That = singular
These / Those = plural.

🎵 *I'm waiting for it, that green light, I want it,
Oh, I wish I could get my things and just let go.*

C ▶ 4.10 Complete with *this*, *these*, *that* or *those*.
Listen, check, and repeat.

1 _____ is my new phone.

2 _____ are my books.

3 What's _____?

4 What are _____?

5 Hey! _____'s my car.

6 _____ are my children.

D ▶ 4.11 Listen and follow the model. Practice the sentences.

This – question   What's this?   *a wallet*   It's a wallet.

E 🎧 **Make it personal** In pairs, test your partner.
1 Show items you have with you, or point at photos in *your* book.

What's this?   It's a pencil.   What are these?   They're keys.

2 Point to items around the classroom or point at photos in *your partner's* book.

What's that?   It's an eraser.   What are those?   They're windows.

③ Vocabulary Colors

A ▶ 4.12 Match the colors to 1–10 in **B**. Listen, check, and repeat.

black **blue** **brown** **green** **gray** **orange** **pink** **red** **yellow** **white**

B In pairs, ask and answer about 1–10.

What's this?   It's a black bike.   What are these?   They're green glasses.

⚠️ **Common mistake**
blue birds
They're ~~birds blues~~.

C 🎧 **Make it personal** In pairs, test your partner using items in the classroom.
How many questions can you ask and answer correctly in five minutes?

What color are those chairs?   They're gray. What color is the whiteboard?   It's white!

4.2

🎵 **Song line:** Turn to p. 180 for notes about this song and an accompanying task.

C Point to the pictures and tell sts to complete the exercise. Play ▶4.10 and tell them to listen and check their answers. Play the track again for sts to repeat.

▶**4.10** Turn to p. 173 for the complete audioscript.

🔑
1 This 2 These 3 this 4 those 5 That's 6 These

D Transformation drill. Point to the speech bubbles and say: *Listen and follow the model*. Play ▶4.11 up to "Your turn" and the first pair of beeps, before and after the student prompt. Pause the track and elicit the question from the whole class (What are these?). Resume playing the track for students to check the answer and listen for the next prompt. After each pair of beeps, pick a different student to respond. Correct any errors, then play the track again. Vary with choral and individual repetition.

▶**4.11** Turn to p. 173 for the complete audioscript.

E 🔵 **Make it personal** In new pairs, sts test each other, performing tasks 1 and 2. Tell sts to take turns asking the questions. Make sure they understand that in 1, they show / point to items with them or in their book; in 2, they point to classroom items or photos in their partner's book. Monitor and make sure sts are showing / pointing correctly. At the end, ask: *What's this / that? What are these / those?* to test the whole class.

③ Vocabulary Colors

A Books closed. Point to an object in the classroom and ask: *What color is that?* Elicit the answer and write the color on the board. Ask sts: *What colors do you know in English?* Write the colors on the board and correct pronunciation.

Books open. Tell sts to look at the color words and say them with you. Then, ask them to do the matching exercise by matching the colors to photos 1–10 in **B**. Play ▶4.12 and tell sts to check answers. Classcheck. Play the track again for sts to repeat.

▶**4.12** Turn to p. 173 for the complete audioscript.

🔑
1 orange
2 pink
3 gray
4 black
5 white
6 blue
7 green
8 yellow
9 brown
10 red

Extra activity Write *What's your favorite color?* on the board and ask one or two sts the question. Then tell all the sts to stand up and walk around the class asking and answering the question with as many people as possible.

Then, tell them to sit down and write down as many classmates' names and their favorite color as they can remember. Ask the st with the most names to read out the names and colors. Congratulate them on their memory skills. Then correct any pronunciation errors you heard during the activity.

B Demonstrate the activity with photo 1, asking a student: *What are these?* (They're orange socks). Point to the speech bubbles and say: *Now you do the same for all the photos*. In pairs, sts ask and answer about the photos. Monitor and help with vocabulary, and listen for good language and errors. As you monitor, write any words they struggle with on the board. Review this vocabulary, the good language, and errors afterwards.

🔄 **Common mistakes** Read with the class and remind sts that adjectives go before nouns and after the verb *be*.

Language tip Sts whose L1 is Spanish or Portuguese often have problems with the order of adjectives and nouns because it's different in their L1. In English, adjectives always come before the noun. To practice this, write a few adjectives and nouns randomly on the board, then have sts work in pairs to make as many correct combinations as they can. Set a short time limit. The pair with the most correct combinations is the winner.

C 🔵 **Make it personal** Point to the speech bubbles and nominate a student to ask you a question about an item in the classroom, e.g. "What color is Jorge's bag?". Write their question on the board, answer it, and ask another question about something else in the classroom. Then say to the class: *Now you do the same*. Make sure sts understand the instructions. Put sts into new pairs and set a time limit of five minutes. Tell them to count all the correct questions and answers they give. After five minutes, ask: *How many questions did you ask and answer correctly?* Congratulate the winning pair.

Extra activity Sts write a description of their classroom using the vocabulary and grammar from lessons **4.1** and **4.2**, e.g. "Our classroom is big. There are twenty black chairs, a whiteboard, and three big tables. It's white and gray. The doors are blue."

4.3 What things do you lose?

1 Reading

A ▶4.13 Read the article and match statements 1–4 to pictures a–d. Guess the pronunciation of the pink-stressed words. Then listen and check.

a

b

c

d

Japanese honesty

(1) Hundreds of people lose personal items in big cities every day, (2) and hundreds of people find these items. In Tokyo, with a population of 33 million, (3) officers at the Lost and Found Center collect hundreds of things every day and catalogue them in a database. (4) The result is 72% of the items are returned to the happy owners! What honest people! Is your country similar or different?

B Reread the question at the end of the text. Choose your answer(s) from 1–5. In pairs, compare. Do you agree?
1 I think it's the same here.
2 I don't think people are honest here.
3 People are honest here too.
4 People don't return items here.
5 Lost and Found centers don't work here.

I (don't) agree with number 1.   *It depends.*

2 Vocabulary Plural nouns (3)

A ▶4.14 Read and listen. Then match photos 1–6 to the underlined words.

Transport for London (TfL) finds 400,000 lost items on the London trains, <u>buses</u>, ☐ and taxis every year. The usual things are ID cards, wallets, cell phones, and keys, but what about the unusual items? Officers find false <u>teeth</u> ☐, <u>toothbrushes</u> ☐, <u>suitcases</u> ☐, personal <u>diaries</u>, ☐ and even <u>fish</u> ☐!

48

4.3 What things do you lose?

Lesson aims: Sts learn about the formation of plural nouns in the context of lost and found items on public transportation. They learn and practice telling the time, and ask and answer questions about quantity.

Function
Listening to and reading an article about Japanese honesty.
Agreeing and disagreeing with opinion.
Asking and answering questions about quantity.
Telling the time.

Language
I think people are honest.
What do you lose? I lose my phone and keys every day!
Excuse me, what time is it, please?
It's 7:45.

Vocabulary: Plural nouns (buses, candies, children, diaries, fish, men, people, suitcases, teeth, toothbrushes, watches, women). Time (It's two fifteen. It's three forty-five.)
Grammar: Plural noun formation. Review simple present.

Warm-up Books open. Ask sts: *What things do you lose?* Say: *I lose my keys and sometimes my phone*. Gesture so they understand the meaning of *to lose something*. Encourage sts to tell you what they lose and write the items on the board. Don't do this for too long as sts do a similar activity in pairs at the end of the lesson.

1 Reading

A Mime finding some money on the floor: you are not sure what to do – take it to the police or put it in your pocket? Act out the scene and ask sts: *What do I do? Do I keep it* (mime putting the money in your pocket) *or take it to the police?* Elicit some answers. Teach the meaning of *honest* and *honesty*, e.g. *Honest people take the money to the police. This is honesty.* Tell sts they're going to read an article about Japanese honesty. Before they start, ask: *Do you think some nationalities are more honest? Which nationalities do you think are very honest?* Tell sts to show their opinion with thumbs up for honest or down for not honest.

Point to the pictures and ask: *Where is it?* (A Lost and Found Center in a train station). Pre-teach the meaning of *officers*, *to return something*, and *owners*. Sts read the article and match statements 1–4 to pictures a–d. Paircheck, then classcheck. Round off the activity by asking sts: *Are Japanese people honest?*

Point to the words with pink letters and ask: *How do we say these words?* Have sts guess the pronunciation with a partner. Then tell them to listen and check the pronunciation, and play ▶ 4.13. Replay the track, pausing after the pink-stressed words for sts to repeat.

Tip Ask sts to identify cognates in the text, e.g. *database, population, catalogue, honest*. Then, tell them to add these to their list of cognates and remind them to make a note of the correct pronunciation.

1 d 2 c 3 a 4 b

B Ask the class the last question in the text: *Is your country similar or different?* Tell sts they're going to choose an answer to the question. Read through sentences 1–5 with sts and clarify the meaning if any sts don't understand.

Tip Many sts confuse the meaning of *It doesn't work*. Clarify the meaning using *function* (*It doesn't function.*) as this is a cognate. While this is not often used in English, it helps to teach the meaning.

Tell sts to choose their answer(s), then tell them to work in pairs. Point to the speech bubbles and ask pairs to compare their answers and say if they agree or disagree. Monitor and help with ideas and language.

2 Vocabulary Plural nouns (3)

A Books closed. Ask sts: *What items do people lose on the subway, train, bus?* Elicit typical items people leave on public transportation and write the vocabulary on the board.

Books open. Point to photos 1–6 and ask: *Do you think these are lost items?* Tell sts to read and listen about items lost on London transportation. Play ▶ 4.14. Ask sts: *Are you surprised?* Use gestures to teach the meaning of *surprised*. Sts complete the matching exercise and paircheck. Classcheck. Play the track again, pausing after the underlined and pink-stressed words for sts to repeat chorally. Tell sts to make a note of new vocabulary.

Language tip Focus on the *meaning of diary*. In sts' L1 *diario / diário* can mean *newspaper*. It is therefore a false friend. As well as building up a bank of cognates using this book, you can point out false friends.

Tip Find a good pronunciation model amongst your sts. Ask them to demonstrate the pronunciation and help the class to pronounce the words correctly.

1 fish   4 false teeth
2 toothbrushes 5 suitcases
3 buses   6 diaries

B Complete the information with the underlined words from **A**.

🎵 *You're dangerous cause you're honest, You're dangerous 'cause you don't know what you want.*

Most plurals = noun + *s*	Some plurals have special spellings.	Some plurals are irregular.
one key, two keys one umbrella, two umbrellas ¹ _____	• Nouns ending in consonant + *y*, change -*y* to -*ies*. one candy, two candies ² _____ • Nouns ending in -*sh*, -*ch*, -*s*, -*z* or -*x*, add -*es*. one watch, two watches ³ _____ ⁴ _____ Pronounce -*es* as an extra syllable /ɪz/.	one man, two men one woman, two women one child, two children one person, two people one tooth, some ⁵ _____ one fish, some ⁶ _____ ➔ **Grammar 4C** p. 78

C In pairs, test your partner. Take turns saying a noun. Your partner says and spells the plural noun.

> *candy*   *candies – C-A-N-D-I-E-S*

D 🎧 **Make it personal** What things do you lose? In pairs, compare.

> *I lose my phone and my keys every day!*

⚠️ **Common mistakes**
~~camera~~ cameras
I have two ~~camera~~.
They are ~~reds~~ pens.

3 Listening Telling the time

A ▶ 4.15 Listen and match conversations 1–6 to the correct clock. Listen again and repeat the times.

> *Excuse me, what time is it, please?*
> *It's seven forty-five.*

08:10 ☐   04:30 ☐   07:45 [1]
11:50 ☐   02:00 ☐   05:15 ☐

B ▶ 4.16 Listen and write the six times. In pairs, compare. Any differences?

C 🎧 **Make it personal** Write more times for your partner to practice saying.

> *What time is it?*   *It's two fifteen.*

D 🎧 **Make it personal** Write five times between 11:05 and 11:55. Listen to your teacher and play **Bingo!**

⚠️ **Common mistake**
time is it / 's the time
What ~~hours are~~?

B Write *diary, toothbrush, fish,* and *suitcase* on the board and ask sts: *How do we say two …,?* pointing to the four words. Direct them to the text in **A** to find the answers. Write the plural forms on the board and underline the plural endings. Tell sts to work in pairs and complete the vocabulary box with the underlined words in **A**. Monitor and help weaker sts. Classcheck and drill the pronunciation of the plural nouns.

🔑 **Common mistakes** Read with the class. Remind sts to add *-s* to form plural nouns. Tell them not to add *-s* to adjectives as they cannot be plural.

Language tip Use Common mistakes to point out other differences between sts' L1 and English. Explain that, unlike their L1, adjectives are never pluralized.

Extra activity To practice the pronunciation of plural nouns, write these sounds on the board:

/s/	/z/	/ɪz/
lipsticks	keys	watches
wallets	umbrellas	glasses
books	phones	
	pills	

Say different plural nouns and ask sts to write them under the correct plural ending.

> 1 one suitcase, two suitcases
> 2 one diary, two diaries
> 3 one bus, two buses
> 4 one toothbrush, two toothbrushes
> 5 teeth
> 6 fish

C Ask a student: *How do you spell teeth?* Ask them not to look at the book. Write the correct spelling on the board. Tell sts they're going to test each other's spelling. Put them into pairs and tell them to decide who is **A** and who is **B**. Give them one minute to look at the words in the box in **B**, and then tell sts **A** to close their books. Sts **B** test them on five words, and then they change roles. Afterward, test the class on different words. Correct any mispronounced letters.

D 👥 **Make it personal** Refer back to the start of the lesson in the Warm-up. Ask: *Can you remember what I lose?* Encourage sts to remember the items you mentioned. Say: *What do you lose?* Put sts into pairs and tell them to ask and answer the question with their partner. Then, put them in new pairs and tell sts to report on their previous partner, then ask and answer the same question with their new partner. Ask sts: *What do we lose? Any unusual things?* Prompt sts to say what they and their partners lose.

🎵 **Song line**: Turn to p. 180 for notes about this song and an accompanying task.

3 Listening Telling the time

A Books closed. Ask sts: *What time is it?* to help you assess their current vocabulary for telling the time. Don't correct them yet. Use the listening to introduce the correct vocabulary.

Note: in this exercise, the time is told using only numbers, not *quarter past, half past,* or *quarter to, twenty past, twenty to,* etc. Tell the time as *eight ten* (8:10), *three fifty* (3:50), etc.

Books open. Point to the photo and speech bubbles. Tell sts they're going to listen and match the conversations to the purple clocks. Show sts that the purple clock showing 7:45 has been completed as an example. In pairs, tell sts to look at the other clocks and guess how to say the time for each clock. Play ▶ 4.15 and tell sts to match the conversations to the correct clocks. Paircheck, then classcheck. Then play the track again, pausing after each time for sts to repeat.

▶ 4.15 Turn to p. 173 for the complete audioscript.

> 2 four thirty   3 eight ten   4 two o'clock   5 eleven fifty
> 6 five fifteen

B Tell sts to listen and write the times. Play ▶ 4.16. Paircheck by asking pairs to compare answers and note any differences. Replay the track and classcheck with answers on the board.

🔑 **Common mistakes** Ask sts to compare how they tell the time in their own language and English. Ask them to work in pairs and discuss similarities and differences. After a few minutes, go over Common mistakes with the class.

▶ 4.16 Turn to p. 173 for the complete audioscript.

> 1 6:25   2 10:40   3 12:05   4 3:20   5 1:55   6 9:35

C 👥 **Make it personal** Write a time on the board and ask a student: *What time is it?* Write their answer out in full, correcting any errors. Tell the sts to write five different times. Point to the speech bubbles and tell sts to practice telling the time in pairs, using the five times they wrote down. Encourage peer correction by asking them to say "Correct!" if their partner is correct, or "Sorry, that's wrong." if their partner is incorrect.

D 👥 **Make it personal** Read the instructions with the class. Monitor and make sure sts are writing correct times before you start playing. Say different times, e.g.: *eleven fifty,* pausing between times so sts can check their numbers. The first student to check all their five numbers shouts "Bingo!"

Extra activity Put sts into groups and ask them to play Bingo again using different times.

4.4 What time do you get up?

1 Reading and vocabulary Typical days

A ▶ 4.17 Read and listen to Leroy's blog entry. Match pictures a–j to the **bold** phrases.

My typical day
Hi guys! Hope we can find a good time to chat and game.

I do virtually the same things every day. I **get up** ☐ at seven o'clock and **check my phone** ☐. You know, social media, read the news … I **have breakfast** ☐ at about 7:40. Then it's time to go to school. I **leave home** ☐ at eight o'clock (my bus leaves at 8:10).

I start school at nine o'clock, **have lunch** ☐ at 12:45, and finish at 3:30. After school, I **go home,** ☐ or **go to the gym** ☐. I'm free from 5 to 7:45.

I **have dinner** ☐ with my family around eight. After dinner, I relax or **study** ☐ – or play video games with you! Finally, I **go to bed** ☐ at around midnight.

What about you? Is your typical day similar or very different?
When is a good time to play?

a

b

f

g

h

4.4 What time do you get up?

Lesson aims: Sts read a blog about a typical day, and review the simple present and telling the time to talk about their typical days.

Function
Reading and listening to a blog post.
Describing someone's typical day.
Asking and answering questions about their typical day.

Language
I do virtually the same things every day.
I start school at nine o'clock.
What time do you get up?
I get up at 6:30 every morning.

Vocabulary: Everyday activities (get up, check my phone, have breakfast, leave home, have lunch, go home, go to the gym, have dinner, study, go to bed). Review telling the time.
Grammar: Simple present

Warm-up To review telling the time, point to the lesson question title and ask sts to walk around the class, asking and answering the question. Tell sts to sit down after they have spoken to everyone and ask: *When does (student's name) get up? Who gets up very early? Who gets up late?*

Correct any errors with telling the time on the board. Then do a quick review by dictating some times and asking sts to write the numerical form, e.g. *It's eight ten* (08:10).

1 Reading and vocabulary Typical days

A Tell sts to look at the text and pictures. Play ▶ 4.17 and tell sts to read and listen to Leroy's blog about his typical day. Tell them to match the pictures to the bold phrases, then paircheck. Classcheck and clarify the meaning of any unknown vocabulary.

Go through the pronunciation of the pink-stressed words and then play ▶ 4.17 again so sts can hear the pronunciation one more time.

Tip Play a quick miming game to test sts on the verbs. Mime a verb and ask sts to guess the action, e.g. *get up*. The student who guesses first mimes the next action for the class to guess. You can play it books open at first and then books closed.

a have breakfast
b check my phone
c have dinner
d get up
e go to the gym
f leave home
g study
h have lunch
i go to bed
j go home

113

B Reread. True (T) or False (F)?
1. Leroy wants to play video games.
2. His typical day is different every day.
3. He reads a newspaper every morning.
4. He goes to the gym every day.
5. He goes to bed at twelve o'clock.

C In pairs. A: Cover the text in **A** and use the pictures to describe Leroy's typical day. B: Help A as necessary. Then change roles.

> He gets up at seven o'clock and he checks his phone.

D Is your typical day similar to or different than Leroy's?

> I get up at six o'clock!   I check my phone at breakfast.   I go to bed at around one thirty!

E 🎧 **Make it personal** In pairs, take turns asking and answering about your typical day. Use the pictures in **A**. How many differences?

> What time do you get up?   What time do you go to school?
> I get up at 6:30 every morning.   I go to school at 7:45.

♪ No one knows about you, about you,
And you're making the typical me break my typical rules,
It's true, I'm a sucker for you.

⏱ **Common mistakes**

~~I take the~~ *have* breakfast / lunch / dinner at …
He gets up at ~~the~~ 7:30 o'clock.
~~At~~ *W* what time do you go to work?

d

e

i

j

B This exercise helps sts understand more details in the text. Tell them to reread the text in **A**, then read sentences 1–5 and decide if they are true or false. Paircheck, then classcheck. Ask sts to correct the false sentences (e.g. His typical day is the same every day.).

> 1 T
> 2 F His typical day is the same every day.
> 3 F He checks his phone every morning.
> 4 F He doesn't go to the gym every day.
> 5 T

C **Common mistakes** Read with the class. Then demonstrate the task with a student. Cover the text in **A**, point to a couple of pictures, and use them to describe Leroy's typical day. Ask the student: *Am I correct?* Point to the speech bubble as an example, then tell sts to work in pairs and take turns using the pictures to remember Leroy's day. Classcheck by pointing to pictures and asking sts to describe them.

Language tip In both Portuguese and Spanish, the equivalent expression for *have breakfast* uses the verb *tomar*, which translates as *take*. Tell sts to memorize the English expression *have breakfast* as a chunk, to avoid making translation errors.

D Ask sts: *Is your day similar to Leroy's?* Point to the speech bubbles and say: *Tell your partner.* Sts talk about their typical day, using the phrases from **A**. Help with vocabulary if necessary. Monitor and listen for good language and errors and go over this at the end.

Extra activity Help sts remember the verb and noun collocations by asking them to write the correct verb for nouns that you dictate. Say the following nouns:

____ *bed* (go to)

____ *sleep* (go to)

____ *your phone* (check)

____ *breakfast* (have)

____ *home* (go, get, leave)

____ *the gym* (go to)

____ *for an exam* (study)

____ *dinner* (make, have)

____ *soccer* (play, watch)

Afterward, ask sts to compare their answers, then classcheck on the board.

E **Make it personal** Ask a couple of students: *What time do you get up?* and *What time do you go to school?* When they have answered, prompt them to ask you the question. Refer sts to the speech bubbles. Put sts into new pairs and tell them to take turns asking and answering about their typical day, using the pictures in **A**. Tell them to keep a note of differences between them, and make sentences (e.g. I get up at seven thirty, but Sara gets up at seven. We have lunch at one o'clock.). When they have finished, ask some pairs to tell the class about their typical days.

Weaker classes Write *What time do you _____?* on the board to help them.

Extra activity Ask sts to imagine they are a famous person and to think about what they do on a typical day. Tell them to make a list of what they do and when, e.g.

I get up at 6:00.

I train from 8:00-2:00.

I check my social media pages at 3:00.

I sleep a little and then go to the gym.

I have dinner with my girlfriend at 9:00.

(A famous footballer)

Put sts into groups of three and have them take turns reading out their typical day for the others to guess who the person is / their job.

Alternatively, you could put sts into pairs and ask them to interview each other as if they are a journalist and a celebrity.

♪ **Song line:** Turn to p. 180 for notes about this song and an accompanying task.

4.5 How do you pronounce *meme* in English?

Skills Pronouncing and spelling cognates

A How many "technology" words do you know in English? Make a list.

> I know a lot … computer, radio, cell phone …

> And what about charger?

B Read the article and underline any words from your list in **A**. Are 1–4 True (T) or False (F)?

> **Common mistake**
>
> There are ~~lot~~ a lot of apps on my cell phone.

HOME   ABOUT   ARCHIVE   SUBSCRIBE

INFORMATION TECHNOLOGY

Information technology (IT) is responsible for a lot of new English words, and many of these are now international. *Electronic mail*, for example, is email, and *applications* (computer and software programs for mobile devices) are *apps*. Other words—blog, gigabyte, smartphone, Wi-Fi and, of course, *Internet*—are now common internationally. Social networks contribute with Facebook, *Twitter* (and tweet—the noun and verb for a post on *Twitter*), and others. And old words get new meanings too—a tablet, for example, is not just another word for a *pill*!

1. Many new words in English are from IT.
2. There aren't a lot of English IT words in other languages.
3. The words *email* and *apps* are abbreviations.
4. There's only one meaning for the word *tablet*.

C ▶ 4.18 Listen and reread. In pairs, do 1–3.
1. Practice the pink-stressed words, and words in italics. Find at least ten cognates.
2. Say which of the cognates have the same spelling in your language.
3. Practice the final consonant sound in the eight highlighted words.

D ▶ 4.19 Listen to a conversation and note the six technology words you hear.

E ▶ 4.19 Listen again. Which tablet is it, a, b, or c?

F **Make it personal** *Spelling test!* In pairs, take turns asking the spelling of the cognates in the article in **B**. One point for each correct answer. Be careful with pronunciation!

> How do you spell technology?

> T - E - C - H …

4.5 How do you pronounce *meme* in English?

Lesson aims: Sts practice pronouncing and spelling cognates related to technology.

Function
Reading and listening to an article about technology.
Pronouncing cognates correctly.
Listening to identify technology words.
Spelling cognates.

Language
Information technology is responsible for a lot of new English words.
How do you spell *technology*?

Vocabulary: Review spelling. Technology cognates (blog, gigabyte, smartphone, WiFi, social networks, email, tablet).

Warm-up Books closed. Write *cognates* on the board and ask sts: *What's a cognate? Can you remember?* Elicit they are words that are similar in English and their L1. Ask: *What cognates do you know?* Tell sts to work in pairs and write down at least five examples. Tell them they cannot look at their notebooks. Sts have come across lots of cognates in the book so far, so should remember some. Write their words on the board. Then, ask them to look at their notebooks and say some more.

ID SKILLS Pronouncing and spelling cognates

A Tell sts to work in pairs. Write *Technology* on the board and ask: *What words do you know about technology?* Tell them to write as many words as they can in two minutes. After two minutes, ask sts: *How many words do you have?* Ask the pair with the most words to read them out and write them on the board. Check pronunciation as you go. Ask the class: *Can you add more words?* Add these words to the board and leave them there for the lesson.

B Tell sts to read the website article and underline any words on the board. Paircheck, then classcheck. Then tell sts to decide if sentences 1–4 are true or false. Classcheck. When the answer is false, ask sts to find the true sentence in the text. Then ask sts: *Are there any cognates in the text?* Elicit a couple of examples. Tell sts they're going to listen to the pronunciation of these words and how they are different in English.

1 T   2 F   3 T   4 F

Common mistakes Read with the class. Remind sts to use *a* with *lot of*. Ask them to list some things in the classroom to practice, e.g. *There are a lot of students. There are not a lot of books.* They could also look out the window, or think of another place, and make sentences.

Language tip Remind sts of the importance of learning the English pronunciaton of cognates, and to use the pink-stressed letters to help them.

C Play ▶ 4.18 and tell sts to read and listen to the text. Tell them to notice if the pink-stressed words are pronounced the same or differently in their language. Paircheck but don't check answers at this stage. Read through instructions 1–3 and check sts are clear on the task. If necessary, elicit an example for each question. Put sts in pairs and tell them to do 1–3. Monitor and help sts with their pronunciation. Go through the answers with the class one question at a time, correcting the pronunciation of any words sts have problems with.

D Tell sts they are going to hear a conversation and they should listen carefully for six technology words. Play ▶ 4.19 and tell them to listen, not write. When the track finishes, tell them to write the technology words they remember. Paircheck and then replay the track. Classcheck.

▶ 4.19 Turn to p. 173 for the complete audioscript.

1 tablet   2 Internet   3 apps   4 emails   5 Facebook
6 Twitter

E Ask sts: *What is the conversation about?* and play ▶ 4.19 again so sts can understand the conversation. Ask a st to describe the conversation afterwards. Ask sts: *Which tablet is it?* and elicit the correct answer. Ask sts: *Do you have a tablet? Do you use it a lot? What do you use it for?*

tablet a

F **Make it personal** Ask sts: *Are you good at spelling? Let's see!* Read through the instructions and point to the speech bubble to clarify the task. Put sts into pairs and say: *Test your partner.* Take turns asking the spelling of the cognates in the article. One point for each correct answer. Monitor pronunciation carefully to make sure sts are pronouncing the words and letters correctly. Afterward, test some sts with words from the lesson.

Extra activity Tell sts to add new cognates from this lesson to their notebook and remind them to make a note of the correct pronunciation.

They could then review the cognates they have learned so far and test each other in small groups. One student says the word in L1 and the other sts race to say the English word with correct pronunciation.

4.5 What color is your wallet?

♫ *Tell me somethin', girl / Are you happy in this modern world? / Or do you need more? / Is there somethin' else you're searchin' for?*

in Action Asking about lost property

A ▶ 4.20 Listen to a conversation. Where exactly are the people? What is the problem? Choose the correct wallet from 1–4.

B ▶ 4.20 Listen again and number the sentences in the order you hear them, 1–8.

- All the money for my vacation! ☐
- Can I help you? ☐
- Do you know where? ☐
- I lost my wallet. ☐
- OK, and what color is the wallet? ☐
- Yesterday? ☐
- Now, let's see what there is in the system. ☐
- It's very big. ☐

C In pairs, complete this part of the Lost and Found report.

D Read AS 4.20 on p. 86. Read to check you have all the correct information in **C**. Do you think the man will be lucky?

E In pairs, practice the dialogue using AS 4.20 on p. 86. Copy the intonation. Then change roles.

F Practice again without the script. Use only the information in **B**.

G 🎤 Make it personal In pairs, role-play a conversation at Lost and Found. Then change roles. Be creative!
- A: Lose an item.
- B: Complete the form in **C**.

Excuse me, is this Lost and Found?

Yes, can I help you?

Yes, I lost my cell phone.

4.5 What color is your wallet?

Lesson aims: Sts listen to a conversation in a lost and found office and practice asking about lost property.

Function
Understanding a conversation about lost property.
Role-playing a conversation at a lost and found office.

Language
Excuse me, is this Lost and Found?
Can I help you? I lost my wallet.
Do you know where? On the train.

Vocabulary: Review colors. Review personal objects.
Grammar: Review simple present and verb *be* ❓

ID in action Asking about lost property

🎵 **Song line:** Turn to p. 181 for notes about this song and an accompanying task.

A Books closed. Show sts items from your bag / purse and ask: *What's this? What are these?* Write the names of the items on the board and model the correct pronunciation. (Suggested items: keys, wallet, ID card, diary, cell phone.) Tell sts they are going to listen to a conversation about a personal item. Play ▶ 4.20 and ask: *Where are they? What item do they talk about, and why?* (Lost and Found, they talk about a lost wallet.)

Books open. Point to the photos of wallets in turn and ask: *What color are they?* Play ▶ 4.20 again and ask sts to check the correct wallet. Paircheck and classcheck.

▶ 4.20 Turn to p. 173 for the complete audioscript.

> wallet 3 (wallet 1 is also green, but it is small)

B In this activity, sts listen for more details. Tell sts to read through the sentences before they listen. Teach the meaning of any unknown vocabulary. Play ▶ 4.20 again and tell sts to number the sentences in order. Paircheck, then classcheck.

> 1 Can I help you?
> 2 I lost my wallet.
> 3 Do you know where?
> 4 Yesterday?
> 5 OK, and what color is the wallet?
> 6 It's very big.
> 7 All the money for my vacation!
> 8 Now, let's see what there is in the system.

C Point to the first row of the Lost & Found report and ask: *What's the item?* (a wallet). Tell sts to complete column one of the chart with the other information. Tell them not to write in column two. Paircheck. Don't check answers yet.

> Item: wallet
> Where: airport
> When: today
> Appearance: very big, green
> Contents: passport, credit cards, $500

D Tell sts to read AS 4.20 on p. 86 to check that their information in **C** is correct. Ask: *Do you think the man will be lucky and get his wallet back?* Encourage sts to speculate.

E Play ▶ 4.20 again and tell sts to listen, reread AS 4.20, and notice the intonation. What happens to intonation when people want to sound polite and helpful? Explain we usually make our voices higher when we want to be polite. Model this with *Can I help you?*, saying it with a high and low voice to exaggerate polite and impolite intonation. Encourage sts to repeat after you.

Tell sts to act out the dialogue, taking turns to be the lost and found officer and the customer. Monitor and help with pronunciation and intonation.

F In pairs, sts turn back to p. 53, and, using only the information in **C**, practice the dialogue again.

G 🎧 Make it personal Point to the instructions and speech bubbles and explain sts are going to do a role-play at a Lost and Found office. If possible, set up the class so customers can walk up to the officers as if they were in the Lost and Found office. Demonstrate the conversation with a confident st. Then put sts into new pairs and ask them to do the role-play. Encourage them to be creative. Monitor, and make sure the sts playing the officer complete the second column of the form in **C**. Then tell sts to change roles and do the role-play again.

> **Weaker students** Give them time to think about what they will say. Encourage them to rehearse the conversation in their heads before they start. This kind of silent rehearsal can help build confidence and better fluency as a result. You could also put some key phrases on the board for these sts.

> **Tip** If you have time, ask sts to repeat the role-play with a different student.

➡ **Workbook** p. 104

➡ Ⓓ **Richmond Learning Platform**

➡ **Writing** p. 54

➡ Ⓓ **Café** p. 55

Writing 4 A description

🎵 *Yeah, I left my wallet in El Segundo
Left my wallet in El Segundo
Left my wallet in El Segundo I gotta get it,
I got-got ta get it.*

A ▶ 4.21 Read Kylee's lost property report. Choose the correct bag 1–3.

LOST PROPERTY REPORT

Fares | Help & contact | More ▼

Name: Kylee Hurst
Email: k.hurst04@usanet.us
Date lost: 02/16/2020

Location:
I lost my bag in Union Station, in the Mexican restaurant or at the Mini Golf.

Description of object:
It's a big green bag. It's really important because my wallet is in it, with my ID, credit card and about $50 too! There's a very expensive tablet in it too! And there are a lot of pens, a notebook and a new blue sweater. Please help me find it because my mom is not very happy with me at the moment!

1

2

3

B True (T) or False (F)?
1. Kylee lost her bag in an airport.
2. She knows exactly where she lost her bag.
3. There's money in the wallet in her bag.
4. Kylee mentions a total of nine items that are in her bag.
5. Kylee's mom and dad are unhappy with her.

C Read *Write it right!* In the report, (circle) two examples of:
- reasons introduced by *because*
- *too* to give extra information
- two adjectives before a noun.

✓ Write it right!

Use *because* to introduce a reason.
*I go to classes **because** I want to learn English.*
Use *too* at the end of a sentence to give additional information.
*I study French **too**.*
To describe a noun using two adjectives, put them **before** the noun.
*I have a **great new** app on my phone.*

D Imagine you lost a bag in Union Station. Answer 1–8.
1. Is the bag big or small?
2. Is it new or old?
3. What color is it?
4. Where and when did you lose it?
5. What items in it are really important?
6. Are there other items in the bag?
7. Are these items new or old? Cheap or expensive? Colors?
8. Why is it important to find the bag today?

E 🔴 **Make it personal** Write a description of your bag for a lost property report.

Before	Use your answers to the questions in **D**. Follow Kylee's model carefully.
While	Include *because* and a reason. Include *too* and extra information. Use two adjectives for the "really important" items.
After	Share your report with a partner. Check her / his report. Send it to your teacher.

Writing 4 A description

♪ **Song line:** Turn to p. 181 for notes about this song and an accompanying task.

A **Books closed.** Ask sts: *What items do people lose on trains and buses?* Write their ideas on the board to revise vocabulary from this unit.

Books open. If you can, display the page in the **Digital Book for Teachers**. Point to the three bags and the lost property report. Tell sts to read the report quickly and decide which bag belongs to Kylee.

1 The green bag

B Tell sts to read sentences 1–5, then reread the report to decide if the statements are true or false. Paircheck, then classcheck, asking sts to correct the false statements. Ask sts: *Do you have a similar experience?* Encourage sts to say what they lost and where.

1 F She lost it in Union Station, in the Mexican restaurant, or at the Mini Golf.
2 F She doesn't know exactly where she lost her bag.
3 T
4 F a total of eight items: wallet, ID, credit card, $50 (money), tablet, pens, a notebook, a sweater
5 F Kylee's mom is unhappy with her.

C Have sts read **Write it right!** Write on the board: *I go to classes because I want to learn English.*, and draw a circle around *because*. Tell sts we use *because* to introduce a reason. Ask sts to find a sentence in the text that uses *because*. Invite a st to read aloud the sentence. Then have sts work on their own to find and circle the other examples. Classcheck. If you are displaying the page, circle the words on the screen / board.

- *because*: It's really important because my wallet is in it; Please help me find it because my mom is not very happy …
- *too*: … and about $50 too; … a very expensive tablet in it too!
- double adjectives: big green bag; new blue sweater

D Say: *Imagine you lost a bag in Union Station*. Ask sts to read 1–8 and answer the questions about their bag. Monitor and help with ideas if necessary.

Tip If you have fast finishers, put these sts into pairs and tell them to ask and answer the questions about each other's bag.

E **Make it personal**

Before Tell sts they're going to write a description of their bag for a lost property report. Ask them to reread Kylee's report and follow the model carefully as they write their own report. Tell them to use their answers in **D** to help them.

While Make sure sts include *because* + reason, *too* for additional information, and two adjectives for important items. Monitor closely as sts write and encourage self-correction of errors you see.

After Put sts into new pairs and tell them to read each other's reports. Ask them to help each other correct any errors they find. Sts then share their texts with you.

Tip Sts could do this writing for homework, and find an image of the lost item. Ask them to bring the text and printed image to the next lesson. Mix up the images and texts and stick them around the room. Ask sts to walk around and try to match each item with its description. Alternatively, you could give each st a text and image (that don't match) and ask them to walk around the room reading out their descriptions until they find the person with the correct image.

4 In the bag

 Café

1 Before watching

A 🔴 **Make it personal** In pairs, list the items you have with you today. Compare with the class. Score one point for each item that only you have.

Apartment keys, my electricity bill ...

B Rory and August have new school supplies. Guess five items in their bags.

I don't know. Maybe pens?

2 While watching

A True (T) or false (F)? Watch to check.
1. Rory's helping because Daniel's not at home.
2. August's cat's name is Garfield.
3. There are three folders.
4. There's a blackboard in one bag.
5. Rory's hungry for a pizza.
6. Daniel keeps a menu in the kitchen.
7. Rory's books are in the kitchen.
8. August's cell phone is on the sofa.

B Number the events 1–7 in the order you hear them.
___ Rory puts his bag on the table.
___ The cat makes a sound.
___ There are many school supplies in the bags.
___ August looks for his cell phone in his room.
___ August and Rory hear the cat.
___ August is hungry.
___ Rory and August sit on the sofa.

C Check the colors you think they mention. Listen again to check, and write the numbers you hear.

Colors	Notebooks	Pens	Erasers	Folders
Black				
Blue				
Green				
Pink				
Purple				
Red				
Yellow				
White				

3 After watching

A Match expressions 1–7 to each situation.

Expressions	Near or with you	Far from you
1 Somewhere over there!		
2 I have two of them right here.		
3 That's where Daniel keeps it.		
4 No, it's not in there.		
5 Maybe over there?		
6 There it is!		
7 And here's my cell phone.		

B Complete 1–6 with *this, that, that's* or *these*.
1. _____ bags are really full.
2. Is _____ yours? What's _____ for?
3. _____ yours. It's for pens, pencils and erasers. And _____ is a bill organizer.
4. And in _____ bag, there is a whiteboard.
5. OK. _____ bag is empty! And my stomach is empty too.
6. It's in the folder in the kitchen. _____ where Daniel keeps it.

C Complete 1–4 with *'s, is* or *are*.
1. There _____ so many school supplies in these bags.
2. When there _____ a sale, you've got to buy!
3. There _____ two notebooks.
4. And in this bag there _____ a whiteboard.

D 🔴 **Make it personal** In pairs, ask and answer about pets. Do you have a pet? What's its name?

I have a cat. Her name is Princess.

There are two pets in my house. We have a cat and a dog.

ID Café 4 In the bag

1 Before watching

A 🔵 Make it personal Show your bag to sts and ask: *What's in my bag today?* Take out a few items (e.g. keys, wallet, phone, etc.) and elicit the words. If you remember, put in a couple of more unusual items, and see if sts know their names. Have sts work in pairs to compare the items they have with them today, and write a combined list. Then have the pairs compare their lists with the class list on the board. They win a point for saying an item that only they have. Monitor and correct pronunciation and any other errors after they have finished.

B Point to the video still and ask: *Who are they?* (Rory and August). Say: *Rory and August have two bags of school supplies. They got them in the sale. Guess what's in the bags.* Sts guess in pairs. Classcheck after they watch ▶4 in **2A** below.

2 While watching

A Tell sts they're going to watch the video of Rory and August. Say: *They're checking what's in the bags. They have school supplies.* Read sentences 1–7 with the whole class and ask sts to say if they are true or false. Play ▶4 for sts to check their answers. Paircheck. Replay the video and classcheck.

1 T
2 F Daniel's cat's name is Carson.
3 F There are two folders.
4 F There's a whiteboard in one bag.
5 F August's hungry for pizza.
6 T
7 F Rory's books are in a bag on the table.
8 F August's cell phone is in the bag.

B Play ▶4 once again for sts to order events 1–7 while they watch. Paircheck. Classcheck with answers on the board.

1 Rory and August sit on the sofa.
2 Rory puts his bag on the table.
3 The cat makes a sound.
4 August and Rory hear the cat.
5 There are many school supplies in the bags.
6 August is hungry.
7 August looks for his cell phone in his room.

C Have sts look at the colors in the chart. Tell to them to check the colors they think are mentioned in the video. Replay ▶4 and ask sts to check their answers and listen for the numbers. Paircheck. Classcheck, replaying the video if necessary.

Colors	Notebooks	Pens	Erasers	Folders
Black		✓		
Blue	✓	✓		
Green				
Pink			✓	
Purple				✓
Red	✓	✓		
Yellow				✓
White				

numbers: 2 notebooks, 2 black pens, 2 blue pens, 2 red pens, 3 pink erasers, 2 rulers

3 After watching

A Read the first expression (Somewhere over there!) with sts and ask / gesture: *Is that far from or near you?* Elicit the correct answer (Far from you) and have sts check the correct column in the chart. Then have them do the same for the other expressions. Play 4 to classcheck.

Expressions	Far from you	Near or with you
1 Somewhere over there!	✓	
2 I have two of them right here.		✓
3 That's where Daniel keeps it.	✓	
4 No, it's not in there.	✓	
5 Maybe over there?	✓	
6 There it is!	✓	
7 And here's my cell phone.		✓

B Sts complete sentences 1–6 with *this*, *that*, *that's*, or *these*. Paircheck. Classcheck with answers on the board.

1 These
2 this, this
3 That's, this
4 this
5 This
6 That's

C Read number 1 and elicit the missing word (are). Sts complete the sentences with *'s*, *is*, or *are*. Classcheck with answers on the board.

1 are   2 's / is   3 are   4 's / is

D 🔵 Make it personal Ask sts: *Do you have a pet?* Elicit answers, and when a student says, e.g.: "I have a dog", ask: *What's its name?* When a student says they don't have a pet, ask: *Do you want to have a pet? Which pet do you want?* Tell sts that if they don't have a pet, they can talk about a friend's or family member's pet. In pairs, sts ask and answer about pets. Monitor and help as needed. Classcheck.

R2 Grammar and vocabulary

A *Picture dictionary.* Cover the words on these pages and remember.

page	
32	10 jobs
33	16 more jobs
34	15 family members
36	9 places of work
41	9 conversation expressions
44	10 personal objects
47	10 colors
48	6 plural nouns
49	6 times
50–51	a typical day

B Make it personal Add *do* or *does* in the correct place. In pairs, ask and answer.
1 Where you live?
2 your father have a job?
3 What your mother do?
4 you live alone, or with other people?
5 you have children?
6 When your family go to bed?

C Match jobs 1–5 to the places. Then ask questions to test a partner.

1 a ph**ar**macist   an office
2 a lawyer   a restaurant
3 a sales clerk   a school
4 a teacher   a drugstore
5 a server   a store

Where does a server work?
In a restaurant.

D ▶R2.1 Complete Meg's description of her family with *this, that, these, those,* or *they*.

1 *These* are my children, Jim and Keira.
2 _____ 're always happy. And 3 _____ is my husband, Greg. He wants to be a chef! 4 _____ 's Angela, his ex-wife, with the burgers, and 5 _____ are their children from Greg's first marriage. 6 _____ visit us a lot. Oh, and 7 _____ 's their enormous dog!

E Make it personal Circle the correct words in 1–5. Then make the sentences true for you.
1 My brother **work / works at / in** a small office.
2 There **is / are** only one child in my family.
3 My aunt **don't / doesn't** live with **your / her** son.
4 My sister **have / has** two children, but she **don't / doesn't** have a dog or a cat.
5 My girlfriend **don't / doesn't** have siblings.

F Write the plurals. In pairs, describe the photos in units 3 and 4 using *There is / are*. Talk about the number of items in the photos.

diary _____   fish _____
dog _____   tooth _____
pill _____   toothbrush _____
shoe _____   bus _____

There are a lot of pills in the photo on page 44.
Yes, and there's a hairdresser on page 32.

G Make it personal In groups, complete the form about a famous character in a popular TV show or movie. Can the class guess who it is?

Age:
Nationality:
Marital status:
Family:
Occupation:
Place of work:
Place of residence:
Your opinion about her / him:
Imagine one or two things she / he does on a typical day:

He's around 30 years old, he's from …
He has a wife and two children …

H Correct the mistakes. Check your answers in units 3 and 4.

Common mistakes
1 She's teacher. She work in Manaus. (2 mistakes)
2 Do you has childrens? (2 mistakes)
3 My fathers live in downtown. (2 mistakes)
4 You work in home? (2 mistakes)
5 Ana get ups at the seven in the morning. (2 mistakes)
6 My boyfriend goes to the bed late. (2 mistakes)
7 John don't live with his mother, he lives with her wife. (2 mistakes)
8 Of what color are this pencil? (2 mistakes)
9 Have a book in the table. (2 mistakes)
10 What time it is? (1 mistake)

Review 2 Units 3-4

Grammar and vocabulary

A **Picture dictionary.** Pairwork. Sts work together to review the main vocabulary items learned in units 3-4. Tell them to look at the pages in the list, cover the words on those pages, and, using the pictures, remember as many of the vocabulary items as they can. Remind sts to use the pink syllables to help with pronunciation. Monitor as sts work and correct pronunciation where necessary.

Tip In order to provide sts with as much fluency practice as possible, expand the activity into mini-dialogues using the key language on the pages listed in the chart. For example, for job vocabulary on p. 32–33, sts can point at photos and ask and answer: "What does he do?" / "He's a (server)."

B 🔵 **Make it personal** Point to question 1 and elicit the missing word and the correct sentence (Where do you live?). Sts complete questions 1–6 with *do* or *does*. Paircheck. Classcheck with answers on the board.

Change partners. In pairs, sts take turns asking and answering questions 1–6. Monitor closely for accuracy and intonation. At the end, test some sts' memory on their partners' answers by asking, e.g.: *(María), What does (Juan's) father do?*

1 Where **do** you live?
2 **Does** your father have a job?
3 What **does** your mother do?
4 **Do** you live alone, or with other people?
5 **Do** you have children?
6 When **do** your family go to bed?

C Ask the whole class: *Where does a server work?* Point to the options and elicit the answer (in a restaurant). Sts match jobs 1–5 to the right places. Then, sts paircheck by asking and answering about the jobs / places of work. Refer sts to the model dialogue in the speech bubbles. Monitor closely for preposition use in places of work phrases. Classcheck. Note any mistakes sts make and give delayed correction / feedback.

1 a drugstore   2 an office   3 a store   4 a school
5 a restaurant

D Ask sts to look carefully at the picture on the smart phone, and say what they can see. Then have them read the text and complete it with the correct words. Paircheck. Play ▶R2.1 to classcheck.

Tip Ask sts if they have photos of family or friends on their cell phones. If they do, ask them to talk about them in small groups or to the whole class.

▶R2.1 Turn to p. 173 for the complete audioscript.

1 These   2 They   3 this   4 That   5 those   6 They   7 that

E 🔵 **Make it personal** Do number 1 with sts. Tell them to choose two words to make a correct sentence, and elicit the answer. Sts circle the correct options in sentences 1–5. Paircheck. Classcheck with answers on the board.

Then model the transformation activity. If you have a brother, say what's true for you, e.g.: *My brother doesn't work in an office*. If you don't have a brother, say: *I don't have a brother*. and point to / change number 2, saying e.g.: *There isn't only one child in my family. I have a sister*. Ask sts to talk in pairs and change the sentences so they are true for them. Ask pairs to find two things in common while they speak. At the end, ask sts: *What do you have in common?*

1 works / in   2 is   3 doesn't / her   4 has / doesn't   5 doesn't

F Write *candy* on the board, say: *One candy, two ...* and let sts finish (candies). Ask *How do you spell that?* and write *candies* on the board as sts spell it for you. Point to the list of words and ask sts to write the plural forms. You can make it a race in pairs, and ask the winners to write the answers on the board when you classcheck. Elicit correct pronunciation of all plural forms.

Point to photo 10 of coins on p. 44. Ask *How many coins are there?* and elicit a full answer from sts (There are a lot of coins.). In pairs, sts describe photos in units 3 and 4 using *There is / are*. Encourage them to use numbers where relevant. Classcheck by having open-pair dialogue, that is, ask sts to ask "How many ...?" questions to classmates from other pairs.

diaries   dogs   pills   shoes   fish   teeth   toothbrushes   buses

G 🔵 **Make it personal** Sts work in groups of three. Each group completes the form about a famous TV or movie character of their choice. Walk around the class and monitor. At the end, refer sts to the speech bubbles. Ask one st from each group to tell the class about their chosen character using the answers in their form. The other groups guess who she / he is.

H Point to Common mistakes and tell sts there are two mistakes in number 1. Copy the sentence onto the board and elicit the corrections from the whole class. Then ask sts to correct sentences 2–10 individually. Remind sts that the number of mistakes is in parentheses. If they're uncertain, encourage them to look back through p. 32–53 to check their answers in units 3 and 4. Classcheck with answers on the board.

1 She's **a** teacher. She work**s** in Manaus.
2 Do you **have children**?
3 My **parents** live **downtown**.
4 **Do** you work **at** home?
5 Ana **gets up** at **seven** in the morning.
6 My boyfriend **goes** to **bed** late.
7 John **doesn't** live with his mother, he lives with **his** wife.
8 **What** color are **these pencils**?
9 **There's** a book on the table.
10 What time **is it**?

Skills practice

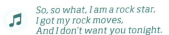
*So, so what, I am a rock star,
I got my rock moves,
And I don't want you tonight.*

R2

A ▶ R2.2 Listen to an introduction to a radio interview with a diplomat and answer 1–3.

1. What's the diplomat's name? _____
2. Where's she from? _____
3. Where does she live? _____

B ▶ R2.3 Listen to the complete interview and check the questions you hear.
- ☐ Where are you from in Brazil?
- ☐ How old are you?
- ☐ How old is your husband?
- ☐ Is Antonio from Rio too?
- ☐ What does he do?
- ☐ Where does he work?
- ☐ Do you have children?
- ☐ What's his name?
- ☐ How old is he?
- ☐ Where do you live here in Bogotá?
- ☐ What do you think of Bogotá and Colombia?
- ☐ What's your favorite thing about Colombia?

C ▶ R2.3 Do you remember the answers? Circle the correct option. Listen again to check.
1. Rosa **is** / **isn't** from Rio de Janeiro.
2. She's **33** / **43** years old.
3. Her husband **is** / **isn't** Brazilian.
4. He's a **diplomat** / **teacher**.
5. He works at **home** / **downtown**.
6. Their **son** / **daughter** is four years old.
7. They **live** / **don't live** in a nice area.
8. Rosa **thinks** / **doesn't think** Colombia and Bogotá are very nice.
9. Her favorite thing about Colombia is the **fruit** / **music**.

D In pairs, role-play the interview. Use the questions in **B** and the information in **C**.

E Read and complete this blog extract with *there's* or *there are*. Read and say the 12 cognate adjectives.

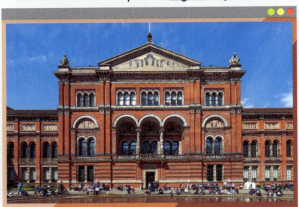

If you're in London, a visit to the Victoria and Albert museum—"the V&A"—is essential. And no, it isn't a museum about Queen Victoria and her husband, Albert! It's the greatest collection of historical and contemporary decorative arts and design in the world.
Situated in glamorous Kensington, _____ magnificent rooms and ultra-modern galleries. In total, _____ 145 galleries, but, with over 4.5 million objects, not all of the V&A's treasures are exhibited every day.
The V&A is incredibly diverse. _____ art from every continent, and _____ fantastic examples of every human activity—fashion, jewelry, ceramics, sculpture, architecture, photography, paintings, and toys. Plus, _____ the famous Great Bed of Ware, constructed in 1590, and big enough for eight people! It's mentioned in Shakespeare's play, *Twelfth Night* (1601)! _____ marvelous clothes from celebrities too, old and new, from rock stars to royals. The V&A teaches you a lot and, best of all, entry is free!

F Reread. True (T) or false (F)? Would you like to go to the V&A museum?
1. The V&A is a museum about the royal family.
2. There isn't any modern art in the museum.
3. It's impossible to see all the V&A's collection in one day.
4. There aren't any objects from Asia.
5. There's an item from Shakespeare's house.
6. Many famous people's possessions are there.
7. It's expensive to go to the V&A museum.

G 🔵 **Make it personal** **Question time.**
In pairs, practice asking and answering the 12 lesson titles in units 3 and 4. Use the book map on p. 2–3. Where possible, ask follow-up questions, too. Can you comfortably ask and answer all the questions?

What do you do?

I'm unemployed. But I study English every day, and I want to work in tourism.

Skills practice

🎵 **Song line:** Turn to p. 181 for notes about this song and an accompanying task.

A Point to the photo and ask: *What can you see?* (A family, parents, and a son.). Tell sts they're going to listen to a radio interview with a diplomat, but they'll just listen to the introduction first. Read questions 1–3 with sts and play ▶R2.2. Paircheck. Classcheck with answers on the board.

▶R2.2 Turn to p. 173 for the complete audioscript.

> 1 Rosa Costa   2 Brazil   3 Bogotá, Colombia

B Tell sts they're going to listen to the interview with the diplomat. Point to the questions and ask sts to listen and check the ones they hear. Allow them 20 seconds to read the questions before you play the track. Play ▶R2.3. Paircheck. Replay ▶R2.3 if necessary. Classcheck.

▶R2.3 Turn to p. 173 for the complete audioscript.

> Where are you from in Brazil?
> How old are you?
> Is Antonio from Rio too?
> What does he do?
> Where does he work?
> Do you have children?
> How old is he?
> Where do you live here in Bogotá?
> What do you think of Bogotá and Colombia?
> What's your favorite thing about Colombia?

C In pairs, sts circle the correct words in sentences 1–9 to answer the questions from **B**. Classcheck with ▶R2.3.

> 1 is   2 43   3 isn't   4 teacher   5 downtown   6 son
> 7 live   8 thinks   9 fruit

D Put sts into new pairs. Sts role-play the interview. Tell sts to use the questions in **B** and refer to the answers in **C**. Change roles. Sts act out the interview once again.

E Point to the blog photo and ask: *What's this?* (A museum) *Where is it?* (In London). Let sts look for information in the text. Pre-teach some museum-related cognates or nouns which are easy to guess, e.g. *sculptures, photographs, paintings*. Write them on the board and drill pronunciation. Point to the photo and ask: *Are there paintings in this museum? Are there sculptures?*

Sts read the text and fill in the blanks with affirmative forms *there's* or *there are*. Paircheck. Write the answers on the board. Then have sts say aloud the underlined cognate adjectives in the text. Ensure they focus on the pink syllables to help with pronunciation.

> there are   there are   there is   there are   there is   There are

F Read sentence 1 with the whole class and ask: *Is it true or false?* (F) Sts decide whether sentences 1–7 are true or false. Paircheck. Classcheck with answers on the board. Then ask: *Would you like to go to the V&A museum? Why or why not?* Encourage and help sts to express their opinions.

> 1 F It's a collection of decorative arts and design.
> 2 F There is contemporary art as well as historical art.
> 3 T
> 4 F There is art from every continent.
> 5 F The Great Bed of Ware is mentioned in a Shakespearean play.
> 6 T
> 7 F Entry to the museum is free.

G **Make it personal** **Question time.** Sts look at the Language map on p. 2–3 and take turns asking and answering the lesson question titles from units 3 and 4. Monitor closely for accuracy and encourage sts to ask follow-up questions when appropriate. At the end, ask them how they felt performing the task: *Do you feel comfortable with all questions? Which ones are easy? Which ones are difficult?*

5

5.1 Do you drink a lot of coffee?

1 Vocabulary Meals, food (1), and drinks

I love dinner. It's my favorite meal.

A ▶5.1 Match photos 1–4 to these sentences. Listen to check. What is your favorite meal of the day?

☐ I eat and drink this for **dinner**. ☐ Americans eat this for **breakfast**.
☐ We usually have this for **lunch**. ☐ This is only **a snack**.

Common mistakes

do
What ~~you~~ have for ~~the~~ lunch?

B ▶5.2 Match items a–l in the photo to these words. Listen, check, and repeat.

☐ **cof**fee	☐ **vege**tables	☐ cheese /tʃiːz/	☐ milk
☐ fruit /fruːt/	☐ beans	☐ eggs	☐ **or**ange juice /dʒuːs/
☐ tea	☐ bread /bred/	☐ meat	☐ soft drinks

C 🎤 **Make it personal** What do you have for breakfast / lunch / dinner? What do you have for a snack? Ask and answer in pairs, then tell the class.

Do you have eggs for breakfast?   *No, I don't. I don't have time in the morning.*

58

Unit overview: In the context of talking about meals, food and drink, and free-time activities, sts learn days of the week and learn and practice using frequency adverbs and object pronouns. They also learn to use possessive 's.

5.1 Do you drink a lot of coffee?

Lesson aims: Sts review the use of the simple present to express opinions about food and drinks and talk about eating habits.

Function
Naming meals, food and drinks.
Talking about meals.
Pronunciation of silent letters.
Listening to an interview.
Reading about nutrition.
Asking and answering about eating habits.

Language
We usually have this for lunch.
What do you have for breakfast?
Which food is good for you?
Jack is a vegetarian.
Do you eat vegetables?

Vocabulary: Food and drinks (coffee, vegetables, cheese, milk, tea, beans, etc)
Grammar: Review simple present

Warm-up Get sts to sit next to classmates they don't usually work with. Assign roles **A** and **B** for each pair and write on the board:

A: Units 1 and 3

B: Units 2 and 4

Ensure sts understand where to find the lesson question titles (always at the start of a lesson). Ask them to choose five lesson question titles from their units. For example, **A** could choose these question titles from units 1 and 3: "What's this in English?" (p. 10), "What's your phone number?" (p. 12), "How are you today?" (p. 15), "What do you do?" (p. 32), and "Do you live near here?" (p. 40).

Allow sts a little time to choose their questions. Then have them work in pairs and take turns asking and answering their questions. Classcheck by having sts ask and answer some questions for the class.

1 Vocabulary Meals, food (1) and drinks

A Books closed. Write *Food* on the board and ask sts to say foods they know in English. Write them on the board in a list, so it will be visible throughout the lesson. Make sure the list includes some items from the main photo. Prompt a couple of words if sts don't suggest any, e.g. mime drinking a coffee or point to the coffee in photo 1. When you have a few items on the board, ask sts: *Do you like (food item)? Do you have it for breakfast, lunch, or dinner?*, teaching the meaning and pronunciation of these words as you go. Teach the meaning of meals, e.g. *We have three meals each day: breakfast, lunch, and dinner. How do you say "meal" in your language?*

Books open. Point to photos 1–4 and tell sts to read the sentences. Have them match the photos to the sentences, and then play ▶5.1 so they can check answers. Classcheck.

1 Americans eat this for breakfast.
2 We usually have this for lunch.
3 This is only a snack.
4 I eat and drink this for dinner.

B Point to the large photo and the list of words on the board and ask sts: *Are any of the foods on the board in the photo?* Ask them to point to the item in the photo and then say the word and letter (e.g. coffee, e). In pairs, sts match items a–l in the photo to the words. Paircheck. Play ▶5.2 for sts to listen and check answers. Then play the track again for sts to listen and repeat chorally. Classcheck with answers on the board.

Common mistakes Read with the class and remind them not to make these mistakes when they speak in the next activity.

a eggs   b cheese   c milk   d tea   e coffee   f fruit
g vegetables   h meat   i beans   j bread   k soft drinks
l orange juice

Tip Get sts to briefly test each other for two minutes. In pairs, sts point to items a–l and take turns asking "What's letter (a)?" and answering. Monitor closely for pronunciation. Correct on the spot. Round off the activity by asking the whole group to cover the words and asking the class: *What's letter a? And b?*, etc.

C Make it personal Point to the speech bubbles and ask some sts questions about what they have for breakfast, lunch, or dinner, e.g. *Do you have meat for lunch? Do you eat cereal for dinner? Do you drink tea in the morning?* Then put sts into pairs and tell them to ask and answer each other. Monitor and correct pronunciation of vocabulary. Ask some sts to tell the class about what their partner eats and drinks.

Extra activity Ask sts to write a food diary for a typical day, e.g. "Breakfast: cereal with milk, orange juice, coffee. Snack: fruit. Lunch: …." Monitor and prompt self-correction of errors.

5.1

♪ *Cause I don't care, when I'm with my baby, yeah,
All the bad things disappear,
And you're making me feel like maybe I am somebody.*

2 Pronunciation Silent letters

A ▶ 5.3 Be careful with "silent" letters. Listen and cross out the silent letters in these words. Listen again and repeat.

> apple   bread   breakfast   cheese   fruit   juice   vegetables

B ▶ 5.4 Listen and write the sentences. In pairs, practice saying them.

3 Listening

A ▶ 5.5 Listen to a couple talking about their meals. Answer 1–3.
1 Which three items in **1B** don't they mention?
2 What do they eat for breakfast and lunch?
3 Do they eat or drink any items that are bad for you?

B 🔴 Make it personal In your opinion, which food and drinks in **1B** are good or bad for you? In pairs, compare.

> I think … is / are bad for you.   I agree. / I disagree. I think … is / are good for you.

Common mistakes

~~The~~ soft drinks are bad for you.

~~The~~ milk is good for you.

My favorite meal is ~~the~~ breakfast.

Don't use *the* with nouns to talk about things generically.

4 Reading

A In pairs, read the nutrition tip and try to pronounce the pink-stressed words.

B Reread and pronounce the highlighted letters /ʃ/ like *shark* and *shorts*.

C ▶ 5.6 Listen and reread to check. Do you agree with the conclusion?

NUTRITION TIP

We all know that milk, beans, vegetables, fruit, and wa ter are good for us. And o ther foods are "bad"—soft drinks, white s ugar, al cohol, for exa mple. But i tems like bread, cheese, eggs, meat, coffee, and tea are contro ver sial. Doctors, s cientists, and nu tri tionists all have different o pinions and say different things. Are these foods and drinks good or bad?

We say it all de pen ds on quan tity. Life is short! We say "Yes" to moder a tion, but "No" to exa gger a tion. What do you think?

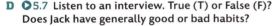

> I agree. Moderation is good.   I disagree. I think bread and meat are bad for you, and the planet!

D ▶ 5.7 Listen to an interview. True (T) or False (F)? Does Jack have generally good or bad habits?
1 Jack is vegetarian.   2 Jack drinks a lot of coffee.   3 He doesn't like bread.

E 🔴 Make it personal In pairs, ask and answer about your eating habits. What do you eat and drink? Do you generally have good or bad habits?

> Do you eat (a lot of) vegetables?   Well, for breakfast I eat … and I drink …

5.1

🎵 **Song line:** Turn to p. 181 for notes about this song and an accompanying task.

2 Pronunciation Silent letters

A Write *fruit* on the board and ask sts: *How do we pronounce this word?* Show the *i* is silent and write the phonemic transcription on the board: /fruːt/. Tell sts to look at the words in the box. Ask: *Which letters are silent?* Elicit ideas but don't correct them. Play ▶5.3 and ask sts to listen and cross out the silent letters. Classcheck then play ▶5.3 again for sts to listen and repeat.

Tip Transcribing the words on the board can help sts to see the pronunciation. Point out that *-le* endings in words are often pronounced /əl/ for example, *apple* /æpəl/.

🔑 bread, breakfast, cheese, fruit, juice, vegetables

B Tell sts they are going to do a dictation. Make sure they are ready and play ▶5.4, pausing after each sentence to give them time to write. Paircheck and then replay ▶5.4. Classcheck on the board. Then, in pairs, sts practice saying the sentences. Monitor and help with pronunciation.

Tip Ask a st to write the sentences on the board and tell the class to say if they agree. Ask: *Is this correct?* Work together as a class to correct any mistakes.

▶5.4 Turn to p. 173 for the complete audioscript.

3 Listening

A Tell sts they are going to listen to a couple talking about the food they eat. Give sts time to read questions 1–3, then play ▶5.5. Sts answer the questions, then paircheck. Replay the track and classcheck.

Common mistakes Read with the class. Remind sts about this rule for *the*. Listen for this error as you monitor in **B** and later in the lesson in **4E**. Correct any errors after sts finish speaking.

Language tip Use Common mistakes to point out the difference between English and their L1. English uses the definite article for specific things, but does not use it for generic / non-specific things. Write some examples on the board to make this clear: *The milk is on the table.* (specific) *Milk is good for you.* (general).

▶5.5 Turn to p. 173 for the complete audioscript.

🔑
1. vegetables, fruit, coffee
2. Breakfast: man: bread, cheese, eggs, and orange juice; woman: tea with milk. Lunch: the woman eats a lot of beans.
3. The woman drinks a lot of soft drinks.

B 👤 **Make it personal** Point to the food words in **1B** and ask: *What food is good for you? What food is bad for you?* Get one or two answers. Point to the speech bubbles, and, in pairs, tell sts to give their opinions about food that is good or bad for you.

Weaker classes Write _____ *is good / bad for you.* on the board to give them support.

Ask some sts to share their ideas with the class. Ask other sts: *Do you agree?* Tell sts they're going to read about foods that are good and bad for you in the next exercise.

4 Reading

A Point to the text and ask sts to read it quickly. Focus on the pink-stressed words. In pairs, sts try to guess the pronunciation. Monitor and help, correcting pronunciation, and then drill the words chorally with the class.

B Ask sts to reread the text. Focus on the yellow highlighted words. Point to the /ʃ/ symbol and ask sts to pronounce it. Then, practice the highlighted words with the class. Tell sts that the letter combination *-tion* is pronounced /ʃən/.

C Play ▶5.6 and ask sts to listen and reread, focusing on the pronunciation of the words in **A** and **B**.

Direct attention to the speech bubbles. Ask a student: *Do you agree with the conclusion?* and prompt them to say if they agree or disagree. Put sts into pairs and tell them to say if they agree or disagree with the nutrition tip. Ask some sts to share their opinions with the class.

D Tell sts they're going to listen to an interview. Say: *Listen to Jack talk about food and drink.* Ask sts to read statements 1–3 before they listen, and then play ▶5.7. Sts decide if the statements are true or false, then paircheck. Replay ▶5.7. Classcheck and ask: *Does Jack have good or bad habits?*

▶5.7 Turn to p. 173 for the complete audioscript.

🔑 1 T 2 F 3 F

E 👤 **Make it personal** Point to the lesson question title and have one st ask another, "Do you drink a lot of coffee?". Refer sts to the model in the speech bubbles. In pairs, sts interview each other about their eating habits, asking "Do you eat / drink (a lot of) …?" Remind sts to use vocabulary learned in this lesson. Monitor for good language and errors and note them on the board. Conduct delayed correction along with positive feedback.

Tip When you write errors or good language on the board, give relevant context and label to show what it is, e.g.

I eat vegetables every day. (good grammar) ✓

vegetables (incorrect pronunciation) ✗

If we don't add enough context and information, it is not clear.

Finish the lesson by asking the class some questions about their eating habits, e.g. *Who has a good diet? What does (student's name) eat?* Then ask: *Do you generally have good or bad eating habits?* and have as many sts as possible tell the class.

5.2 What's your favorite food?

1 Vocabulary Food (2)

A ▶5.8 Match photos a–p to these words. In pairs, guess their pronunciation. All the <mark>highlighted</mark> letters are pronounced /ə/ like b<mark>a</mark>nan<mark>a</mark>s and pajamas. Listen, check, and repeat.

- [ ] b<mark>a</mark>nan<mark>a</mark>s
- [ ] beef
- [ ] carr<mark>o</mark>ts
- [ ] chicken /tʃɪkɪn/
- [ ] Chinese
- [ ] fish
- [ ] French fries
- [ ] grapes
- [ ] hot dogs
- [ ] Italian
- [ ] Japanese
- [ ] lettuce /letɪs/
- [ ] oranges
- [ ] pizz<mark>a</mark>
- [ ] p<mark>o</mark>tatoes
- [ ] t<mark>o</mark>matoes

B 🗣 **Make it personal** Cover the words in **A**. In pairs, ask and answer *Do you like …?* using the photos. Any differences between you?

Do you like grapes? *Yes, I do!* *I don't like grapes. I prefer wine!*

5.2 What's your favorite food?

Lesson aims: Sts continue to practice the simple present by asking and answering about food and drinks they like / dislike.

Function
Reading online forums.
Listening to interviews about food preferences.
Producing the /ə/ sound.
Talking about foods and drinks you like / don't like.

Language
My partner and I like variety.
She likes chicken. She doesn't like vegetables.
I love fish. Do you like fish? No, I hate it!

Vocabulary: Food (bananas, beef, carrots, chicken, Chinese food, fish, French fries, grapes, hot dogs, Italian food, Japanese food, lettuce, oranges, pizza, potatoes, tomatoes). Very much, not much, not really, not at all.
Grammar: Simple present + *like, love, don't like, hate*

Warm-up Books closed. Ask some sts: *Do you like Chinese food? What about Italian food?* Put sts into pairs and ask them to ask and answer "Do you like …?" questions about different types of food. Monitor and listen for good language and pronunciation errors, and go over this once sts have finished speaking.

1 Vocabulary Food (2)

A Books open. Point to the photos of food and tell sts to cover the food vocabulary. In pairs, sts try to name any food items they know. After one or two minutes, tell them to uncover the vocabulary and complete the matching exercise together. While they're doing this, have them guess the pronunciation of the words. Play ▶5.8 and tell sts to listen and check answers. Classcheck.

Write /ə/ on the board and show sts how to make the sound. Tell them to relax their mouth and sigh. Tell them to keep the same sound but make it short. Tell them this is the schwa and it is a very common sound in English. You can also refer sts to the **Sounds and usual spellings** chart on p. 82 for further examples of the schwa. Write *banana* /bənænə/ on the board and help them say the word correctly. Then, ask them to try saying the other words with yellow highlighted letters. Play ▶5.8. Pause after each word and have sts repeat.

> a tomatoes b potatoes c carrots d lettuce e grapes
> f bananas g oranges h beef i chicken j fish k pizza
> l hot dogs m French fries n Japanese o Italian
> p Chinese

B Make it personal Ask some sts: *Do you like bananas?* Elicit short answers (Yes I do. / No, I don't.). Tell sts to cover the words in **A**. In pairs, they ask and answer *Do you like …?* about the foods in the photos. Afterward, ask sts: *Do you and you partner like the same foods?* Elicit some replies and reformulate their answers to "We like …" Then elicit some differences (e.g. I like Chinese food. Elena doesn't like Chinese food. She prefers Mexican food.) Help sts form the sentences if they find it difficult.

2 Listening

♪ *I love it when you go crazy,*
You take all my inhibitions,
Baby, there's nothing holding me back.

A ▶5.9 Read the forum and match food groups 1–5 on p. 60 to the posts. Listen to the interviews to check. Are you similar to the people?

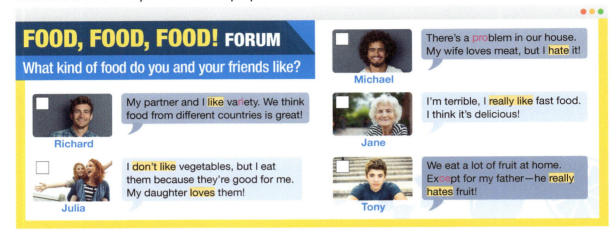

B 🎙️ **Make it personal** Do you know three more food or drink words in English? In pairs, compare.

I know mangoes. It's similar to Portuguese!

Common mistakes
I like very much the chicken.
He like the banana. → doesn't
She not like the fruit.

3 Grammar *like / love / don't like / hate*

A Complete the scale with the highlighted phrases in **2A**.

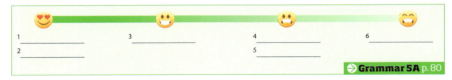

→ Grammar 5A p. 80

B True (T) or False (F) for you? Change the verb in the false sentences to make them true.
1 I like bread and cheese.
2 I love pizza.
3 I really hate black coffee.
4 I don't like fast food.
5 I really like Italian restaurants.
6 I hate fish.

C ▶5.10 Listen and follow the model. Practice the sentences.

I don't like Italian food. – he   He doesn't like Italian food.

D 🎙️ **Make it personal** Complete the sentences for you. In pairs, compare. Any similarities or differences?

1 I love _____ and _____.
2 I like _____, but I don't like _____.
3 I really hate _____.
4 I really like _____.
5 My best friend likes _____, but he / she hates _____.
6 In _____, people usually eat _____ on weekends.

What kind of food do you love?
I love fish, but I really hate chicken!

2 Listening

A Point to the five forum posts. Read aloud the question ("What kind of food do you and your friends like?") and say: *Let's see what Richard says.* Read his post with the class, point to the groups of food 1–5 in the photos on p. 60 and elicit the correct group for Richard. Sts continue with the activity, matching the remaining posts to the correct group of photos. Paircheck. Play ▶5.9 to classcheck answers. Then ask some sts if they are similar to any of the people on the forum.

▶5.9 Turn to p. 173 for the complete audioscript.

```
Richard 5
Julia 1
Michael 3
Jane 4
Tony 2
```

B **Make it personal** Ask: *Do you know three more food or drink items in English?* Refer sts to the speech bubble. Tell sts to write three more food or drink words they know in English. Encourage them to think about words that are cognates.

In pairs, sts compare their food / drink items. Ask sts: *What food does your partner know?* and write the words in a list on the board, correcting any pronunciation errors.

Tip You could ask sts to look online for food cognates. If they search online "food cognates English (insert their own language)", they will find websites with cognates.

Tell them to check the pronunciation of words they find in online dictionaries, and encourage them to add the words to their cognates list, making a note of the pronunciation.

♪ **Song line:** Turn to p. 181 for notes about this song and an accompanying task.

3 Grammar *like / love / don't like / hate*

A Read **Common mistakes** with the whole class. Point out that these mistakes are the result of translating directly from their L1. Remind them of English word order in the first sentence, and that they must use an auxiliary verb in negatives and questions. Test sts and challenge them to transform the sentences in the box. Elicit the negative form of "I like chicken very much." and "He likes bananas.", and the affirmative form of "She doesn't like fruit." and write the sentences on the board.

Point to the scale and ask sts to match the verbs (*love*, *like*, *don't like* and *hate*) to the emojis. Read the instructions with the class and ask them to complete the scale with the six highlighted phrases from **2A**. Paircheck, then classcheck.

There is more information on these verbs in Grammar 5A on p. 80.

```
1 loves
2 really like
3 like
4 don't like
5 hate
6 really hates
```

B Ask sts: *Do you like cheese? Or do you love cheese?* Write on the board: *I love / really like / like / don't like / hate cheese.* Drill the sentences, encouraging sts to add emphasis to *love* and *hate*. Point to sentence 1 and ask one or two sts to say if it is true or false for them. When a st says it is false, tell them to change the verb so that the sentence becomes true for them. Tell sts to read sentences 1–6 and change the verbs so the sentences are true for them. Put them in pairs and ask them to compare answers. Monitor and correct any errors in grammar or pronunciation.

Tip After they finish speaking, ask sts to think about errors they think they made. Tell them to write their errors down in a notebook, next to the corrections. This might help them to better monitor their language when they speak and be aware of errors. If they struggle with this, ask them to try to notice their errors the next time they speak.

C Transformation drill. Point to the speech bubbles and say: *Listen and follow the model.* Play ▶5.10 up to "Your turn" and the first pair of beeps, before and after the student prompt. Pause the track and elicit the response from the whole class (He hates fish.). Resume playing the track for sts to check the answer and listen for the next prompt. After each pair of beeps, pick a different student to respond. Correct any errors, then play the track again for sts to practice.

▶5.10 Turn to p. 174 for the complete audioscript.

D **Make it personal** Ask sts to read the sentences and complete them with their own food preferences. Tell them to use the vocabulary on p. 60 and help with other food vocabulary if necessary. When they have finished, point to the speech bubbles and demonstrate the speaking activity with a confident st. Then have sts do the same in pairs.

Monitor and make a note of good language. Write it on the board at the end so you finish the lesson on a positive note. Praise good pronunciation, vocabulary, and grammar.

Extra activity Ask sts to write their own forum posts about their food likes and dislikes, based on the structures in sentences 1–4, e.g. "We like pizza but we hate other fast food." "We love pasta!" "Sandra likes fish but I don't." etc.

They could display these texts in the classroom as a record of the lesson.

5.3 What do you usually do on Friday evenings?

1 Vocabulary Days of the week and free-time activities

A ▶5.11 Complete the days on the calendar. Listen to the poem to check.

a **Mon**day
b **Tues**day
c **Wednes**day
d **Thurs**day
e ___ ___ iday
f ___ ___ urday
g ___ ___ nday

I love Wednesdays and Sundays—I watch soccer on TV!

For me, it's Friday. The weekend starts!

B ▶5.11 Listen again and repeat the days. Then answer 1–5.

Which day(s) ...
1 have a capital letter?
2 has three syllables?
3 have silent letters?
4 have the same first letter in your language?
5 are your two favorite days?

C ▶5.12 Match activities 1–7 to photos a–g in **A**. Listen, check, and repeat.

1 ☐ go to the **mo**vies
2 ☐ go to the mall
3 ☐ go to church
4 ☐ play **so**ccer
5 ☐ watch TV
6 ☐ take a dance class
7 ☐ cook

2 Reading

A ▶5.13 Read the posts and match the people to three of the photos a–g in **1A**. Then listen and complete the posts with the days of the week.

WEEKENDS AROUND THE WORLD – WHAT DO YOU DO ON WEEKENDS?

MAYA GARCÍA
Here in Barranquilla, Colombia, sports like cycling, swimming, and a lot of others are very **po**pular! I'm usually very **ac**tive on weekends. I play soccer or **base**ball with my friends on ¹_____ morning, and in the afternoon we play **vi**deo games or go to the gym.

LEE KON
We live in Seoul, South Korea, and we never stay home on ²_____ or ³_____ evenings. We see friends on the weekend. We **some**times go to a **re**staurant, or go to the movies. In Seoul, there are a lot of movie theaters, and you can to go to the movies 24 hours a day!

GIL LÓPEZ
I'm from Madrid in Spain. I **al**ways go to church on ⁴_____ **du**ring the day, but in the evening, I stay home. I listen to music, or I read a book. It depends how tired I am.

5.3 What do you usually do on Friday evenings?

Lesson aims: Sts use the simple present and learn and practice frequency adverbs to talk about what they do on different days of the week.

Function
Listening to a poem about the days of the week.
Reading / Listening to people talk about their weekends.
Asking and answering questions about weekends.

Language
What do you do on weekends?
We sometimes go to a restaurant or to the movies.
What do you usually do on Friday evenings?

Vocabulary: Prepositions and days of the week / times of the day. Weekend activities (cook, go to church / to the mall / to the movies, play soccer, take a dance class, watch TV).

Grammar: Advebs of frequency (always, usually, sometimes, never)

Warm-up Ask sts to go to **Sounds and Usual Spellings** on p. 83. Focus on Consonants. Sts work in groups of three or four. Ask them to cover the words and look at the pictures only. Sts take turns pointing and naming the pictures for all consonant sounds. Monitor closely for accuracy. Classcheck briefly.

1 Vocabulary Days of the week and free-time activities

Books closed. Elicit / Check if sts know any days of the week. If technology is available, show sts the current week's calendar and conduct your presentation from there. If not, write the dates for the ongoing week, Mon–Sun, e.g.: *5/21, 5/22, 5/23*, etc.

Point to the current day and say, e.g.: *Today's (Monday)*. Point to the following day and say: *Tomorrow's (Tuesday)*. Elicit the rest of the days.

A Books open. Point to the calendar and ask sts to complete the days with the missing letters. Tell sts they're going to listen to a poem about the days of the week. Say: *Listen and check*. Play ▶5.11. Classcheck with answers on the board.

▶5.11 Turn to p. 174 for the complete audioscript.

e Friday
f Saturday
g Sunday

B Play ▶5.11 again and ask sts to listen and repeat the days. Ask questions 1–5 to different sts in the class, writing answers on the board. Drill pronunciation of all days and indicate the syllables as you / sts say them. Raise your hand at the first syllable of all days to indicate the stress. Do this twice. Play ▶5.11 again and have sts repeat the days only. If sts are curious about the poem, refer them to AS 5.11 on p. 87 and read it with the whole class.

▶5.11 Turn to p. 174 for the complete audioscript.

1 all of them
2 Saturday
3 Tuesday, Wednesday

Extra activity The spelling of days of the week can be confusing, so ask sts to work in pairs and test each other on the spelling. They take turns saying a day and spelling it aloud as quickly as possible. Tell them to try to do this faster and faster, until they can spell the days quickly and easily.

C Tell sts to read activities 1–7. Point to photo a in **A** and elicit the activity it shows (watch TV). Then tell sts to complete the matching exercise. Paircheck. Tell sts to listen to check their answers and notice the pronunciation of the activities. Play ▶5.12 and classcheck. Play the track again for sts to listen and repeat.

Tip Focus on the vowel sounds in *movie* and *soccer*. Both are spelled with *o* but are pronounced differently. Point out that *movie* and *cook* have different vowel sounds, but *soccer* and *watch* have the same vowel sound. Drill the pronunciation of activities both chorally and individually.

▶5.12 Turn to p. 174 for the complete audioscript.

1 d 2 f 3 g 4 b 5 a 6 e 7 c

2 Reading

A Focus on the heading of the social network group page. Say: *These people are talking about their weekends*. Tell sts to read Maya García's post. Ask: *What does she do on weekends?* (plays soccer or baseball, plays video games or goes the gym). Point to the photos in **1A** and ask: *Which photo?* Elicit "b" (play soccer).

Have sts do the same for the other two posts. Tell them not to fill in the blanks yet. Paircheck, then classcheck. Drill pronunciation of all the activities.

Point to the gaps in the posts and say: *Listen and complete*. Play ▶5.13, then paircheck. Replay the track and classcheck.

Maya: b
Lee: d
Gil: g
1 Saturday
2 Friday
3 Saturday
4 Sunday

B **Reread and complete 1–5 with *on*, *on the*, or *in the*.**
1 _____ weekend   2 _____ weekends   3 _____ Monday
4 _____ Monday afternoon   5 _____ morning / afternoon / evening

♪ *I wanna rock n roll all night and party every day.*

C **Find and circle nine more free-time activities in the posts in A.**

D 🟢 **Make it personal** Study Common mistakes, then, in pairs, compare your weekends with the posts. Any big differences or similarities?

I don't go to the gym on Saturday.   *I go to the movies on weekends.*

⚠ **Common mistakes**

We take a class ~~in~~ **on** Friday evening.
I go to ~~the~~ school ~~the~~ **on M**monday.
I listen ~~/~~ **to** music ~~all the days~~ **every day**.
~~Usually I~~ **I usually** stay ~~in~~ home after ~~the~~ work.

③ Grammar Frequency adverbs

A **Look at the examples in the grammar box and circle the correct word in the rule. Reread the posts in 2A and underline the frequency adverbs.**

100%	I **always** go to the gym on Tuesday.
	We **usually** eat in a restaurant on weekends.
	We **sometimes** go to a bar in the evening.
0%	My friends and I **never** stay home on Saturday night.

Frequency adverbs usually go immediately **before** / **after** the main verb.

➡ **Grammar 5B** p. 80

B ▶5.14 **Put the words in 1–5 in order to make sentences. Listen, check, and repeat. Are they true for you?**
1 I / remember / to / usually / my / homework / do / class / before
 I usually remember to do my homework before class!
2 the movies / we / go / always / Friday / evening / on / to
3 read / I / the / sometimes / on / a / book / weekend
4 my family and I / Sunday / go / to / a / restaurant / on / usually
5 never / I / watch / Saturday / on / TV / morning

C ▶5.15 **Listen and follow the model. Practice the sentences.**

We play soccer on Friday. – Always   *We always play soccer on Friday.*   *Never*   *We never play soccer on Friday.*

D 🟢 **Make it personal** In pairs, ask, answer, and complete the table for your partner. Compare with another pair. Any big differences?

What do you usually do on weekends?

	Morning	Afternoon	Evening
Friday			
Saturday			
Sunday			

What do you usually do on Friday evening?   *I sometimes watch TV.*

B Ask sts: *What's correct? On weekend? On the weekend? In the weekend?* (on the weekend). Tell them to complete 1–5 and paircheck. Classcheck with answers on the board.

> 1 on the
> 2 on
> 3 on
> 4 on
> 5 in the

C Point to the posts in **2A** and ask sts to find and circle nine more free-time activities. Classcheck, correcting pronunciation as you check the answers.

> cycling, swimming, play baseball, play video games, go to the gym, see friends, go to a restaurant, listen to music, read a book

D **Make it personal** Read **Common mistakes** with the class. Ask sts: *Do you do the same things as Maya, Lee, and Gil on weekends?* Refer sts to the speech bubbles, then elicit similar comparisons from three or four sts. Put sts into pairs and have them take turns comparing their weekends with those in the posts. Monitor to make sure sts are comparing their weekend activities with those in the posts.

Language tip Use Common mistakes to point out the errors that sts may make as a result of direct translation from their L1. Tell them to use the preposition *to* with verb *listen*, and to remember to say *every day* in English (not *all the days*, which is an incorrect translation from their L1).

When they have finished, ask some sts to tell the class about their partner. Don't correct any errors in open class, but make a note of them to check later in the lesson. Then ask sts if there were any big differences or similarities.

Weaker classes Write a few of the sts' examples (that you elicited at the start of the exercise) on the board and leave them there for this pairwork task.

♪ **Song line:** Turn to p. 182 for notes about this song and an accompanying task.

3 Grammar Frequency adverbs

A Point out the frequency scale in the grammar box, with *always* at 100% and *never* at 0%. Ask sts to guess a percentage for *usually* (e.g. 80%) and sometimes (e.g. 40%). The exact figures aren't important, but make sure sts understand that *usually* is an activity we do much more frequently than an activity we do *sometimes*. Drill pronunciation of the first four sentences in the box. Then tell sts to circle the correct word in the rule. Classcheck.

Then refer sts to the posts in **2A** and tell them to find and underline all the frequency adverbs.

> before
> Underline: usually, never, sometimes, always

B Point to sentence 1 and the example answer. Point out the position of the frequency adverb. Sts complete the ordering exercise. Paircheck. Play ▶5.14 to check answers. Classcheck with answers on the board. Replay ▶5.14 for choral repetition of all sentences. Ask: *Are the sentences true for you?* Point to one of the sentences on the board, and ask: *True?* Ask different sts to reply "true" or "false". When a student says "false", ask them to change the frequency adverb in the sentence so that it is true for them. Write the new sentence on the board. In pairs, have sts do the same for the other sentences.

> 2 We always go to the movies on Friday evening.
> 3 I sometimes read a book on the weekend.
> 4 My family and I usually go to a restaurant on Sunday.
> 5 I never watch TV on Saturday morning.

C Transformation drill. Point to the speech bubbles and say: *Listen and follow the model.* Play ▶5.15 up to "Your turn" and the first pair of beeps, before and after the student prompt. Pause the track and elicit the response from the whole class (She usually stays home on Sunday.). Resume playing the track for sts to check the answer and listen for the next prompt. After each pair of beeps, pick a different student to respond. Replay the track and ask the whole class to listen and say the sentences.

▶5.15 Turn to p. 174 for the complete audioscript.

D **Make it personal** Drill the question *What do you usually do on weekends?* Point to the chart and elicit the question for "Friday evening." Refer sts to the speech bubbles for support. In pairs, sts take turns asking, answering, and completing the chart for their partner. Refer sts to the weekend activities in **2A**. Monitor and help with other vocabulary if necessary. Classcheck by having sts report their partners' answers to the whole class. Ask questions, e.g.: *What does (partner's name) usually do on Saturday morning?* Monitor closely for use of 3rd person -s at this stage. Then have sts compare their completed charts with another pair. Invite sts to tell the class about any big differences.

As you monitor the activity, make a note of good language and common errors you hear. After sts have finished, write a mixture of the good language and errors on the board. Put sts into pairs or groups of three and ask them to identify the correct sentences and the errors. Have them correct the errors. Go through this together as a class at the end, and correct the errors on the board.

Extra activity Ask sts to write about a fantasy weekend. They can imagine whatever they like, e.g. they are a famous person, or they are in a country / city they have always dreamed of visiting. They write a description of their fantasy weekend using adverbs of frequency. Afterward, ask sts to work in groups and read each other's descriptions. Encourage them to comment on what they like about the descriptions.

5.4 Do you like Rihanna's music?

1 Listening

1. Ryan Gosling's movies
2. Stephen Colbert's show
3. James Bond's car
4. _____'s autobiography
5. _____'s racket
6. _____'s tattoo
7. _____'s trophy

8. _____'s house

A Read and complete the newsfeed entries with photo captions 1–3.

ENTERTAINMENT NEWS   Friday, April 17

☐ Michelle Obama on (2) this Friday.
☐ People all over the world admire (___), the Aston Martin DB5.
☐ Collection of (___) released as a boxset this weekend.

B ▶ 5.16 Listen to two friends talking about the entertainment news. Which photos do they mention? Do you agree with their opinions?

2 Grammar Possessive 's

A Read the grammar box and (circle) the correct answer in 1 and 2. Then match the people to their possessions in photos 4–8 in **1A**.

Use a name or a noun + 's for the possessive.	's can mean *is* or the possessive.
I like Ryan Gosling's movies.	1 He's my brother. ('s = ***is*** / the *possessive*)
My sister's car is red.	2 Tessa's mother works downtown. ('s = *is* / ***the possessive***)

→ **Grammar 5C** p. 80

The U.S. President   Naomi Osaka   Michelle Obama
The soccer team   Calvin Harris

B ▶ 5.17 Listen and follow the model. Practice the phrases.

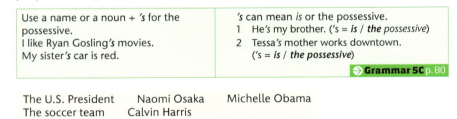

The movies of Ryan Gosling   *Ryan Gosling's movies*   *Possessive adjective*   *His movies*

C ⬤ **Make it personal** Write the names of three people in your family and the first letter of a possession for each person. In pairs, guess who it is and what the possession is.

Jorge, B.   *Is Jorge your brother's name?*   *Yes, it is!*   *Is it Jorge's bottle? Banana? Bus?*

5.4 Do you like Rihanna's music?

Lesson aims: Sts learn possessive 's, and use object pronouns to talk about celebrities and their favorite brands. They also listen to two friends talk about movies and TV shows.

Function
Reading about entertainment news.
Listening to a conversation between two friends.
Describing people and their possessions.
Sharing opinions about different topics.

Language
I like Ryan Gosling's movies.
Is Jorge your brother's name?
What do you think of Lady Gaga's songs?
I like them.

Vocabulary: Review adjectives (excellent, great, boring)
Grammar: Possessive 's. Object pronouns.

Warm-up Write the five scrambled questions below on the board. In pairs, sts have three minutes to order the words.
1) do / evenings / usually / what / you / Friday / on / eat / ?
2) you / usually / mornings / what / do / do / on / Saturday / ?
3) do / your / do / you / always / homework / ?
4) eat / usually / do / you / breakfast / what / for / ?
5) the / do / sometimes / a / have / afternoon / snack / in / you / ?

Classcheck with answers on the board. In pairs, sts take turns asking and answering all five questions. At the end, ask some sts to tell the class about their partners, e.g. "Pedro usually eats bread and cheese for breakfast."

1 Listening

A Point to photo 1 and ask: *Do you like Ryan Gosling? Do you know this movie?* Then point to photo 2 and ask: *Who is the woman on Stephen Colbert's show? Who's her husband?* Tell sts to read the newsfeed entries and complete them with photo captions 1, 2, or 3. Classcheck and ask: *Do you like James Bond movies?*, encouraging sts to use the verbs *like, love, don't like,* or *hate* from lesson **5.2**.

> People all over the world admire (3) James Bond's car ...
> Collection of (1) Ryan Gosling's movies released ...

B Tell sts to look at the rest of the photos and say what they see. Don't give answers at this point as sts will discover more in the listening. Tell sts to listen to friends talking about entertainment news, and note the photos they mention. Play ▶5.16 once or twice. Paircheck, then classcheck. Ask sts if they agree with the two friends.

> **Tip** If sts find the listening difficult, direct them to the transcript on p. 87 and play ▶5.16 again so they can read and listen at the same time.

▶5.16 Turn to p. 174 for the complete audioscript.

> 1, 2, 4

2 Grammar Possessive 's

A Draw sts' attention to the 's in the photo captions in **1A**. Elicit other examples with sts' names and their belongings, and write them on the board, e.g. *This is Juan's bag. This is his bag. That's Maria's book. That's her book.* Then, have sts read the grammar box and as a class, complete the rules by circling the correct options.

Tell sts to match the people in the box to photos 4–8 in **1A**. Paircheck, then classcheck.

There is more information on possessive 's in Grammar 5B on p. 80.

> 1 is   2 the possessive
> 4 Michelle Obama
> 5 Naomi Osaka
> 6 Calvin Harris
> 7 The soccer team
> 8 The U.S. President

B Transformation drill. Point to the speech bubbles and say: *Listen and follow the model.* Play ▶5.17 up to "Your turn" and the first beeps and student prompt. Pause the track and elicit the response from the whole class (Naomi Osaka's racket). Resume playing the track for sts to check the answer and listen for the next prompt. After each prompt, pick a different st to transform the sentence and occasionally have the whole class do it. Replay the track if you're working with a very large group.

▶5.17 Turn to p. 174 for the complete audioscript.

C **Make it personal** Model the task on the board with your own family and possessions. Write a name and letter on the board and say: *Jorge is in my family. Guess who it is!* (brother, father, son, etc.) Point to the letter and say: *This is one of Jorge's possessions. What do you think it is?* Have sts ask you questions to find out what the possession is. Refer them to the speech bubbles to clarify the task. Put sts into new pairs and have them do the same. Give feedback after the activity on good language and errors.

3 Grammar Object pronouns

♪ *Only hate the road when you're missing home,
Only know you love her when you let her go,
And you let her go.*

A ▶5.18 Read the questions and circle the correct words. Listen, check, and repeat.

Questions ?		Answers ⊕ ⊖	
What do you think of	Lady Gaga?	I love I (don't) like	she / him / her.
	the *Twilight Saga* **books**?		it / them / he.
Do you like	LeBron James?		him / her / he.
	Mexican **food**?		it / they / them.

→ **Grammar 5C** p. 80

B ▶5.16 Complete the dialogue with object pronouns. Listen again to check.
Ella Look! A collection of Ryan Gosling's movies are on boxset this weekend.
Luke Really? That's great! I like ¹_____ a lot. He's a great actor. I think his movies are excellent.
Ella Hmmm. I don't like ²_____ much.
Luke What?! They're fantastic! And what's on TV?
Ella Do you like Stephen Colbert's show?
Luke Yes, I do. I really like ³_____. Why?
Ella Well, Michelle Obama is on his show tonight.
Luke Michelle Obama? Again? I think Colbert loves ⁴_____!
Ella Well, the show is about Michelle's new book.
Luke Her autobiography? Oh, maybe I can read ⁵_____.

C ▶5.19 Listen and follow the model. Practice the sentences.

I like Adele.   *I like her.*   *I never watch American movies.*   *I never watch them.*

D Complete the mini dialogues. Then in pairs, practice them.
1 **A** This is my car. Do you like _____?
   B It's great! I like _____ very much!
2 **A** What do you think of the *Star Wars* movies? Do you like _____?
   B No, I really hate _____. I think they're boring.
3 **A** I love Billy Eilish. What do you think of _____?
   B She's fantastic. I like _____ a lot.
4 **A** What do you think of Chris Evans?
   B I like _____ a lot. I think he's an excellent actor.

⊘ Common mistakes

What do you think of J Lo? I like ~~she~~. *her*
It's ~~the car of my mother~~. *my mother's car*
Do you like baseball? I love. *it*

Do you like McDonald's burgers?
Yes, I like them a lot but I prefer Burger King burgers.

E 🟢 **Make it personal** In pairs, ask for and share opinions about these celebrities and your favorite brands of the items in the photos.

♫ **Song line:** Turn to p. 182 for notes about this song and an accompanying task.

3 Grammar Object pronouns

A Ask the whole class: *What do you think of Lady Gaga? Do you like her?* Point to the options "she / him / her" in the grammar box and elicit the correct answer (I like / don't like her.). Sts circle the correct words in the other answers. Paircheck. Play ▶5.18 to classcheck and repeat the answers.

▶5.18 Turn to p. 174 for the complete audioscript.

There is more information on possessive *'s* in Grammar 5B on p. 80.

> her
> them
> him
> it

B Tell sts this is the dialogue from **1B** on p. 64. Ask them to read the dialogue quickly before completing it with the correct object pronouns. Paircheck and then play ▶5.16, pausing after each gap to classcheck the answer.

▶5.16 Turn to p. 174 for the complete audioscript.

> 1 him
> 2 them
> 3 it
> 4 her
> 5 it

C Transformation drill. Point to the speech bubbles and say: *Listen and follow the model.* Play ▶5.19 up to "Your turn" and the first beep and prompt. Pause the track and elicit the response from the whole class (I sometimes eat it.). Resume playing the track for sts to check the answer and listen for the next prompt. After each prompt, pick a different st to respond. Encourage sts to mimic the sentence stress so they emphasize the key words and use the schwa in the correct places.

▶5.19 Turn to p. 174 for the complete audioscript.

D Elicit the answers to mini-dialogue 1. Then have sts complete the dialogues with *him, her, it,* or *them.* Paircheck. Classcheck with answers on the board. In new pairs, sts role-play the mini-dialogues. Monitor closely for intonation. At the end, have four different pairs of sts role-play a mini-dialogue each.

Common mistakes Read with the class and identify the mistakes (use of object pronouns and possessive *'s.*)

> 1 it, it
> 2 them, them
> 3 her, her
> 4 him

E **Make it personal** Point to the photo of the burger. Have two sts read the dialogue in the speech bubbles to the whole class. In pairs, sts ask and answer questions about the people and items in the photos. Monitor and go over any good language or errors you heard at the end.

Extra activity Ask sts to suggest other celebrities and brands, and write their ideas on the board. Tell sts to repeat the activity with a new partner, using the items on the board.

5.5 Do you eat a lot of fast food?

ID Skills Noticing sound-spelling combinations

A ▶5.20 What food can you see in photos a–d? Listen, read, and match the photos to restaurant recommendations 1–4.

1 Jane
Check out the cheeseburgers at this place. Great meat, delicious cheese, and amazing mayonnaise. I really recommend them.
★★★★★

2 Rick
I don't usually like ice cream, except for this one. I love their double chocolate cones. My sister likes the vanilla one with mango sauce!
★★★★☆

3 Viv
They open at six a.m. and I come here for breakfast every day! The fresh fruit salad with yogurt is fantastic. Their exotic juices are incredible too!
★★★★☆

4 Yuri
On weekends, my girlfriend and I always eat here. Their hot dogs and French fries are the best in the city, and the portions are very generous too!
★★★★★

Was this review helpful? 👍 👎

B Reread the recommendations in **A**. True (T) or False (F)? Correct the false sentences.
1. Jane likes cheeseburgers.
2. Rick likes vanilla ice cream.
3. Viv doesn't usually have breakfast at home.
4. Viv really likes fruit.
5. Yuri and his girlfriend eat hot dogs on Mondays.

C ▶5.21 Look at the pictures and say the pairs of words. Write the underlined words from **A** under the correct picture. Listen to check.

dʒ — b — v — r — j

generous ___ ___ ___ ___

D In pairs, say the five other consonant pairs marked **P** and **S** in the Sounds and usual spellings chart on p.82–83. Read the example words under the chart and notice the different spellings.

E 🎧 **Make it personal** *Story time!* Write a sentence with one of the consonant pairs in **C** or **D**. Challenge the class to pronounce it perfectly!

The vet drives a van.   A red rock on the road to Rio.

5.5 Do you eat a lot of fast food?

Lesson aims: Sts use the simple present to ask and answer questions about food, and notice sound and spelling combinations.

Function
Noticing sound–spelling combinations.
Reading recommendations about food.
Pronouncing the sounds /dʒ/ /b/ /v/ /r/ /j/ correctly.

Language
Jane likes cheeseburgers.
Their exotic juices are incredible.
Viv really likes fruit.

Vocabulary: Food items (cheeseburgers, French fries, fruit salad, hot dogs, ice cream, juice, mayonnaise, mango sauce, yogurt, vanilla)
Grammar: Review simple present

Warm-up Point to the photos / texts a–d in **A** say: *This is a website where people make comments about restaurants and food they eat. Do you read restaurant or café reviews online?* Briefly explore the photos. Elicit what food the sts can see in them.

ID SKILLS Noticing sound-spelling combinations

A Point to the texts and have sts match them to photos a–d. Tell sts to listen and read to check their answers, and play ▶5.20. Classcheck. Point to the photos and ask the class: *What do you like to eat or drink?*

a 2   b 3   c 4   d 1

B Asks sts to reread the reviews in **A**. Read aloud sentence 1 and ask: *Is it true or false?* (true). Sts decide if sentences 1–5 are true or false, and correct the false sentences. Paircheck. Classcheck, correcting the false sentences on the board.

1 T
2 F He only likes this chocolate ice cream.
3 T
4 T
5 F They eat hot dogs on weekends.

C Point to the five pictures with phonemic symbols and ask: *What can you see in the pictures for each sound?* (jump, jeans, bird, bike, vet, van, red rock, yellow yacht). Show sts how to make the sounds. You can also refer sts to the **Sounds and usual spellings** chart on p. 83 for pictures and instructions on how to make the sounds.

Language tip Sts may have trouble with /dʒ/ as it is not in some L1s, such as Spanish. To help them make this sound, ask them to say /tʃ/, and then make it voiced – they can do this by making their vocal chords vibrate. If they don't know how to do this, use /p/ and /b/ as examples, which are easier to demonstrate. Tell sts to put their hands on their throats when they say the two sounds, and feel the vocal chords start and stop between /b/ and /p/ respectively. Spend some time getting sts to practice the four sounds. If they have mobile devices, they can record a video of their mouths making the sounds and watch it back to see if they have the correct position. They can also help each other, working in pairs to practice the sounds.

Tell sts to look at the underlined words in **A** (including the writers' names) and write them under the correct picture. Play ▶5.21 so they can check answers. Replay and tell them to listen and repeat each word.

▶5.21 Turn to p. 174 for the complete audioscript.

/dʒ/: Jane, juices
/b/: cheeseburgers, breakfast, best
/v/: vanilla, Viv, very
/r/: really, recommend, Rick
/j/: mayonnaise, yogurt, Yuri

D Tell sts to turn to the **Sounds and usual spellings** chart on p. 82–83, and practice the consonant sounds. Look at the spellings together and have sts practice saying the words.

Tip Put sts into new pairs and ask them to test each other on the spelling. They take turns saying the words and spelling them (orally or in writing), without looking at the book.

E 🔵 **Make it personal** Sts write alliterative sentences with the consonant sounds in this activity. Show them the speech bubbles and ask some sts to say the sentences. Tell them to look at the words in **C** and on p. 82–83 and make their own sentences using one of the consonant pairs. Monitor and help with language and ideas. Sts take turns coming to the board to write their sentences, then challenging the class to say it. They can nominate individuals to say the sentence or ask the whole class.

Tip If you have a large class, do this activity in groups of four or five where they take turns showing the group their sentence for the others to say.

Extra activity Put sts into new groups of three. Sts take turns dictating their sentences. The other two sts have to listen and write the sentences and then practice saying them.

5.5 Anything to drink?

*Anything you want, you got it.
Anything you need, you got it.
Anything at all, you got it. Baby!*

Remember words and expressions with their opposites or associations.
For example:
For here? – To go?
Yes, please. – No, thanks.
large – small
with – without
eat – drink
ice – lemon
cream – sugar

Common mistakes
Anything ~~for~~ to drink?
For here or ~~for~~ to go?

ID in Action Ordering food

A ▶5.22 What do they order? Listen and match conversations 1 and 2 with two of food trays a–c.

B ▶5.23 Match questions 1–5 to the answers. Listen, check, and repeat.

1 Can I help you?
2 **A**nything to drink?
3 Large, **me**dium, or small?
4 Cream and sugar?
5 Anything else?

☐ A tea, please.
☐ Large, please.
1 A hot dog, please.
☐ No, thanks.
☐ Just sugar, please.

C ▶5.24 Circle the correct words. Listen to check. In pairs, cover all the words and practice the dialogue.

ATTENDANT	CUSTOMER
Can I help you?	A hamburger and French fries, **please / thanks**.
Anything to **eat / drink**?	**A / An** cola.
Large, medium, or small?	**Medium. / Small.**
With ice?	**Yes, please. / No, thanks.**
Anything **else / to drink**?	**Yes, please. / No, thanks.**
For here or to go?	**For here. / To go.**
That's $12.95.	There you are. **Thanks. / Thanks a lot.**

D 🎤 **Make it personal** In pairs, role-play. Then change roles.
A: You go to a fast-food restaurant.
B: You're the server. Take the order.

Can I help you?
A ..., please.

5.5 Anything to drink?

Lesson aims: Sts practice ordering food in a fast-food restaurant.

Function
Asking for and giving information about a food order.

Language
Can I help you?
A cola, please.
Large, medium, or small?
Small, please.

Vocabulary: Phrases for ordering food and drinks
Grammar: Shortened sentences (ellipses) (Would you like anything to drink? = Anything to drink?)

ID in action Ordering food

Song line: Turn to p. 182 for notes about this song and an accompanying task.

A Point to the main photo and ask: *Where is this?* (fast-food restaurant) *Do you like fast food?* Tell sts to listen to the first conversation and match it with one of the trays a–c. Play conversation 1 on ▶ 5.22, repeating it if necessary. Paircheck, then classcheck quickly. Do the same for conversation 2.

▶ 5.22 Turn to p. 174 for the complete audioscript.

1 c   2 b

B Read aloud question 1, *Can I help you?* and ask sts to say the answer (A hotdog, please.) Sts then match the other questions to the correct answers. Paircheck. Play ▶ 5.23 to check answers, then play it again for sts to repeat.

▶ 5.23 Turn to p. 175 for the complete audioscript.

2 A tea, please.
3 Large, please.
1 A hot dog, please.
5 No, thanks.
4 Just sugar, please.

C Ask sts to read the dialogue and circle the correct words. Play ▶ 5.24 to paircheck answers. Then replay ▶ 5.24 for choral repetition. Tell sts to change partners and practice reading the dialogue aloud. Then, tell sts to cover all the words and practice the dialogue using the pictures only.

Refer sts to the information box with *opposite* and associated phrases. Elicit who says the phrases and then practice them quickly by eliciting the other phrase, e.g.

T: *For here?* Sts: "To go?"

T: *No, thanks.* Sts: "Yes, please."

 Common mistakes Read with the class. Point out we use *to* in English, where they might use *for* in their L1.

Language tip Tell sts that the words *for* and *to* are translated the same in their L1, but that they have different usages in English. Give them some examples of usage to make sure sts understand (e.g. *go to school, go for a run*).

▶ 5.24 Turn to p. 175 for the complete audioscript.

Attendant: drink, else
Customer: please, A, Small, Yes, please., No, thanks., To go., Thanks a lot.

D **Make it personal** Put sts in new pairs and tell them **A** is the customer and **B** is the server. If possible, arrange the seating so that servers and customers are sitting opposite each other. Sts role-play ordering food and taking the order at a fast-food restaurant. Monitor and help if necessary. Then, sts change roles and act out the dialogue once again.

Tip You could ask sts to improvise by creating their own menus. Ask them to write menus quickly with their favorite fast food and use these for the role-plays. They could use each other's menus to extend the activity.

→ **Workbook** p. 109

→ ⓘⅅ **Richmond Learning Platform**

→ **Writing** p. 68

→ ⓘⅅ **Café** p. 69

Writing 5 A reply on social media

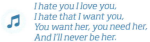

*I hate you I love you,
I hate that I want you,
You want her, you need her,
And I'll never be her.*

A ▶ 5.25 Read Claudia's reply to a social media post. Check the photos of the food on her pizza. Answer 1 and 2.

1   Who doesn't like "Chickibeans Pizza"?
2   Do they all eat *churros*?

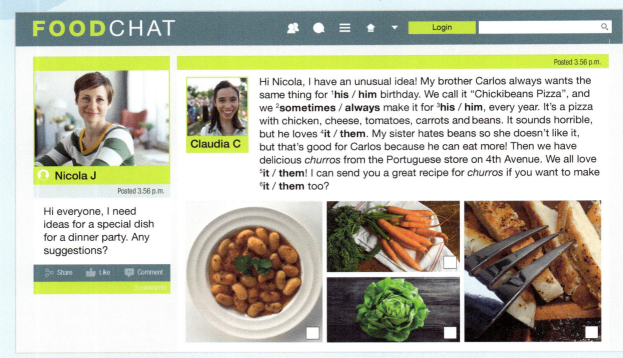

B Reread and choose the correct word in 1–6.

C Read *Write it right!* and (circle) one example of each of the six rules in Claudia's reply.

> ✅ **Write it right!**
>
> Use capital letters:
> 1 for names
> 2 street names
> 3 nationalities
> Use commas (,):
> 4 after an introduction
>   *Hello Nicola, here's a dish I love.*
> 5 for items in a list
> 6 Don't use *the* to talk about food in general.
>   *I don't really like pasta.* NOT ~~I don't really like the pasta.~~

D Match questions 1–4 to answers a–d.

1   What's the name of your dish?
2   Who usually makes it, and when?
3   What are the important ingredients?
4   Who really likes it? Who doesn't like it? Why?

a ☐ There are a lot of different recipes. I use onions, garlic, olive oil, tomatoes, saffron, and a lot of seafood and fish.
b ☐ All my family love it, except my sister because she's a vegetarian.
c ☐ It's *paella*.
d ☐ My dad usually makes it on weekends.

E 🗨 **Make it personal** Write a reply to Nicola's social media post.

Before	Think of a special dish, and answers to 1–4 in **D**. Use a dictionary for words you don't know in English.
While	Follow the rules in *Write it right!* Offer to send Nicola the recipe.
After	Check your reply carefully with a partner. Post it to your class.

68

Writing 5 A reply on social media

♪ **Song line:** Turn to p. 182 for notes about this song and an accompanying task.

A If possible, display the text using the **Digital Book for Teachers**. Point to the website page and ask sts: *What's this?* (a forum or blog about food.). Tell sts to read Nicola's post and ask: *What does she want?* (an idea for a special dish). Point to the photos of food and ask: *What food can you see?* Write answers on the board. Then, tell sts to read the text and answer questions 1 and 2. Paircheck, then classcheck. Ask: *Would you eat this pizza? Do you like churros?*

1 Claudia's sister. 2 Yes.

B Point to the first pair of bold words in the text and elicit the correct word from the class (his). Then have sts work individually to choose the correct words in the rest of the text. Classcheck.

1 his 2 always 3 him 4 it 5 them 6 them

C Have sts read **Write it right!** and ask them to find an example of each of the six rules in the text. If you are displaying the text, ask a student to come and circle the items on the screen / board. Classcheck.

Possible answers:
1 Nicola, Claudia, Carlos
2 4th Avenue / Fourth Avenue
3 Portuguese
4 Hello Nicola, here's a dish I love.
   Hi everyone, I need ideas …
5 chicken, cheese, tomatoes, carrots …
6 beans, *churros*

D Ask sts: *What's your idea for a special dish?* Elicit some ideas from the class quickly. Help with vocabulary if necessary and write the dishes on the board. Tell sts to read questions 1–4 and match them to answers a–d. Paircheck, then classcheck. Then ask different sts the questions and help them to express their own answers using a–d as a basis.

1 c 2 d 3 a 4 b

E **Make it personal** Tell sts they're going to write a reply to Nicola's post.

Before Tell sts to think of a special dish and their own answers in **D**. Ask sts to make a note of vocabulary they need for their dish and encourage them to use a dictionary to find unknown vocabulary.

While Sts write their reply to Nicola's post. Remind sts to use the punctuation rules in **Write it right!** as they write. Monitor and prompt self-correction of punctuation. Don't pick sts up on every language error you see.

After Ask sts to work with a partner to check each other's work for punctuation. Then, ask them to post their texts around the room so you can do a gallery reading activity. After sts have read all the texts, ask: *What dishes do you like the most?*

5 It's about taste

1 Before watching

A Complete the dialogue with these words.

| hungry | ~~looks~~ | pay for |
| tastes | try | vegetarian |

A: Wow, that chicken sandwich ___looks___ good.
I'm _____. Can I _____ it by credit card?
Thanks.
Mmm. It _____ delicious. Really great! Do you want to _____ it?
B: No, thanks. I'm a _____.

B Put the foods in the correct columns. Which do you eat every week?

beef	bread	breadsticks	burgers	chicken
dessert	fish	French fries	fruit	meat
pasta	rice	salad	vegetables	

Vegetarian foods	Non-vegetarian foods

I eat fruit every day, but I never eat dessert.

C 🔘 **Make it personal** *Schedules* In pairs, guess your partner's answers to 1 and 2.
1 How many hours a week do you work, study, and sleep?
2 When are your days off?

> *I work from 8:30 a.m. to 5:30 p.m., from Monday to Friday. That's 45 hours a week.*

2 While watching

A Look at the photo and the chart. In pairs, try to guess Genevieve's weekly schedule. Then watch until 2:15 and check the days Genevieve does these things.

	Mo	Tu	We	Th	Fr	Sa	Su
1 work							
2 go to class							
3 go to the gym							
4 take singing lessons							
5 practice singing							
6 practice guitar							
7 a day off							
8 study							

B Watch again to check and write her work and class times. What does she want to do on Saturday mornings and evenings?

Times	Work	Class
Monday & Wednesday	_9_ – _4_ & ___ – ___	___ – ___ & ___ – ___
Tuesday	___ – ___	
Thursday	___ – ___ & ___ – ___	*in the afternoon*

C Complete extracts 1–4 with the words.

| always | every day | four days a week |
| usually | weekends | |

1 What hours do you _____ work?
2 I practice singing and guitar _____.
3 I work _____ and _____, so I understand.
4 Are you _____ so busy?

D True (T) or false (F)?
1 Rory manages the schedule at ID Café.
2 He doesn't have a day off.
3 Genevieve likes her schedule.
4 Rory works to pay for school.
5 Genevieve and Rory like to be busy.

E Watch the complete video and ⓒircle the correct word or phrase.
1 Rory puts the dinner specials on the menu in the **morning** / **afternoon**.
2 Today's special is **Midwestern burger** / **Kentucky chicken** and French fries.
3 **Genevieve** / **Rory** doesn't eat beef.
4 Genevieve likes **everything on the menu** / **only the salads and sandwiches**.
5 **Rory** / **Genevieve** loves the desserts.
6 **The cook tries** / **Rory and the cook try** everything before it goes on the menu.

3 After watching

A 🔘 **Make it personal** Role-play a similar schedule interview. If you have a job, talk about yourself. If not, A: You're Rory. B: You're Genevieve. Then change roles.

So, what hours do you usually work?

ID Café 5 It's about taste

1 Before watching

A **Books closed.** Ask sts: *Are you vegetarian? Do you eat beef / chicken / fish?* Play a quick game with them. You say a food item they know, and ask: *Is it OK for vegetarians?* Explain they need to raise their hands if the food item is OK for vegetarians. Say: *beef, bread, potatoes, vegetables, fish, French fries, hamburger.*

Books open. Ask sts to complete the dialogue, then paircheck and classcheck. Tell sts to practice the dialogue quickly, paying attention to pronunciation.

> looks   hungry   pay for   tastes   try   vegetarian

B Sts put the foods in the correct categories. Classcheck. Read aloud the speech bubble, then ask sts: *Which foods do you eat every week?* They tell each other in pairs. Ask some sts to tell the class.

> **Vegetarian foods:**
> bread   pasta
> breadsticks rice
> dessert   salad
> French fries vegetables
> fruit
>
> **Non-vegetarian foods:**
> beef
> burgers
> chicken
> fish
> meat

C 🟢 **Make it personal** Tell sts they're going to talk about each other's weekly schedule. Ask sts questions 1 and 2 and elicit answers. Refer sts to the speech bubble. In pairs, sts take turns asking and answering the questions. Monitor closely for accuracy. At the end, ask a few sts to report their partner's answers.

2 While watching

A Point to the photo and ask the class: *Who are they?* (Genevieve and Rory). Ask: *Where do they work?* (a café). Point to the chart and, in pairs, have sts try to guess quickly the days that Genevieve does the different activities. Tell sts they're going to watch a video of Genevieve and Rory talking about their weekly schedule.

Play ▶5 until 2:15. Ask: *When is Genevieve's day off?* and see if they can remember from the video. Elicit / Drill pronunciation for all days of the week in the chart. Read the list of activities and tell sts to check the correct days for each while they watch the video again. Play ▶5 until 2:15 again. Paircheck, then classcheck.

	Mo	Tu	We	Th	Fr	Sa	Su
1 day off					✓		
2 go to class	✓		✓	✓			
3 go to the gym		✓					
4 take singing lessons		✓					
5 sing	✓	✓	✓	✓	✓	✓	✓
6 study						✓	✓
7 work	✓	✓	✓	✓		✓	

B Direct sts to the table and ask them to remember Genevieve's work and class times if they can. Play ▶5 again and ask sts to complete the chart with the times. Pause when necessary to give them time to write. Classcheck.

> Mon & Wed: Work 9–4 & 9–11; Class 4:45–6:30 & 7–8:30
> Tues: Work 3–11
> Thurs: Work 11–3 & 8–11
> Genevieve wants to work in the café on Saturday mornings and sing there on Saturday evenings.

C Tell sts to read 1–4 and look at the words in the box. Do number 1 with the class, and then ask sts to complete 2–4. Classcheck.

> 1 usually
> 2 every day
> 3 four days a week, weekends
> 4 always

D Read sentence 1 and ask: *True or false?* (true). Tell sts to decide if the other sentences are true or false. Play ▶5 until the end, and classcheck with answers on the board.

> 1 T   2 F   3 F   4 T   5 T

E Tell sts to read sentences 1–6, then play ▶5 again for them to circle the correct words / phrases. Classcheck, playing the video again and pausing if / when necessary.

> 1 morning
> 2 Midwestern burger
> 3 Genevieve
> 4 only the salads and sandwiches
> 5 Rory
> 6 Rory and the cook try

3 After watching

A 🟢 **Make it personal** Demonstrate the task with a st who has a job. Ask her / him questions to find out about her / his schedule. Write the questions on the board to help sts in their role-plays. Put sts into new pairs and tell them to do similar role-play interviews. Tell them that if they don't have a job, they can be Rory and Genevieve. Monitor for good language and go over this afterward.

To finish, ask sts if they enjoyed watching the ID Café videos and what characters and stories they liked best.

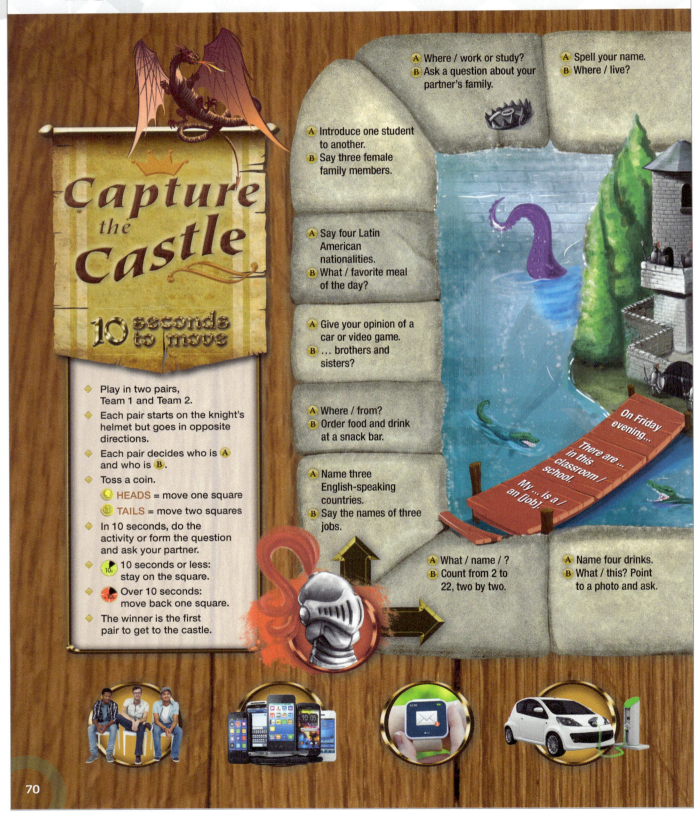

Review 3 Capture the Castle

 Song line: Turn to p. 183 for notes about this song and an accompanying task.

Split the class into groups of four. Within their groups, sts form two teams (Team 1 and Team 2) of two to compete against each other. In each pair, have sts decide who is **A** and who is **B**. Explain that to win the game, they have to be first to reach the castle gate.

Read the instructions on p. 70 with the whole class. Point to the knight's helmet on the bottom left of the page and tell sts this is the starting point. Tell them the teams go in opposite directions, following the direction of one of the two arrows. Point to the coins in the instructions box and explain that if they get heads, they move one square, and if they get tails, they move two.

 heads **tails**

Explain there's a time limit for each activity / square. When a pair is performing an activity, the other team should monitor the time. If they exceed the time limit of 10 seconds, sts are penalized and have to move back one square. If not, they stay on the same square until they toss the coin again.

In each square a team stops on, **A** does activity A; **B** does activity B. The winning team is the first to complete the full circuit and cross the bridge to the castle gate. Monitor closely for accuracy and offer help whenever necessary.

At the end, ask all groups: *Which square was the most difficult?*

Topics	Reference	Expected language production
A: Name three English-speaking countries. B: Say the names of three jobs.	p. 18/19 p. 32/33	A: The U.S., Australia, the UK / Britain … B: lawyer, doctor, university professor …
A: Where / from? B: Order food and drink at a snack bar.	p. 9 p. 67	A: Where are you from? (B: I'm from …) B: A hamburger and a cola, please.
A: Give your opinion of a car or video game. B: … brothers and sisters?	p. 21 p. 34/35	A: I think *FIFA 20* is a fantastic video game. B: Do you have brothers or sisters? (A: Yes, I do. I have … / No, I don't.)
A: Say four Latin American nationalities. B: What / favorite meal of the day?	p. 18/19 p. 58	A: Argentinian, Venezuelan, Brazilian, Mexican … B: What's your favorite meal of the day? (A: Breakfast.)
A: Introduce one student to another. B: Say three female family members.	p. 9 p. 34/35	A: Mariana, this is Eduardo. B: mother, sister, daughter …
A: Where / work or study? B: Ask a question about your partner's family.	p. 36/37 p. 34	A: Where you do work? Where do you study? (B: I work in an office.) B: What does your mother do? / Do you have a big family?
A: Spell your name. B: Where / live?	p. 13 p. 36	A: S-O-U-Z-A. B: Where do you live? (A: I live in Copacabana.)
A: How old / your …? B: Name three European countries.	p. 26 p. 18/19	A: How old is your father? (B: He's 60 years old.) B: Spain, Portugal, France …
A: When / meet friends? B: Give your opinion of an actor.	p. 62/63 p. 21	A: When / How often do you meet friends? (B: On weekends. / Every evening.) B: I think Ben Affleck is a fantastic actor.
A: Name four personal objects you have with you. B: What / usually do / weekends?	p. 44/45 p. 62/63	A: a pen, a book, a phone, an ID card … B: What do you usually do on weekends? (A: I usually go to the beach.)
A: Count from 3 to 33, three by three. 3, 6 … B: Name four kinds of fruit or vegetables.	p. 19/23 p. 58/60	A: 3, 6, 9, 12, 15, 18, 21, 24, 27, 30, 33 B: bananas, apples, carrots, potatoes …
A: … children? B: Name? From? Job?	p. 34/35 p. 7/9 p. 18/19	A: Do you have children? (B: Yes, I have a son / daughter. / No, I don't.) B: What's your name? Where are you from? What's your job?
A: What kind / food / like? B: Name three male family members.	p. 58/60/61 p. 34/35	A: What kind of food do you like? B: I like Italian food. B: father, brother, son …
A: Say six colors. B: What / phone number?	p. 19 p. 13	A: blue, red, yellow, green, orange, brown … B: What's your phone number?
A: Say three alternate days of the week. B: Give your opinion of a singer or sports celebrity.	p. 62 p. 16	A: Monday, Wednesday, Friday … B: I think Simone Biles is an awesome gymnast. She's an inspiration.
A: Name four personal objects you don't have with you. B: When / watch movies?	p. 44/46 p. 62/63	A: a flash drive, a laptop, a marker, a dictionary … B: When do you (usually) watch movies? (A: Every weekend.)
A: … married? B: Spell the name of your city.	p. 13 p. 12	A: Are you married? (B: Yes, I am.) B: B-O-G-O-T-Á.
A: Give your opinion of a book or movie. B: How old / you?	p. 20/21 p. 13	A: I think *Toy Story 4* is a very funny movie. B: How old are you? (A: I'm 19.)
A: Name four drinks. B: What / this? Point to a photo and ask.	p. 58/60 p10/11	A: orange juice, cola, water, coffee … B: What's this? / What are these? (A: It's a car. / They're wallets.)
A: What / name / ? B: Count from 2 to 22, two by two.	p. 6/7 p. 7/19	A: What's your name? B: 2, 4, 6, 8, 10, 12, 14, 16, 18, 20, 22

Grammar Unit 1

1A *a / an* and *the*

Dora is **a** teacher.   She's **an** excellent teacher.
 is **a** book.   It's **an** English book.
New York is **a** city.   It's **a** big city.

Use **a / an** for a non specific person, place, or thing = "one."

Use **a** before a consonant sound:
- **a** <u>m</u>an, **a** <u>ch</u>air, **a** <u>b</u>ook.

Use **an** before a vowel sound:
- **an** <u>a</u>pple, **an** <u>e</u>mail, **an** <u>i</u>con, **an** <u>o</u>pera, **an** <u>u</u>rgent email.

Exception:
- **a** <u>u</u>niversity, **a** <u>u</u>niform (the *u* is pronounced with a consonant sound /juː/)

a / an = singular = **a** tablet.

The teacher is Dora.   Where is **the** elevator? (singular)
Welcome to **the** New  School of English.   **The** museums in DC are fantastic. (plural)

Use **the** for:
- a specific noun: **the** President, **the** capital city
- singular or plural: **the** Natural History Museum, **the** museums.

1B Verb *be* ⊕ ⊖

The verb *be* has three forms: *am, is, are.*

⊕	Contractions	⊖	Contractions
I **am** single.	I**'m** single.	I **am not** married.	I**'m not** married.
You **are** married.	You**'re** married.	You **are not** single.	You**'re not** / **aren't** single.
It **is** a problem!	It**'s** a problem!	It **is not** good.	It**'s not** / **isn't** good!

You = singular and plural
You're **a** student = one
You're student**s** = two or more

Use contractions when you speak or write informal texts.
Note: Don't contract *am + not.* Remember the subject.
I'm not. **NOT** ~~I amn't.~~
I'm Mexican. **NOT** ~~Am Mexican.~~

1C Verb *be* ❓

Yes / No questions & Short answers

❓ Be + Subject	⊕ S + be	⊖ S + be + not
Are you married?	Yes, I **am**.	No, I**'m not**.
Is it a 5G phone?	Yes, it **is**.	No, it**'s not**. /
Is this your pen?		No, it **isn't**.

Invert the subject (S) and the verb (V) to form a question.
Are you Peruvian? **NOT** ~~You are Peruvian?~~
Yes / No questions have a short answer.
Note: Don't contract ⊕ short answers.
Are you American? Yes, I am. **NOT** ~~Yes, I'm.~~

Wh- questions

❓ Wh-Question + be + S	Full Answer	Short Answer
Where are you from?	I **am** / I**'m** from Brazil.	Brazil.
How are you?	I **am** / I**'m** fine, thanks.	Fine, thanks.
What's your name?	It **is** / It**'s** Marcos.	Marcos.
What's this?	It **is** / It**'s** a tablet.	A tablet.

Form a **Wh-** question with **Wh-** question word + *be* + S.
Where are you from? **NOT** ~~From where are you?~~
Answer **Wh-** questions with information.
Contraction: **What's, Where's, How's.**
Note: Don't contract *Wh-* questions + *are.*
Where are ...? or How are ... ? **NOT** ~~Where're ...? How're ...?~~

Unit 1

1A

1 Circle the correct words.
1. Look at **a** / **the** photo in **a** / **the** book.
2. What's **an** / **the** eraser?
3. This is **an** / **the** apple. It's for **a** / **the** teacher.
4. "W" is **a** / **the** letter in **an** / **the** English alphabet.
5. Buenos Aires is **a** / **the** great city. It's **a** / **the** capital of Argentina.

2 Complete 1–5 with **a** / **an** where necessary.
1. This is _____ book.
2. Pedro and Mariana are _____ students.
3. Is this _____ credit card or _____ ID card?
4. I have _____ dog called Maya and _____ energetic cat called Luna.
5. Is this _____ letter "O" or _____ zero?

3 Correct the mistake in 1–5.
1. I'm student.
   I'm a student.
2. You're from U.S.
3. I'm from the Brazil.
4. This is the my friend.
5. Shhhh! Teacher is here.
6. The parking lot is in the Terminal 2.

4 Write **the** where necessary.
1. _The_ book is on _____ table.
2. _____ teacher _____ is _____ in _____ classroom.
3. Look _____ at _____ photo _____ and _____ repeat _____ sentences.
4. What's _____ email _____ of _____ school?
5. This _____ is _____ President of _____ Colombia.

1B

1 Complete with **am**, **are**, or **is**.
1. ID _____ an English book.
2. I _____ from Peru. This _____ my friend from Italy.
3. You _____ a student.
4. This _____ my email address.
5. _____ this an eraser?

2 Make sentences 1–5 negative. Use contractions where possible.
1. This is a book. _____
2. You're my friend. _____
3. I'm from Europe. _____
4. This is my car. _____
5. You're my favorite teacher. _____

1C

1 Match the questions and answers.
1. Are you single?   □ No, it's a tablet.
2. Is this an English class? □ I'm from Egypt.
3. Where are you from?   □ Yes, it is.
4. Are you from France?   □ No, I'm not.
5. Is this a computer?   □ Yes, I'm from Paris.

2 Complete the dialogue 1–9 with the correct form of **be** (+ or –)

Jorge Hi. I ¹_____ Jorge. Nice to meet you.
  a [_____]
Linda My name ²_____ Linda. Nice to meet you too.
Juan Hello, Linda! ᵇ [_____]
Linda Hi, Juan. I ³_____ fine, thanks.
Juan Cool!
Linda Juan, this ⁴_____ Jorge.
Jorge Nice to meet you. ᶜ [_____]
Juan I ⁵_____ from Mexico. And you? ⁶_____ you from Spain?
Jorge Yes, I ⁷_____!
Juan Cool! Hey Linda, ᵈ [_____]?
Linda It ⁸_____ my flash drive. It ⁹_____ for my documents.
Juan Cool!

3 Now write **Wh-** questions in the boxes to complete the dialogue. Use contractions where possible.

157

Grammar Unit 2

2A Verb *be*

	Contractions	
	+ S + *be*	**−** S + *be* + *not*
Singular	I'm You're He's / She's / It's	I'm not You're not / You aren't He / She / It's not He / She / It isn't
Plural	We're You're They're	We're not / We aren't You're not / You aren't They're not / They aren't

American.
20 years old.
from China.

Use verb *be* to:
- describe people and things.
- talk about age and nationality.

To ask about age, use **How old** + verb *be*.

How old	is	he / she / it? Bill / Shakira / your car?
	are	you / we / they? Fred and George / your dogs?

Yes / No questions

	? *Be* + S	**+** S + *be*	**−** S + *be* + *not*
Singular	Is *he* / *Bill* American? Is *she* / *Shakira* a musician? Is *it* / *a spider* an insect?	Yes, *he* is. Yes, *she* is. Yes, *it* is.	No, *he's* not. / No, *he* isn't. No, *she's* not. / No, *she* isn't. No, *it's* not. / No, *it* isn't.
Plural	Are *they* / *The Killers* British?	Yes, *they* are.	No, *they're* not. / No, *they* aren't.

Wh- questions (Where … from?)

	? *Wh*-Q + *be* + S		**+** S + *be* + information	
Singular	Where	is *he* / *Bill* is *she* / *Oprah* is *it* / *your car*	from?	He's She's It's	Mexican. from Mexico.
Plural		are *they* / *the Simpsons*		They're	

Use **who** for people.
- *Who's Bill Gates?*

Use **what** for ideas, animals or things.
- *What's your address?*

The 3rd person singular has three forms: *he*, *she*, *it*.
The 3rd person plural has one form: *they*.

2B Personal pronouns

The seven personal pronouns in English are:
I, you, he, she, it, we, they.

Use:
- *he* for a man
- *she* for a woman
- *it* for an idea, an animal, or a thing
- *you* for singular or plural
- *we* and *they* for plural.

2C Adjectives

Elle Fanning is **an** excellent **actor**.
Is Ricardo **a** good **teacher**?
We're **happy students**.
Dua Lipa and Drake are **fantastic musicians**.

In English, **adjectives** go before **nouns**.
NOT ~~She's an actor excellent.~~

Adjectives have only one form for singular and plural, and no gender.
NOT ~~We're happys students.~~

Form:

Use noun +*s* to form plurals: *a book, two books; a pen, two pens.*
- *They're good students.*
- *I'm 30 years old.*

Use *a* / *an* before occupations (singular).
- *I'm a student.*
- *He's an Argentinian actor.*

Unit 2

2B

1 Circle the correct option.
1. Bob and I **am** / **are** students. **Are** / **We're** good friends.
2. **Are** / **Is** James Bond American?
3. I think iPads **are** / **is** incredible!
4. A **Are** / **Is** you and your teacher American?
   B My teacher **'re** / **'s** American, but I **'m** / **'s** Canadian.
5. A How old **are** / **is** Jim and Tim?
   B They **'re** / **'s** 17.

2 Insert verb *be* where appropriate. Use contractions.
1. A you a good soccer player?
   B No, I not. But I a big soccer fan!
2. Paul 25 years old, and he an excellent teacher!
3. This movie not good. It terrible!
4. A Rihanna and Ed Sheeran British?
   B No, they not. She from Barbados and he British.
5. A How old you and your friends?
   B I 22 and they 21.

3 Put 1–8 in order to make questions. Then match them to the answers.
1. old / Lucy / 18 / is / years / ?
2. Jackie / who / 's / ?
3. Japan / your / friend / is / from / ?
4. are / your / names / what / ?
5. how / is / Luis / old / ?
6. Juan / is / a / musician / ?
7. Julie / and / Celia / are / your names / ?
8. from / where / 's / Samira / ?

☐ He's 18.
☐ Yes, they are.
☐ She's from Turkey.
☐ She's my teacher.
☐ No, he isn't. He's from Portugal.
☐ Yes, he is. He's an actor too.
☐ No, she isn't.
☐ Julie and Celia.

4 Look at the ID cards. Complete 1–8 with **'s**, **is**, or **isn't**. Use contractions where possible.
1. How old _____ Mario?
2. Mario _____ 23 today. It _____ his birthday!
3. Mario _____ Mexican. He _____ Spanish. He _____ from Bilbao.
4. Celine _____ 21 years old. She _____ only 18.
5. This _____ Celine Soucy. She _____ Canadian.
6. A _____ Angela really 21?
   B Yes, she _____. Look! This is her ID card.
7. Angela _____ Brazilian. She _____ from Monterrey.
8. Celine _____ a teacher. She _____ an English student at the iD School of English.

2B

1 Substitute the underlined words in 1–5 with pronouns.
1. <u>Laura</u> is a teacher.
2. <u>Pedro and I</u> are from Honduras.
3. <u>Emma Watson and Daniel Craig</u> are British celebrities.
4. <u>My car</u> is Chinese.
5. <u>Mexican movies</u> are fantastic!

2 Complete 1–5 with personal pronouns.
1. A Are _____ students?
   B Yes, _____ are.
2. This is Ana. _____ 's my Paraguayan friend.
3. Fred and Maria are Cuban. _____ 're very similar. _____ 're 25, _____ 're single, and _____ like rap music.
4. A Is this an Android phone?
   B No, _____ 's not. _____ 's an iPhone.
5. A Where's Rosa from?
   B _____ 's from Costa Rica. _____ 's a beautiful place.

2C

1 Correct the mistakes in 1–5.
1. Imagine Dragons are a rock band famous.
2. This is my car new.
3. *Ad Astra* and *Avengers: Endgame* is excellents movies.
4. We not goods baseball players.
5. A This is important exercise.
   B Yes, is.

2 Order 1–5 to make sentences.
1. is / fantastic / Ben Affleck / actor / a / American
2. this / urgent / an / e-mail / is
3. excellent / games / *Zombies* and *Dishonored* / are / video
4. a / Brazilian / soccer / Neymar / is / player
5. my / is / musician / Billie Eilish / favorite

159

Grammar Unit 3

3A Possessive adjectives

I'm a student. This is **my** course book.
You're my friend. Give me **your** address.

He's married. **His** wife is Rosa.
She lives downtown. This is **her** house.

We work a lot. **Our** office is very busy.
They're dogs. **Their** names are Don and Bel.

The seven possessive adjectives in English are:
I → My   You → Your   He → His   She → Her   It → Its   We → Our   They → Their

3B Simple present: *I / you / we / they*

	⊕ Subject + Infinitive	
I	have a dog.	
You	live in Rio de Janeiro.	
We	work in a bank.	
They	⊖ S + Auxiliary (do) + not + I	
My friends	do not / don't	have a car. / live in Berlin. / work in a store.

Use the simple present to talk about facts and routine.
The forms for *I / You / We / They* are exactly the same in ⊕, ⊖ and ?.
Contraction: *do not* = *don't*
Use the auxiliary verb *do* to form negatives and questions.
▸ We **don't** know. NOT ~~We no know.~~
▸ **Do** you understand? NOT ~~You understand?~~
Use *in* + city, part of a city, and buildings.
▸ I live **in** NYC, and I work **in** a school **in** Soho.
Use *at* + home:
▸ Do you work **at** home?

Yes / No questions: ASI

A	S	I	⊕ S + A	⊖ S + A + not
Do	you we they	live in NYC? work? have a car?	Yes, I you we they do.	No, I you we they don't.

Wh- questions: QASI

Q	A	S	I		
Where	do	you we they your parents	live? work?	I You We They	live downtown. work in a hospital.
What	do	you	do?	I	'm a doctor.

3C Simple present: *he / she / it*

	⊕ S + I	
He	has a dog.	
Tom	lives in Quito.	
Your son	works in a hospital.	
She	⊖ S + A (do) + not + I	
Berta	does not	have a cat.
Your sister	doesn't	live in London. work in a bank.

	⊕ S + I	
The café	has Internet access.	
It	⊖ S + A (do) + not + I	
	does not / doesn't	have a printer.

Form:
⊕ Use *he, she* and *it* + infinitive + *s*.
⊖ Use *does + not* (= *doesn't*) + infinitive.
He doesn't study. NOT ~~He no studies.~~
Does he have a car? NOT ~~Has he a car?~~

Yes / No questions: ASI

A	S	I	⊕
Does	he / Leo / your son she / Ana / your sister it / your cell phone	live near here? work at home? have 5G?	Yes, he / she / it does.
			⊖ No, he / she / it doesn't.

Form:
⊕ Use *Does* + Subject + Infinitive

Wh- questions: QASI

Q	A	S	I	
What	does	he / Ed / your son it / your cell phone	do? have?	He works in a school. It has a good camera.

Simple present verbs have only two forms: the infinitive and the 3rd person form (*he / she / it*).
The 3rd person = verb + *s* (see spelling rules on p.78)
Exceptions: *have* → *has*   *do* → *does*

Unit 3

3A

1 Correct the mistakes.
1. This is my sister Jane, and this is she's husband.
2. His 20 years old, and he's brother is 22.
3. Do you live with you're parents?
4. Where are Daniel and he's wife from?
5. Their my children. They're names are Diego and Alejandra.
6. We don't know he. He's not us friend.
7. She's married. She lives with your husband.

2 Circle the correct option.
1. Jack's not happy. **He's / His / Your** parents are very strict.
2. Emma's really cool! Look at **his / her / she's** new jeans!
3. Nice to meet you. Is this **he's / his / your** son?
4. My husband and I live with **your / our / their** son and **his / her / our** wife.
5. Isabel and Carlos are new to the city. **Their / They're / They** children go to the local school.

3B

1 Complete 1–4 with the verbs and *in* or *at* where necessary. Then match them to photos a–d.

have (×2)   (not) have (×2)   (not) like
live (×2)   study   work (×2)

1. I _____ a lot because I _____ a lot of exams. I _____ time to see my friends. It's horrible.
2. We _____ two children. They're beautiful! We _____ an apartment and I _____ home.
3. I _____ a restaurant, but I _____ my job.
4. We _____ alone and we _____ children, but we're very happy.

3C

1 Circle the correct form.
1. **Do / Does** Johnny **work / works** in Mexico City?
2. My friends **have / has** two children.
3. Celia and her sister **don't / doesn't** live alone. Their mother **live / lives** in their house too.
4. Oscar **don't / doesn't** work freelance. He **work / works** for an online company.
5. Where **do / does** he **work / works**?

2 Complete 1–5 and a–e with *do*, *don't*, *does* or *doesn't*. Then match the questions and answers.
1. _____ you have a big family?
2. _____ Mireya work downtown?
3. _____ your children study in Chicago?
4. _____ you and your husband work at home?
5. _____ Rodrigo want to be a hairdresser?

a. ☐ Yes, they _____.
b. ☐ No, I _____.
c. ☐ Yes, he _____.
d. ☐ No, she _____.
e. ☐ Yes, we _____.

3 Read the answers and complete the questions.
1. A Where _____?
   B I work in a drugstore.
2. A _____ alone?
   B No, we live with our father.
3. A _____ your grandparents _____?
   B No, they don't. They're retired.
4. A What _____ your siblings _____?
   B My sister's a cashier and my brother's at college.
5. A _____ exactly?
   B We live in downtown Philadelphia. It's a great city. _____ _____ know it?

 a
 b
 c
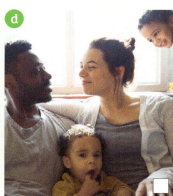 d

Grammar Unit 4

4A There + be

There's a charger in my bag.
There isn't a teacher in the classroom.
Is there a subway station on this street?
Use **There + be** to indicate the existence of something.
NOT ~~It's a charger in my bag.~~

There are two cars in the garage.
Are there a lot of apps on your phone?

Singular		
➕	There is / There's	an umbrella in my car. one credit card in my bag.
➖	There isn't	a coin in my purse.
❓	Is there	a good show on TV tonight? a cell phone in your bag? a virus on your computer?
Short Answers	➕ Yes, *there is*. ➖ No, *there isn't*.	

Plural		
➕	There are	two umbrellas in my car.
➖	There aren't	a lot of students here today.
❓	Are there	computers in the classroom? mints in your purse? keys in your bag?
Short Answers	➕ Yes, *there are*. ➖ No, *there aren't*.	

Contractions: there is = there's, there is not = there isn't, there are not = there aren't
But *there are* NOT ~~there're~~

4B this / that / these / those

		Singular	Plural
Here	🧍	What's **this**? **This** is a cell phone. **This** book is good.	What are **these**? **These** are earphones. **These** students are incredible.
There	🧍	What's **that**? **That's** your ID. **That** woman is my teacher.	What are **those**? **Those** are your keys. **Those** tablets are new.

Use *this / these* for items with you, near you, or "here".
NOT ~~What's that here?~~
Use *that / those* for items with other people, distant from you, or "there".
NOT ~~What are these there?~~

4C Plural nouns

Regular plurals

+ -s	consonant + y = - y + -ies	s, sh, ch, x + -es
a pen – pen**s**	a dictionary – dictionar**ies**	a class – class**es**
a book – book**s**	a country – countr**ies**	a toothbrush – toothbrush**es**
an actor – actor**s**	a nationality – nationalit**ies**	a beach – beach**es**
a cell phone – cell phone**s**	a city – cit**ies**	a church – church**es**
a key – key**s**	a celebrity – celebrit**ies**	a box – box**es**
a photo – photo**s**	a baby – bab**ies**	a bus – bus**es**
a month – month**s**	an activity – activit**ies**	Pronounce *-es* as an extra syllable: /ɪz/
a year – year**s**		
a comb – comb**s**		

The plural of most nouns = noun + s

Irregular plurals

Different forms

a man – **men**
a woman – **women**
a child – **children**
a person – **people**
a wife – **wives**

Unit 4

4A

1 Order the words to make sentences.
1. twenty / are / there / students / in / class / our
2. police officers / are / there / in / New York City / excellent
3. charger / is / on the table / there / white / a
4. rulers / on / the desk / are / there / two
5. there / a / ring / 's / box / in the

2 Complete 1–5 with *'s*, *is*, *isn't*, *are* or *aren't*.
1. There _____ a black camera here. _____ it your camera?
2. There _____ a lot of students in this class. There _____ only one.
3. _____ there a lot of people in your family?
4. A _____ there a new photo of you on Facebook?
   B Yes, there _____! It's me and my mom.
5. All the restaurants in my city are expensive! There _____ one cheap restaurant!

4B

1 Complete 1–5 with *this*, *these*, *that* or *those*.

1. What are _____? Candies? — No, they're pens!

2. _____ watches are beautiful!

3. Is _____ a cell phone? — No, it's a mini tablet.

4. _____ red apple is delicious!

5. _____'s a really good movie!

4C

1 Change sentences 1–5 to the plural.
1. What's that? Your new diary?
2. This is a slow bus!
3. That's a beautiful fish.
4. Is this your blue toothbrush?
5. This isn't a camera, it's a cell phone.

Grammar Unit 5

5A like / love / don't like / hate

really hate — hate — don't like — like — really like — love

Use these verbs to talk about how we feel about things.
Use plural forms with countable nouns.
- I *hate* apples. **NOT** ~~I hate apple.~~
- She really *likes* eggs.

Don't use *the* + nouns to talk about things in general.
- He *doesn't like* chicken. **NOT** ~~He doesn't like the chicken.~~
- We *love* oranges. **NOT** ~~We love the oranges.~~
- My dad doesn't like soccer.
- I hate Mondays!

5B Frequency adverbs

Frequency	What do people do on Sundays?
100% ↑ ↓ 0%	I *always* go to church. We *usually* watch a movie. My brother *sometimes* goes to the gym. Donna *never* stays home.

Use these adverbs to say how frequently things occur.
Frequency adverbs usually go:
- before **main verbs**: I *always watch* soccer on Sundays.
- after verb **be** and **auxiliaries**: She *is never* late.
  She *doesn't usually* study for exams.

Prepositions:
Use *in* + *the* with parts of the day.
- I always eat fruit **in** the mornings.
- Do you watch TV **in** the evenings?

Use *at* + times and night.
- My dad works at night. He starts at 10 p.m. and finishes at 6 a.m.

Use *on* with the weekend, days, or days + parts of the day.
- My mother works **on** the weekend.
- I never eat meat **on** Fridays.
- We study English **on** Thursday evenings.

5C Possessive 's & object pronouns

Possessive 's
Use *'s* to indicate possession.
The *teacher's* phone. (singular, one teacher, one phone)
The *teachers'* phones. (plural, two teachers, plural phones)
The *children's* phones. (irregular plural)
Beyoncé's music. **NOT** ~~The music of Beyoncé.~~

Subject	Object	
I	me	I love you. Do you love *me*?
You	you	You're a terrible person. I don't like *you*.
He	him	Bruce Springsteen is OK. I like *him*.
She	her	What do you think of Pink? Do you like *her*?
It	it	Japanese food is OK, but I don't often eat *it*.
We	us	We're here. Please, listen to *us*!
They	them	My parents are great. I live with *them*. There are good movies on TV, but I never watch *them*.

Use **object pronouns**:
- to substitute people and things when they are the object of a sentence.
- usually **after** a verb or preposition.

Do you use social media? Yes, I use *it* a lot. **NOT** ~~I use a lot.~~
Do you like Shawn Mendes? Yes, I love *him*! **NOT** ~~I love!~~

Unit 5

5A

1 Correct the mistakes.
1. Mark don't like a Chinese food.
2. My children don't eat vegetables for the lunch.
3. Does your mother drinks coffee for the breakfast?
4. I not like meat very much, but my brother do.
5. What kind of fruit do your daughter likes?
6. Do your childs like the soccer?

2 Use the prompts to write sentences / questions.
1. I / hate / carrots
2. My sister / not like / cheese
3. you / like / swimming ?
4. I / really like / Italian / food
5. your son / like / black coffee ?
6. I / love / fish / but / my brother / not like / it / very much
7. you / eat / a lot of / meat ?

5B

1 Look at Gina's schedule. Complete a–e with *in* or *on*. Then match 1–5 to a–e.
1. Gina sometimes goes to the gym
2. She always goes to the grocery store
3. She always goes to church
4. She never watches TV
5. She usually works

a ☐ _____ Saturday mornings.
b ☐ _____ the weekends.
c ☐ _____ the afternoons.
d ☐ _____ Sunday afternoons.
e ☐ _____ Sunday mornings.

	Sunday	Monday	Tuesday	Wednesday	Thursday	Friday	Saturday
9:00 12:00	church	gym	book	book	book	gym	grocery
13:00 18:00	gym	work	work	work	work	work	work
18:00 22:00	cinema	TV	TV	TV	TV	TV	movie

2 Order the words to make sentences.
1. the / they / cook / food / special / weekends / on / always
2. never / we / go / on / to / school / Sundays
3. watch / in / always / TV / evenings / the / I / don't
4. the / do / you / go / to / movies / on / weekends / the ?
5. Chinese / at / they / eat / never / food / home
6. on / often / mornings / play / Sunday / soccer / Scott / doesn't
7. the gym / go / sometimes / to / Saturdays / the / I / on
8. every / they / class / day / a / take / do?

5C

1 Correct the mistakes in the answers in 1–5.
1. A Do you like Taylor Swift?
   B No, I don't like she. She's music is terrible.
2. A Do your children like Disney movies?
   B Yes, they love. They watch it every day.
3. A What do you think about Ryan Reynolds?
   B He's a good actor. I like he!
4. A Do you like the *Avengers* movies?
   B We don't like it. We hate superhero movies.
5. A What do you think about Thai food?
   B I really like them. Let's go to a Thai restaurant now.
6. A Does your boyfriend like Selena Gómez?
   B Yes, he loves. Personally, I don't like she!

2 Complete 1–5 with *him*, *her*, *it*, or *them*. Then circle five possessive *'s* in the conclusion.
1. Mary loves her boyfriend, but he doesn't love _____.
2. Her brother's very intelligent, but she never listens to _____.
3. Mary likes apples a lot, but she never eats _____.
4. She really likes coffee. She drinks _____ a lot.
5. Her dogs are terrible. We don't like _____.

Conclusion
Mary's boyfriend's not in love with her. Mary's brother's very intelligent, but she ignores this. Mary's favorite fruit is apple, and coffee's Mary's favorite drink. Finally, Mary's dogs aren't very nice.

Sounds and usual spellings

S Difficult sounds for Spanish speakers
P Difficult sounds for Portuguese speakers

▶ To listen to these words and sounds, and to practice them, go to the pronunciation section on the Richmond Learning Platform.

Vowels

/iː/	three, tree, eat, receive, believe, key, B, C, D, E, G, P, T, V, Z
/ɪ/	six, mix, it, fifty, fish, trip, lip, fix
/ʊ/	book, cook, put, could, cook, woman
/uː/	two, shoe, food, new, soup, true, suit, Q, U, W
/ɛ/	pen, ten, heavy, then, again, men, F, L, M, N, S, X
/ə/	bananas, pajamas, family, photography

/ɜr/	shirt, skirt, work, turn, learn, verb
/ɔr/	four, door, north, fourth
/ɔ/	walk, saw, water, talk, author, law
/æ/	man, fan, bad, apple
/ʌ/	sun, run, cut, umbrella, country, love
/ɑ/	hot, not, on, clock, fall, tall
/ɑr/	car, star, far, start, party, artist, R

Diphthongs

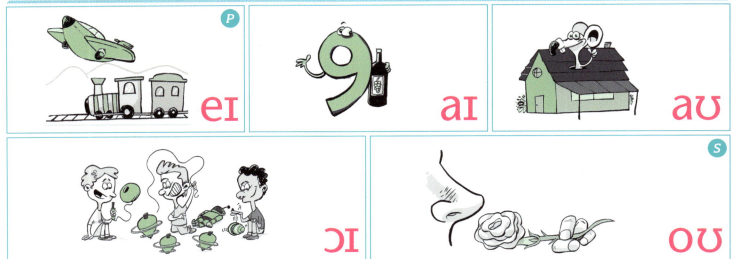

/eɪ/	plane, train, made, stay, they, A, H, J, K
/aɪ/	nine, wine, night, my, pie, buy, eyes, I, Y
/aʊ/	house, mouse, town, cloud

/ɔɪ/	toys, boys, oil, coin
/oʊ/	nose, rose, home, know, toe, road, O

Sounds and usual spellings

☐ Voiced
☐ Unvoiced

Consonants

/p/	pig, pie, open, top, apple
/b/	bike, bird, describe, able, club, rabbit
/m/	medal, monster, name, summer
/w/	web, watch, where, square, one
/f/	fish, feet, off, phone, enough
/v/	vet, van, five, have, video
/θ/	teeth, thief, thank, nothing, mouth
/ð/	mother, father, the, other
/t/	truck, taxi, hot, stop, attractive
/d/	dog, dress, made, adore, sad, middle
/n/	net, nurse, tennis, one, sign, know
/l/	lion, lips, long, all, old
/s/	snake, skate, kiss, city, science
/z/	zoo, zebra, size, jazz, lose
/ʃ/	shark, shorts, action, special, session, chef
/ʒ/	television, treasure, usual
/k/	cat, cake, back, quick
/g/	goal, girl, leg, guess, exist
/ŋ/	king, ring, single, bank
/h/	hand, hat, unhappy, who
/tʃ/	chair, cheese, kitchen, future, question
/dʒ/	jeans, jump, generous, bridge
/r/	red, rock, ride, married, write
/j/	yellow, yacht, university

Audioscript

Unit 1

◉ 1.1

T = Teacher S = Student

T Hello. Welcome to the New ID School of English. I'm Isadora, your teacher.
S Hi, Isadora.
T What's your name?
S My name is Luiza.
T Nice to meet you, Luiza.
S Nice to meet you too, Isadora.
T Please call me Dora.

◉ 1.2

T = Teacher S = Student

T I'm Isadora. What's your name?
S My name is Alejandro. Please call me Alex.

◉ 1.3

M = Mariana = Pedro

M Hello, I'm Mariana.
P Hi Mariana.
M Please, call me Mari. What's your name?
P My name is Pedro.
M Nice to meet you, Pedro
P Nice to meet you too, Mari.

◉ 1.4

One, two, three o'clock, four o'clock rock,
Five, six, seven o'clock, eight o'clock rock,
Nine, ten, eleven o'clock, twelve o'clock rock,
We're gonna rock around the clock tonight.

◉ 1.5

1 The computer – six
1 Bye bye – four
1 The banana – one
1 The coffee – five
1 The radio – nine
1 The passport – three
1 The cell phone – twelve
1 The restaurant – ten
1 The taxi – eleven
1 The hospital – seven
1 The chocolate – two
1 The guitar – eight

◉ 1.6

1 Complete the exercise.
2 Listen to the dialogue.
3 Look at the photos.
4 Read the text.
5 Repeat the words.
6 Say the sentence.

◉ 1.7

T = Teacher S = Student V = (other) Voice

T Listen to the dialogue. The sentence.
S Listen to the sentence.
T Read the sentence. The text.
S Read the text.
T Your turn. Listen to the dialogue. The sentence.
V Listen to the sentence.
T Look at the exercise. The photos.
V Look at the photos.
T Read the exercise. The dialogue.
V Read the dialogue.
T Say the numbers. The sentence.
V Say the sentence.

◉ 1.8

M = Mariana P = Pedro L = Luiza

M Hi, Pedro!
P Hello, Mari. Good to see you.
M Yes, you too. Pedro, this is my friend, Luiza.
P Nice to meet you, Luiza.
L Nice to meet you too. Please call me Lu.
P OK, and where are you from, Lu? São Paulo?
L No, I'm not. I'm from Curitiba. And you?
P I'm from Santiago.

◉ 1.9

T = Teacher S = Student V = (other) Voice

T Where are you from? Santiago.
S I'm from Santiago.
T Where are you from? Lima.
S I'm from Lima.
T Your turn. Where are you from? Santiago.
V I'm from Santiago.
T Where are you from? Quito.
V I'm from Quito.
T Where are you from? Brasilia.
V I'm from Brasilia.
T Where are you from? La Paz.
V I'm from La Paz.
T Where are you from? Montevideo.
V I'm from Montevideo.

◉ 1.11

P = Pedro D = Dora

P Dora, what's this in English? Is it a pen?
D No, it isn't. It's a pencil.
P Ah, yes, thanks. And what's this in English?
D It's an eraser. What's this?
P I don't know.
D Let's look in the dictionary.
P OK ... Ah, yes, it's a marker. Thanks.
D You're welcome.

◉ 1.13

1 A Hello, José. Where are you from?
   B I'm from Bogotá.
2 A What's this in English? Is it a pen?
   B No, it isn't a pen. It's a marker.
3 A Are you Dora, the teacher?
   B No, I'm not. I'm a student too.
4 A Are you from Brazil?
   B Yes, I am. I'm from Salvador.

◉ 1.14

T = Teacher S = Student V = (other) Voice

T What's this in English? A pen.
S It's a pen.
T What's this is English? An apple.
S It's an apple.
T Your turn. What's this in English? A chair.
V It's a chair.
T What's this is English? An eraser.
V It's an eraser.
T What's this is English? A car.
V It's a car.
T What's this is English? A computer.
V It's a computer.

◉ 1.15 Notice *th* = /ð/ or /θ/. Notice /eu/ and /iː/.

D = Doctor M = Mr. Jones

D Now, Mr. Jones, please read the letters and numbers in line one.
M A-H-J-K-8.
D OK. Line two?
M B-C-D-E-G...
D And then?
M P-T-V-Z-3.
D And line three?
M Uh ... F-L ... M-N ... uh ... S-X ... 7?
D Good and line four?
M Uh ... I-Y-5-9 ...
D Good, and the final line?
M O? No, no. Q. Q-U-W. And, uh ... R? No, no, 2? I don't know!
D That's OK. Thank you!

◉ 1.18 Notice /æ/ and /j/.

Part 1

D = Daniel A = Angela

D Hi Angela!
A Hi! ... Hmmm, Sorry ... Oh ... are you in my English class?
D At the New ID School of English? Yes, I am. My name's Daniel.
A Ah, yes, of course. I recognize you. How are you?
D I'm fine, thanks. How are you?
A I'm fine, too. Please, sit down.
D Thanks. Coffee?
A Yes. Yes, please. Thank you.

Part 2

A ... good idea. Let's meet and study together.
D OK! What's your phone number?
A It's 78190366.
D And, what's your name? Angela ...?
A Ochoa. Angela Ochoa.
D Can you spell that, please?
A O-C-H-O-A. It's a Mexican name.
D Oh, are you on WhatsApp?
A Yes, I am. Message me.
D OK. Yes. So ....see you soon!
A Yes and thanks for the coffee. Bye.

◉ 1.19

A Angela D = Daniel

1 A Are you in my English class?
   D At the New ID School. Yes, I am.
2 A How are you?
   D I'm fine, thanks.
3 D What's your phone number?
   A It's 78190366.
4 D What's your name?
   A It's Ochoa. Angela Ochoa.
5 D Can you spell that, please?
   A O-C-H-O-A. It's a Mexican name.
6 D Are you on WhatsApp?
   A Yes, I am. Message me.

◉ 1.20

1 A What's this in English?
   B It's an eraser.
2 A Are you married?
   B No, I'm single.
3 A How are you today?
   B I'm OK, thanks.
4 A What's your name?
   B Paulo.
5 A Where are you from?
   B I'm from Cordoba.
6 A What's your phone number?
   B It's 631 ... er, sorry. I don't remember.
7 A Where's my cell phone?
   B It's on the table.

Audioscript

1.21
T = Teacher S = Student V = (other) Voice
- T Double -2-7-4-3-6-9-0. Question.
- S What's your phone number?
- T It's an eraser. Question.
- S What's this in English?
- T Your turn. Double 2-7-4-3-6-9-0. Question.
- V What's your phone number?
- T Emilia. Question.
- V What's your name?
- T I'm from New York City. Question.
- V Where are you from?
- T I'm OK, thanks. Question.
- V How are you today?

1.23 Notice spelling of final /m/ and the intonation in the questions.
R = Receptionist A = Antonio
- R Next!
- A Good morning. How are you? ↘
- R Fine, thanks. What's your name, please? ↘
- A Chaves. Antonio Chaves.
- R Is that C-H-A-V-E-Z? ↗
- A No, C-H-A-V-E-S.
- R Oh, are you from Caracas? ↗
- A No, I'm from Rio de Janeiro.
- R What's your email address, please? ↘
- A It's toni.ch@gvr.com.
- R Can you repeat that, please? ↗
- A Sure! Toni—that's T-O-N-I, dot C-H, at G-V-R dot com.
- R Thanks. And what's your phone number? ↘
- A 21 8977 4053.
- R Thank you. OK, here's your student ID card.
- A Thanks. Bye.
- R Goodbye.

1.26 Notice /u/, /uː/, and final /d/.
1. A Hello! It's so good to see you!
   B Oh, hi ...
2. A Good evening. A table for two?
   B Yes, please.
3. A OK, I'm off. Good night, everyone.
   B Bye!
   C Good night!

1.27
1. How are you?
2. What's your name?
3. Bye! See you!
4. What's your email address?
5. Where are you from?
6. Hello! Good evening!
7. What's your phone number?

Unit 2

2.1
1. Brazil. Brazilian. B-R-A-Z-I-L-I-A-N.
2. China. Chinese. C-H-I-N-E-S-E.
3. The UK. British. B-R-I-T-I-S-H.
4. Mexico. Mexican. M-E-X-I-C-A-N.
5. Spain. Spanish. S-P-A-N-I-S-H.
6. The U.S. American. A-M-E-R-I-C-A-N.
7. Venezuela. Venezuelan. V-E-N-E-Z-U-E-L-A-N.

2.2
T = Teacher S = Student V = (other) Voice
- T Where are you from? Brazil.
- S I'm from Brazil. I'm Brazilian.
- T Where are you from? Argentina.
- S I'm from Argentina. I'm Argentinian.
- T Your turn. Where are you from? The U.S.
- V I'm from the U.S. I'm American.
- T Where are you from? China.
- V I'm from China. I'm Chinese.
- T Where are you from? Spain.
- V I'm from Spain. I'm Spanish.
- T Where are you from? Mexico.
- V I'm from Mexico. I'm Mexican.
- T Where are you from? The UK.
- V I'm from the UK. I'm British.

2.3
- W Are you from Australia?
- M Yes, I am.
- W Ah, you're a woman. You aren't a man.
- M Correct.
- W Are you an actor?
- M No, I'm not. OK, I'm a woman. I'm Australian. I'm not an actor. I'm a musician! Who am I?
- W I know! You're Sia. She's a fantastic musician.

2.4
g	thirteen	b	seventeen
c	fourteen	f	eighteen
h	fifteen	d	nineteen
a	sixteen	e	twenty

2.5 Notice /ɜr/ and s = /z/.
And this is apartment fourteen.
Nineteen kilos. Wow!
Only here: on channel seventeen ...
Thirteen liters.
Twenty dollars, please.
Fifteen miles per hour.
You're eighteen! Happy birthday!
Sixteen kilometers is ten miles.

2.6 Notice the pronunciation and spelling of /n/ and /ng/.
A = Anna B = Ben
- A OK, I read the headlines, and you guess the photos. OK?
- B Sure!
- A Drake Song is Big Hit.
- B The ... song? Oh, of course ... Photo 6?
- A Yeah! Uh ... Fans View Luis Fonsi's Pop Video 6 Billion Times!
- B That's photo 7!
- A Yes! Good! 100% Electric Car is Incredible Success.
- B Photo 4.
- A Yep. Multi-million Dollar Contract for Soccer Player.
- B It's photo 3, obviously.
- A Uh-huh. But who is he?
- B He's Kylian Mbappé!
- A Ah yes. I think he's from Madrid - or Barcelona?
- B No! He isn't Spanish. He's from Paris. He's French.
- A Oops! OK, next: New Movie of Famous Comic book.
- B Ah, that's easy! It's Avenger's: EndGame. Photo 1.
- A Wooh, yes! Oscar for Best Female Actor.
- B Photo 5!
- A No! She's Taylor Swift. She's a musician, not an actor.
- B Of course! It's photo 2. I love Emma Stone. The movie is fantastic.
- A Hmm, it isn't bad. And the next headline: Musician Posts Political Comments on Instagram.
- B OK, that's Taylor Swift. Photo 5.
- A Right! You're a genius!
- B Hmpf!

2.7
T = Teacher S = Student V = (other) Voice
- T Taylor Swift is a musician.
- S She's a musician.
- T A Porsche is a car.
- S It's a car.
- T Your turn. Justin Trudeau is a politician.
- V He's a politician. Despacito is a song.
- V It's a song.
- T Chris Hemsworth is an actor.
- V He's an actor.
- T Black Panther is a movie.
- V It's a movie.
- T Jennifer Lawrence is an actor.
- V She's an actor.

2.8 Notice the pronunciation of t and th.
A = Anna B = Ben
- A Look! Drake's song is a big hit.
- B Yes! I think it's a fantastic song! And the video is incredible.
- A Mm, I agree. Is he your favorite musician?
- B I think he's good, but my favorite musician is Taylor Swift. I love her!
- A And who's your favorite actor?
- B Emma Stone, 100 per cent.
- A Yeah, I think she's a good actor too!
- B OK, and what's your favorite movie?
- A Uh... that's difficult. I don't know ... Avengers: End Game, I think.
- B NO!!! I think it's a terrible movie! Three hourszzzzzzzzz!

2.9
T = Teacher S = Student V = (other) Voice
- T She's a very good politician. Terrible.
- S She's a terrible politician.
- T He.
- S He's a terrible politician.
- T Your turn. He's a bad actor. Fantastic.
- V He's a fantastic actor.
- T She.
- V She's a fantastic actor.
- T It's a horrible song. Incredible.
- V It's an incredible song.
- T Video game.
- V It's an incredible video game.

2.10
A = Anna B = Ben
- A Look at this photo.
- B What's her name? Oh, I don't remember. She's a fantastic actor.
- A Yes, and she's a model too! Is she from Peru?
- B No, she isn't! She's from Colombia. Oh, what's her name?!
- A Sorry, I don't remember. Hey, what's this?
- B It's a berimbau, a musical instrument.
- A Wow! Is it Chinese?
- B No, it isn't! It's from Brazil.
- A What's the name again?
- B A berimbau. Oh, and she's Sofía Vergara.
- A Yes, correct!

2.11

T = Teacher S = Student V = (other) Voice

T She's Brazilian. Question.
S Is she Brazilian?
T Negative.
S She isn't Brazilian.
T Your turn. It's a fantastic song. Question.
V Is it a fantastic song?
T Negative.
V It isn't a fantastic song.
T He's an incredible actor. Question.
V Is he an incredible actor?
T Negative.
V He isn't an incredible actor.

2.12

20 tablets
30 things
40 photos
50 phones
60 students
70 seconds
80 trains
90 notebooks
a hundred hamburgers

2.13 Notice unvoiced /θ/ and the connections.

A W This car's twenty-three years_old and_it's horrible!
   M How old is_it? Twenty-three? Wow, that's_ old. Very, very old!
B W How old are_you today?
   M I'm thirty-eight.
   W Happy birthday!
C W How old is_she?
   M She's forty-nine!
D M Look_at that chair. It's_an antique. How old is_it?
   M It's_about ninety-five years old, I think. And it's beautiful!

2.14

T = Teacher S = Student V = (other) Voice

T Twelve plus three.
S Fifteen.
T Twenty-four plus ten.
S Thirty-four.
T Your turn. Twenty-one plus six.
V Twenty-seven.
T Thirty three plus eleven.
V Forty-four.
T Fifty-four plus two.
V Fifty-six.

2.16

T = Teacher S = Student V = (other) Voice

T What's the opposite of hot?
S cold
T What's the opposite of beautiful?
S ugly
T Your turn. What's the opposite of cheap?
V expensive
T What's the opposite of big?
V small
T What's the opposite of old?
V new
T What's the opposite of friendly?
V unfriendly
T What's the opposite of unhappy?
V happy

2.18

T = Teacher S = Student V = (other) Voice

T They're friendly. Negative.
S They aren't friendly.
T Question.
S Are they friendly?
T Your turn. The restaurants are expensive. Question.
V Are the restaurants expensive?
T Negative.
V The restaurants aren't expensive.
T We're hot. Negative.
V We aren't hot.
T Question.
V Are we hot?
T Are the rooms big? Negative.
V The rooms aren't big.
T Positive.
V The rooms are big.

2.21 Notice voiced /ð/, /ɪ/, and /iː/.

W = Woman M = Man

W Look. It's Ryan Gosling; he's a fantastic actor.
M Where's he from?
W I think he's from the U.S.
M Are you sure?
W Hmmm. No, he's Canadian!
M What city is he from?
W He's from London. There's a London in Canada too! It's in Ontario.
M Really?! And how old is he?
W He's around 38.
M Is he married?
W Yes, he is ... I think. And his wife, or his girlfriend, is an actor, too.
M And who are the girls?
W They're Girls Generation. They're a K Pop band.
M K Pop? Where are they from?
W They're from Seoul in South Korea, of course!
M How old are they?
W I don't know. No idea!
M Are they married?
W Hmmm, no. I don't think they are.
M And who's she?
W I'm not sure, but she's, uh, familiar...
M Hmmm, wait. I know! She's a tennis player!
W You're right! She's Simona Halep.
M Halep? Where's she from?
W She's Romanian. She's from Constanta in Romania, and she's around 30. And I think she's married.

2.22

T = Teacher S = Student V = (other) Voice

T How old – she
S How old is she?
T Where from – she
S Where is she from?
T Your turn. How old – he
V How old is he?
T Where from – he
V Where is he from?
T How old - they
V How old are they?
T Where from - they
V Where are they from?

2.23 Notice the intonation in the questions.

1 M Where's he from? ↘
   W I think he's from the U.S.
2 M Are you sure? ↗
   W Hmm. No, he's Canadian!
3 M How old is he? ↘
   W He's around 38.
4 M Is he married? ↗
   W Yes, he is.
5 M How old are they? ↘
   W I don't know. No idea.
6 M She's a tennis player.
   W You're right. Number one in the world.

Review 1

R1.1

1 What's your name?
   My name's Carmen.
2 How old are you?
   I'm 23 years old. And you?
3 Are you married?
   Yes, I am. But I don't have children.
4 What's your phone number?
   My cell? It's 41-8777-4883.
5 Who's Greta Thunberg?
   She's a young activist from Sweden.
6 Is Robert Pattinson from the UK?
   Yes, he is. He's from London.
7 Where are the Backstreet Boys from?
   They're from Orlando. They're American.
8 Is this a pen or a pencil?
   It's a mechanical pencil!

R1.2

Camila Mendes is an American actor. She's from Virginia, USA, but her family are from Brazil. Camila is a very beautiful woman, and she's in a number of movies. But she's internationally famous for her part in the teen drama series *Riverdale* as Veronica Lodge. In the series, Veronica is the daughter of Hiram Lodge, the richest man in Riverdale. Camila is also a graduate of the New York University Tisch School of the Arts. She speaks English and fluent Portuguese.

R1.3

E = Eddy P = Paul S = Sandra

E Good evening, Paul. Good to see you.
P Hello, Eddy. How are you?
E I'm fine, thanks. Paul, this is my friend Alessandra.
P Nice to meet you, Alessandra.
S Nice to meet you. Please, call me Sandra.
P Where are you from, Sandra? Italy?
E Yes, you're right. She's Italian.
P Are you from Rome?
S No, I'm from Siena.
P Wow! Siena's a beautiful city!
S Yes, I agree!

R1.4 Notice dark /l/ vs. normal /l/.

R = Receptionist P = Pablo

R Next!
P Good morning.
R Hello. What's your name, please?
P I'm Pablo Castillo.
R Please spell your name.
P OK. It's C-A-S-T-I-L-L-O.
R Where are you from, Mr. Castillo?
P I'm Chilean, from Valparaíso.
R Are you married?
P Yes, I am.
R How old are you, please?

P   I'm 36.
R   OK, thank you. And what's your phone number, please?
P   312-8977-0346.
R   And your email address?
P   It's pabloc@qhy.net.
R   Thank you.

Unit 3

▶ 3.1 Notice a = /æ/ or /ɑ/.

Don't miss FANTASTIC FAMILIES! Tonight, the topics are TV series characters and their jobs. What does your favorite TV character do? Is he or she a bank cashier, a doctor, an engineer, a police officer, a university professor? Watch *Fantastic Families* this evening at eight o'clock on KYZ TV.

▶ 3.2 Notice the rhyming words.

H = Host   T = Tessa   P = Paul   G = Gloria
F = Fred   M = Maria   R = Roger   S = Sophia
J = James

H   Good evening, ladies and gentlemen, and welcome to *Fantastic Families*. I am Louie Green. And here are tonight's *Fantastic Families* – the Smiths and the Andersons. Hello, everyone, how are you tonight?
All Good evening. / Hi. / Fine. / Great.
H   Here's team A, The Smiths. What are your names, and what do you do?
T   My name's Tessa. I'm a hairdresser.
H   Hah! Brilliant! Tessa, the hairdresser!
P   I'm Paul and I'm a sales clerk. And this is my wife, Gloria.
G   Yes, that's right! And I'm a lawyer.
H   What? Gloria, the lawyer?
F   Hello, everybody. I'm Fred. I'm a server.
H   Thank you! What about *Fantastic Families* team B, The Andersons? What are your names, and what do you do?
M   I'm Maria. I'm an engineer.
H   Maria, the engineer!
M   And this is my husband ...
R   Thank you, Maria, dear. My name's Roger, and I'm a police officer.
S   I'm a bank cashier. My name's Sophia.
H   No way! Sophia, the cashier too?
J   I'm James, and I'm very happy to be here.
H   Great, James! And what do you do?
J   Oh, sorry! I'm an IT professional.
H   Thank you all! And now let's start our quiz with the first question ...

▶ 3.3 Notice the /ə/.

1
Ladies and gentlemen of the jury. This is impossible.
Answer She's a lawyer.
2
OK, that's one hundred, two hundred, three hundred and fifty-five dollars. Thank you. Have a nice day!
Answer She's a bank cashier.
3
OK, here you are. One coffee, one tea and a mineral water with lemon.
Answer He's a server.
4
A   OK, say "Ah!"
B   Aaaagh.
A   Good, good, Thanks. OK, Relax. You're OK. No problem there.

Answer She's a doctor.
5
OK, just a little more here and a little more and ... There! Beautiful!
Answer He's a hairdresser.
6
A   Uh, this shirt? It's one hundred dollars. It's beautiful, isn't it?
B   Yes, I like it. Do you have it in black?
A   Yes, we do. One moment. Here you are.
Answer She's a sales clerk.
7
OK, OK. Good morning, everybody. The topic for today is "the history of feminism".
Answer She's a university professor.
8
Yes, yes, yes! It works. This new program works! I'm rich!
Answer He's an IT professional.
9
Stop! Hey, you! Stop right there! Stop that man! Stop! Got you. Right, you are coming with me!
Answer She's a police officer.

▶ 3.4 Notice the sentence stress and reductions.

H = Host   P = Paul

H   OK, the next topic is television. Here's question one. Ready? In the famous NBC sitcom, *Friends*, do you remember *Friends*? In *Friends*, what does Ross Geller do? Is he: a) a university professor, b) an actor or c) a lawyer? Yes! Paul?
P   He's a university professor. Letter a.
H   That's absolutely correct! David Schwimmer plays Ross Geller, a university professor at New York University. Question two is about the USA Network series *Suits*. Ready? What do Jessica Pearson, Harvey Specter and Louis Litt do in *Suits*? Are they: a) IT professionals, b) doctors or c) lawyers? Yes! Sophia?
S   b! They're doctors!
H   No, they aren't! Yes, Tessa?
T   They're lawyers, obviously! Letter c!
H   Yes, they are, Tessa! The characters are lawyers. The next question is about ...

▶ 3.5

T = Teacher   S = Student   V = (other) Voice

T   Ross Geller – university professor
S   He's a university professor.
T   Jennifer Lawrence – actor
S   She's an actor.
T   Your turn. Messi and Ronaldo – soccer players
V   They're soccer players.
T   Lady Gaga - musician
V   She's a musician.
T   Scotty from Star Trek – engineer
V   He's an engineer.
T   Serena and Venus Williams – tennis players
V   They're tennis players.
T   Chief Wiggum from the Simpsons – police officer
V   He's a police officer.

▶ 3.8

W   Mother
W   Father
W   Parents
M   Wife
M   Husband
M   Couple
W   Daughter
W   Son

W   Children
M   Sister
M   Brother
M   Siblings
W   Grandmother
W   Grandfather

▶ 3.9 Notice the intonation in questions.

1   W2   Do you have children? ↗
    W3   Yes, I do. I have a son.
    W2   What's his name? ↘
    W3   His name's Daniel.
2   M   Do you live alone? ↗
    W   No, I don't. I live with my grandmother.
    M2   What's her name? ↘
    W4   Her name's Elizabeth.
3   M   Do you have a big family? ↗
    W4   No. I don't have siblings. I'm an only child.

▶ 3.10

1   W1   Do you have children?
    W2   Yes, I do. I have a son.
2   W3   Do you live alone?
    M1   No, I don't. I live with my grandmother.
3   M2   Do you have a big family?
    W4   No, I don't have siblings. I'm an only child.

▶ 3.11

T = Teacher S = Student V = (other) Voice

T   Children – question
S   Do you have children?
T   Children – negative
S   I don't have children.
T   Your turn. A daughter - question
V   Do you have a daughter?
T   A daughter - positive
V   I have a daughter.
T   A daughter - negative
V   I don't have a daughter.
T   live alone – question
V   Do you live alone?
T   live alone - positive
V   I live alone.
T   live alone – negative
V   I don't live alone.

▶ 3.12 Notice the connections.

A lot of people don't have_a job. But on today's program we talk to people who have not_one, but_two jobs. Where do they work? In_a school and_in_a restaurant? In_a hospital and_a drugstore? Or_in_a travel_agency and_ in_a bank or_an_office? Do they work downtown? Do they work_at home? Let's listen to their stories.

▶ 3.13 Notice /ɜr/ and the spelling of /w/ at the beginning of words.

W   What do you do, Hanna?
W2   I have two jobs. I'm a personal assistant and a sales clerk.
W   A personal assistant? Do you work in an office?
W2   Yes, I work in a lawyer's office. But only in the mornings.
W   And where do you work as a sales clerk?
W2   I work in a drugstore—I work there in the afternoons.
W   Which do you prefer?
W2   Oh, personal assistant. It's very interesting.
W   And what do you do, Victor?
M   I'm a web designer. And I'm a server too.
W   I see. Where do you work as a web designer?

M Well, I'm freelance, and I work at home. It's very convenient!
W And a server? Do you work in a bar?
M No, not a bar. I work in an Italian restaurant. It's a difficult job with a lot of stress.

▶ 3.14 Notice the connections.
W2 I work_in_a drugstore.
W2 Do you work_in_an_office?
M   I work_at_home.
M   I work_in_a restaurant.

▶ 3.15
1 Do you work at home?
2 Do you want to be a doctor?
3 Do you live here?
4 What do you do?
5 Where do you work?
6 Where do you want to work?

▶ 3.16
T Work – question.
S **Where** do you **work**?
T An office.
S I **work** in an **office**.
T Work – question.
S Where do you work?
T A bank.
S I work in a bank.
T Your turn. Work – question.
V Where do you work?
T Downtown.
V I work downtown.
T A restaurant.
V I work in a restaurant.
T An office.
V I work in an office.
T A hospital.
V I work in a hospital.
T At home.
V I work at home.

▶ 3.17 Notice /ð/ and the intonation at the end of the sentences and questions.
W Where are you from, Natesh?
M I'm from Islamabad, Pakistan. ↘
W And you live here in New York City, right? ↗
M Yes, that's right. I live in Queens. ↘
W Do you live alone? ↗
M No, no. I live with my parents and my brother, Arul. ↘
W What do your parents do? ↘
M My parents don't work. They're retired. ↘
W And your brother? ↗ What does your brother do? ↘
M My brother doesn't have a job. ↘ He's ... uhm ... unemployed. ↘
W Oh. OK. Are you married, Natesh? ↗
M No, I'm not, but I have a girlfriend. Her name's Reva. ↘ She's from India. ↘
W I see ... You're a limo driver, ↘ right? ↗ Where do you work? ↘
M I work in the Manhattan area, thirteen hours a day. ↘
W That's a lot, isn't it? ↗ And what do you think of your job? ↘
M Oh, I think it's very interesting! I love my limo! ↘

▶ 3.18
1 M Where's he from?
   W He's from Pakistan.
2 M Where does he live?
   W He lives in New York City.
3 M Does he live alone?
   W No, he lives with his family.
4 M Does he have a sister?
   W No, he doesn't. He has a brother.
5 M Is he married?
   W No, but he has a girlfriend.
6 M What does he do?
   W He's a limo driver.
7 M Where does he work?
   W He works in Manhattan.
8 M Does he like his job?
   W Yes, he does. Very much.

▶ 3.19
T = Teacher S = Student V = (other) Voice
T I live alone – He
S He lives alone.
T I have a brother – She
S She has a brother.
T I don't work downtown – He
S He doesn't work downtown.
T I don't live with my parents. – She
S She doesn't live with her parents.
T Your turn. I work at home. – She
V She works at home.
T I don't have a sister. – He
V He doesn't have a sister.
T I don't live with a friend – She
V She doesn't live with a friend.
T I work in a restaurant. – He
T He works in a restaurant.

▶ 3.21
W = Laura M = Charlie
W Fantastic party!
M Yes, it is ...
W Hi. My name's Laura.
M Oh, hello. I'm Charlie. Charlie Brown. Yes, really. Charlie Brown. Nice to meet you, Laura.
W Nice to meet you too, Charlie. Do you live near here?
M No. I live downtown. What about you?
W I live near here.
M Uh-huh. And what do you do, Laura?
W I don't work at the moment. I'm unemployed, but I'm a university student.
M I see. Uh, what do you study?
W I study Information Technology – IT.
M Oh, that's interesting. I'm an IT professional!

▶ 3.22 Notice the sentence stress and weak forms.
W **Fantastic party**!
M **Yes**, it **is** ...
W **Hi**. My **name**'s **Laura**.
M Oh, **hello**. I'm **Charlie**. Charlie **Brown**. **Yes**, really. Charlie **Brown**. **Nice** to **meet** you Laura.
W **Nice** to **meet** you **too**, **Charlie**. Do you **live** near here?
M **No**. I live **downtown**. **What** about **you**?
W I **live near** here.
M And **what** do **you** do, **Laura**?
W I **don't work** at the **moment**. I'm **unemployed**, but I'm a **university student**.
M I **see**. **What** do you **study**?
W I **study Information Technology**—IT.
M Oh, **that's interesting**. I'm an **IT professional**!
W **Really**? That's a coincidence! **Where** do you **work**?
M I **work** for a **bank**.

W **Cool**! Are you **married**, **Charlie**?
M **No**, I ...
W Do you **live alone**? Do you have a **girlfriend**?
M ... I **live** with my **partner**.
W Oh, I **see** ... Well, OK. Great talking to **you**. Bye!
M Bye ...

Unit 4

▶ 4.1 Notice /ɑ/ and /ə/.
W1 Vero, what's in that purse?
W2 Oh, you know. Everything! Hmm ... there's my wallet, obviously! There are a lot of coins ...
W1 Coins? Why?
W2 Oh, I collect them - you know - coins from different countries!
W1 Er, OK ...!
W2 Yeah, and there are always mints in my bag, oh, and my pills. And there's an umbrella – it rains a lot here! My lipstick, a comb, and a charger too ... Oh wait, where's my cell phone?
W1 Is this your cell phone?
W2 Yes! Thank you!

▶ 4.5
1 This is an umbrella.
2 This is a wallet.
3 This is an ID card.
4 This is a lipstick.
5 This is a comb.
6 These are pills.
7 These are mints.
8 These are keys.
9 This is a charger.
10 These are coins.

▶ 4.6
T = Teacher S = Student V = (other) Voice
T = There's a book on the table. Pens.
S = There are pens on the table.
T = There's a charger in the car. Classroom.
S = There's a charger in the classroom.
T = Your turn. Umbrella. Purse.
V = There's an umbrella in my purse.
T = Pills. Bathroom.
V = There are pills in the bathroom.
T = Car. Garage.
V = There's a car in the garage.
T = Sweater. Closet.
V = There's a sweater in the closet.

▶ 4.7 Notice final /k/, /t/, and /d/.
W Look!
M Where?
W There. On the red seat. What's that?
M Uh ... it's a bag.
W Oh no!
M Yes. Open it!
W No! You open it.
M Why?
W To find a name – an ID card?
M OK. Uh, let's see. Hmm ... What's this?

▶ 4.8 Notice the spelling of the /ɪ/ and /iː/ sounds.
M OK. Uh, let's see. Hmm ... What's this?
W Let me see. Oh, they're glasses.
M Obviously! What else ... keys ... and a cell phone. And what are these? Are they pills?
W No, they're candies.
M Huh, OK. Look, what are those?
W Let me see. They're headphones.

Audioscript

M Ah, of course. Bluetooth headphones. Cool.
W Is there a wallet in the bag?
M No, no wallet, ... but look here ... what's this?
W Yeah! It's an ID card!
M Hm-mm and it has a name on it. And a photo. Linda Sánchez. Great!

▶ 4.9

1 W What's that?
   M It's a bag.
2 M What's this?
   W It's an ID card.
3 W What are these?
   M They're candies.
4 M What are those?
   W They're headphones.

▶ 4.10

1 This is my new phone.
2 These are my books.
3 What's this?
4 What are those?
5 Hey! That's my car.
6 These are my children.

▶ 4.11

T = Teacher S = Student V = (other) Voice
T This. Question.
S What's this?
T A wallet.
S It's a wallet.
T Your turn. These. Question.
V What are these?
T Headphones.
V They're headphones.
T Those. Question.
V What are those?
T Keys.
V They're keys.
T That. Question.
V What's that?
T An ID card.
V It's an ID card.

▶ 4.12

1 orange socks
2 pink shorts
3 a gray clock
4 a black bike
5 white dogs
6 a blue notebook
7 green glasses
8 yellow taxis
9 brown pills
10 a red lipstick

▶ 4.15 Notice /f/, /v/, and th.

1 W Excuse me, what time is it, please?
   M It's seven forty-five.
2 M What time is your English class?
   W It's at four thirty every day.
3 W What time does the movie start?
   M It starts at eight ten.
4 M What time is lunch?
   W It's at two o'clock.
5 W What time is your flight?
   M It's at eleven fifty.
6 M What time is it in Tokyo right now?
   W Wow! It's very early. It's five fifteen in the morning.

▶ 4.16

What time is it?
1 It's six twenty-five.
2 It's ten forty.
3 It's twelve oh-five.
4 It's three twenty.
5 It's one fifty-five.
6 It's nine thirty-five.

▶ 4.19 Notice /b/ and /p/.

W Hey, is that a new tablet?
M Yes, it is. Do you like it?
W Wow! It's beautiful!
M It has 5G Internet access.
W Cool. How many apps does it have?
M Oh, I don't know. A lot! But there's an app for emails, one for Facebook, another one for Twitter ...
W Oh, no ...! So you're online all the time!
M Is that a problem?
W Yes! It's probably impossible to talk to you now!

▶ 4.20 Notice the sentence stress and reductions.

A = Lost property Assistant   T = Tourist
T Excuse me. Is this Lost and Found?
A Yes, it is. Can I help you?
T Ah, good. Yes. I lost my wallet.
A OK. Do you know where?
T Here. In the airport.
A When? Today?
T Yes. Today.
A Yesterday?
T No! Today!
A Sorry! OK, and what color is the wallet?
T It's green.
A And is it big or small?
T It's very big. My passport and credit cards are in it. Oh, and around 500 dollars too. All the money for my vacation!
A Oh no. I'm sorry. Now, let's see what there is in the system.

Review 2

▶ R2.1

These are my children, Jim and Keira. They're always happy! And this is my husband, Greg. He wants to be a chef! That's Angela, his ex-wife, with the burgers, and those are their children from Greg's first marriage. They visit us a lot. Oh, and that's their enormous dog!

▶ R2.2 Notice final /n/ and spellings of /m/.

And here is Helen Rivers with today's edition of *Common People, Uncommon Lives*. Today, Helen interviews Rosa Costa, not a celebrity, but another common person with an uncommon life. Ms. Costa is a Brazilian diplomat living in Bogotá, Colombia, for the past three years. Over to you, Helen!

▶ R2.3 Notice /h/ and /r/.

H = Helen   R = Rosa
H Thank you, Johnny. I'm Helen Rivers and I'm here in Bogotá with Rosa Costa. Hello, Rosa.
R Hello, Helen. Nice to talk to you.
H So you're a Brazilian diplomat, right?
R That's right.
H Where are you from in Brazil?
R I'm from Rio de Janeiro.
H How old are you, Antonio?
R I'm 43.
H Are you married?
R Yes, I am. My husband's name's Antonio.
H Is Antonio from Rio too?
R No, he's from Montevideo, Uruguay.
H What does he do? Is he a diplomat too?
R No, Antonio's an English teacher.
H Really? Where does he work?
R In a big school downtown.
H Do you have children?
R Yes, we have a son. His name's Marcel.
H How old is he?
R He's four years old.
H Where do you live here in Bogotá?
R We live in Chicó, a very nice part of the city.
H What do you think of Bogotá and Colombia?
R Oh, I think Colombia is a beautiful country, and Bogotá is an excellent city to live in.
H What's your favorite thing about Colombia?
R My favorite thing? Hmmm. I think it's the fruit!
H The fruit?!
R Yes. And my favorite Colombian fruit is lulo. It's delicious!

Unit 5

▶ 5.4

1 Do you like apple juice?
2 I like fruit, but I don't like vegetables.
3 I like bread and cheese for breakfast.

▶ 5.5 Notice the spelling of /iː/ and /ɛ/ sounds.

M Breakfast is my favorite meal. I eat a lot. Usually bread, cheese, eggs and orange juice. What about you?
W I just drink tea with milk.
M Really? No food? No protein?
W Well, I eat a lot of beans at lunch.
M No meat?
W No, meat is not good for you.
M Oh.
W What?
M Nothing.
W What?
M Well ...
W What?
M Soft drinks are very bad for you too, but you drink a lot of soft drinks, don't you?
W Hmmm. Well, I guess nobody is perfect.

▶ 5.7 Notice the silent letters and /dʒ/ sound.

W Do you eat a lot of meat, Jack?
M No, I don't.
W What about vegetables?
M I eat a lot of vegetables, and fruit too.
W Do you drink a lot of coffee?
M No, but I drink a lot of fruit juice.
W Do you eat bread?
M Yes. Usually at breakfast, with cheese. I love it!

▶ 5.9 Notice the sentence stress and reductions.

R = Reporter
R Richard, what kind of food do you and your friends like?
M1 Well, my partner and I like variety. We think food from different countries is great!

173

R What **kind**? Do you like **Peruvian food**, for example?
M1 Yes, very much! And we love **Italian food**, **Chinese**, **Japanese** ... In fact, we like **all food**!
R Great, thanks. And **what** about **you**, Julia?
W1 I don't like **vegetables**, but I eat them because they're good for me. My **daughter loves** them!
R What **kind** of **vegetables** does she **like**? Does she like **tomatoes**?
W1 Yes, she does. **Tomatoes**, **potatoes**, **carrots**, **lettuce** ... She's only eight, but I think she's a vegetarian.
R Michael, **what** kind of **food** do you like?
M2 There's a **problem** in our **house**. My **wife** loves **meat**, but I **hate** it!
R **Does** she like all **kinds** of **meat**?
M2 She likes **beef** and **chicken** ... Hmm ... And **fish** ... Yuck! But it's OK because we're **really in love**!
R **Good luck**! Now Jane, what about **you**? What kind of **food** do you like?
W2 I'm **terrible**, I really like **fast food**. I think it's **delicious**!
R Really? What's your **favorite**?
W2 All of it! I like **pizza**, **hot dogs** ... And **French fries**! Oh, **French fries**!
R Ha ha! Eat some **vegetables** too! And Tony, **what** about **you** and **your family**?
M3 We eat a lot of **fruit** at home. Except for my **father** — he really **hates fruit**!
R And what kind of **fruit** do you like?
M3 Me? Uh ... I don't know ... Uh ... **Grapes**, **bananas**, **oranges** ... It's just fruit.

○ **5.10**

T = Teacher S = Student V = (other) Voice
T I don't like Italian food. — He
S He doesn't like Italian food.
T She loves fast food. — We
S We love fast food.
T We really like bananas — She
S She really likes bananas.
T Your turn. They hate fish. — He
V He hates fish.
T She likes vegetables. — You
V You like vegetables.
T I really hate hot dogs. — He
V He really hates hot dogs.

○ **5.11** Notice *o* and *u* = /ʌ/ and *ue* = /uː/.

Monday, no fun day.
Tuesday, blues day.
Wednesday, a little gray.
Thursday, good day.
Friday, hurray!
Saturday, we play!
Sunday, we relax all day!

○ **5.12**

On Monday I watch TV.
On Tuesday I play soccer.
On Wednesday I cook.
On Thursday I go to the movies.
On Friday I take a dance class.
On Saturday I go to the mall.
On Sunday I go to church.

○ **5.15**

T = Teacher S = Student V = (other) Voice
T We play soccer on Friday. Always.
S We always play soccer on Friday.
T Never.
S We never play soccer on Friday.
T Your turn. She stays home on Sunday. Usually.
V She usually stays home on Sunday.
T We to the mall on Thursday. Sometimes.
V We sometimes go to the mall on Thursday.
T He takes a class on the weekend. Never.
V He never takes a class on the weekend.
T I cook dinner for my family. Always.
V I always cook dinner for my family.

○ **5.16** Notice *s* = /s/ or /z/ and the intonation in the questions.

W Look! A collection of Ryan Gosling's movies are on boxset this weekend.
M Really? ↗ That's great! I like him a lot. He's a great actor. I think his movies are excellent.
W Hmmm. I don't like them much.
M What?! They're fantastic! And what's on TV? ↘
W Do you like Stephen Colbert's show? ↗
M Yes, I do. I really like it. Why? ↘
W Well, Michelle Obama is on his show tonight.
M Michelle Obama? ↗ Again? ↗ I think Colbert loves her!
W Well, the show is about Michelle's new book.
M Her autobiography? ↗ Oh, maybe I can read it.

○ **5.17**

T = Teacher S = Student V = (other) Voice
T The movies of Ryan Gosling.
S Ryan Gosling's movies.
T Possessive adjective.
S His movies.
T Your turn. The racket of Naomi Osaka.
V Naomi Osaka's racket.
T Possessive adjective.
V Her racket.
T The trophy of the soccer team.
V The soccer team's trophy.
T Possessive adjective.
V Their trophy.

○ **5.18**

W What do you think of Lady Gaga?
M I love her.
W Do you like the Twilight Saga books?
M I like them.
W What do you think of LeBron James.
M I don't like him.
W Do you like Mexican food?
M I love it.

○ **5.19**

T = Teacher S = Student V = (other) Voice
T I like Adele.
S I like her.
T I never watch American movies.
S I never watch them.
T I don't like Justin Bieber.
S I don't like him.
T Your turn. I sometimes eat Japanese food.
V I sometimes eat it.
T What do you think of Robert Pattinson?
V What do you think of him?

T I really hate tomatoes.
V I really hate them.
T I love hot dogs.
V I love them.

○ **5.21**

jump
jeans
Jane
generous
juices
/dʒ/
bird
bike
cheeseburgers
breakfast
best
/b/
vet
van
Viv
vanilla
very
/v/
red
rock
Rick
really
recommend
/r/
Yuri
yellow
yacht
mayonnaise
yoghurt
/j/

○ **5.22**

S = Server C = Customer
1
S Can I help you?
C1 A cheeseburger, please.
S Fries?
C1 No, thanks.
S Anything to drink?
C1 Yes, a cola.
S Large, medium or small?
C1 Large.
S With ice?
C1 No, thanks.
S Anything else?
C1 No, thanks.
S For here or to go?
C1 For here.
S That's $5.99
C1 There you are. Thanks.
2
S Can I help you?
C2 A hot dog and French fries, please.
S Anything to drink?
C2 Yes. A small coffee.
S Cream and sugar?
C2 Just sugar, please.
S Anything else?
C2 No, thanks.
S For here or to go?
C2 To go.

Audioscript

◐ 5.23 Notice the **silent letters** and the spelling of /ɛ/ and /iː/.

S = server   C = customer

1 S Can I help you?
   C1 A cheeseburger, please.
   S Fries?
   C1 No, thanks.
   S Anything to drink?
   C1 Yes, a cola.
   S Large, medium or small?
   C1 Large.
   S With ice?
   C1 No, thanks.
   S Anything else?
   C1 No, thanks.
   S For here or to go?
   C1 For here.
   S That's $5.99.
   C1 There you are. Thanks.
2 S Can I help you?
   C2 A hot dog and French fries, please.
   S Anything to drink?
   C2 Yes. A small coffee.
   S Cream and sugar?
   C2 Just sugar, please.
   S Anything else?
   C2 No, thanks.
   S For here or to go?
   C2 To go.

◐ 5.24

A Can I help you?
B A hamburger and French fries, please.
A Anything to drink?
B A cola.
A Large, medium, or small?
B Small.
A With ice?
B Yes, please.
A Anything else?
B No, thanks.
A For here or to go?
B To go.
A That's $12.95.
B There you are. Thanks a lot.

Songs

1.1

🎵 **Song line:** *Welcome to the new age, Whoa, oh, oh, oh, oh, whoa, oh, oh, oh, I'm radioactive, radioactive.*
Song: *Radioactive*, released in 2012
Artist: Radioactive
Lesson link: welcome / verb *be*
Notes: This song was released as the band's second single and it opens the band's debut album, *Night Visions*. The song is about realizing that the world is changing and embracing change.

Before the class, write the song line from the top of p. 7 on the board with the first and the last words missing:

_____ to the new age, Whoa, oh, oh, oh, oh, whoa, oh, oh, oh, I'm radioactive, _____.

As sts arrive in class, ask them not to open their books, and start the class by asking them to look at the board. As they do, ask them: *What is this?* Make sure they realize that this is the song line from this lesson, but with the first and last words missing. If necessary, hum the line for sts to remember the song or search the web before class for an instrumental audio or video clip of the song line. Then, ask sts to work in pairs to complete the song line. Play the song line for them and have them listen and check. Finally, have volunteers share their answers and sing the song line if they want to.

1.2

🎵 **Song line:** *Listen to the Mariachi play at midnight. Are you with me, are you with me?*
Song: *Are you with me?*, released in 2014
Artist: Lost Frequencies (Belgian)
Lesson link: verb *be*
Notes: This song was first recorded by country artist Easton Corbin, in 2012. Only two years later, the Belgian DJ released this deep house remix version, which reached the top 10 in several European countries.

Before the class, write the song line from the top of p. 9 on the board, but with the words in the wrong order as follows:

the Mariachi / Listen to / play at midnight. / with me / Are you, with me / are you?

As sts arrive in class, ask them not to open their books, and start the class by asking them to look at the board. As they do, ask them: *What is this?* Explain that this is the song line from the lesson, but that the words are in the wrong order. They have to work in pairs to try to put the words in order to form the song line. When they're ready, have volunteers come to the board to write it in the correct order. Encourage the other sts to correct anything that they believe is incorrect. Finally, ask: *Do you know this song line? Can you sing it?*, and encourage sts to sing the song line if they want to.

1.3

🎵 **Song line:** *Oh, oh, I'm an alien, I'm a legal alien, I'm an Englishman in New York.*
Song: *Englishman in New York*, released in 1987
Artist: Sting (British)
Lesson link: indefinite articles
Notes: Sting wrote this song about famous gay author Quentin Cris and his experiences when he moved from London to NYC in 1986. The Black Eyed Peas sampled this song on their song *Union*, in 2005.

Before the class, write the song line from the top of p. 11 on the board, but with three mistakes with indefinite articles for sts to identify. Do not highlight the mistakes as in the suggestion below:

Oh, oh, I'm a alien, I'm an legal alien, I'm a Englishman in New York.

As sts arrive in class, ask them not to open their books, and start the class by asking them to sit in pairs and look at the board. Ask: *Do you know this song? Can you sing this line?* Encourage sts to answer and sing the song line if they want to. Next, explain that the song line on the board has three mistakes, and they have to work in pairs to find and correct them. When the pairs are ready, have volunteers come to the board to correct the mistakes. Encourage the whole class to discuss and say whether they agree or not with the corrections being made. Finally, sts open their books to check their corrected version against the actual song line. Tell sts that in this lesson they will learn about the use of indefinite articles.

1.4

🎵 **Song line:** *A B C, it's easy as 1 2 3, as simple as do re mi, A B C, 1 2 3, baby you and me girl.*
Song: *ABC*, released in 1970
Artist: The Jackson 5 (American)
Lesson link: the alphabet
Notes: Michael Jackson was just 11 years old when The Jackson 5 released this song. In this schoolyard theme, Michael sings about giving private lessons to a young lady. The song was launched in February, and in April it went to number one in the charts, beating *Let It Be*, by The Beatles.

At any time during the lesson, have sts read the song line at the top of p. 13 and ask: *Can you recognize this song? Can you sing this line?* Encourage sts to answer and sing the line if they want to. Next, ask: *Can you find the link of the song with the lesson?* Have sts sit in pairs, and tell them to scan the pages of the lesson in order to find out the link between the song and the lesson. Allow sts a few minutes to do this and, when they are ready, have volunteers share their answers. At this stage they should be able to identify that the link of the song line with the lesson is the alphabet. Finally, you can encourage sts to share any other songs that they can think of which have spelling in them.

1.5

🎵 **Song line:** *Baby, we don't stand a chance, it's sad but it's true, I'm way too good at goodbyes.*
Song: *Too Good at Goodbyes*, released in 2017
Artist: Sam Smith (British)
Lesson link: goodbye
Notes: In this song, Sam Smith states that he has been hurt in the past, and that now he's got used to saying goodbye. So, when the next goodbye moment arrives, he will be better prepared for it.

At any time during the lesson, have sts look at the song line at the top of p. 15 and ask: *Do you know this song? Can you sing this line?* Encourage sts to answer and sing the line if they want to. Then, ask: *What is the link of this song line with the lesson?* Have sts work in pairs to scan the pages of the lesson and find the link. Ask volunteers to share their answers with the whole class. Finally, ask what other songs about saying goodbye they can think of. Encourage sts to work in pairs to come up with as many songs as they can that mention the word goodbye. Explain that they should be able to sing or hum the part of the song in which the word appears. Allow sts a few minutes to do this, then have them count the number of songs they've thought of, and ask the pair with the most songs to sing or hum their songs. If all songs are correct, they win. You can check a few songs with the word goodbye on this link: https://www.lyrics.com/lyrics/goodbye.

Songs

Writing 1

♪ **Song line:** *Beautiful people. Drop top, designer clothes. Front row at fashion shows. "What d'you do?" And "Who d'you know?" Inside the world of beautiful people.*
Song: *Beautiful People*, released in 2019
Artist: Ed Sheeran (British) ft. Khalid
Lesson link: *beautiful* (opinion words)
Notes: In this song, both Sheeran and Khalid, sing about not feeling comfortable in the *beautiful people's* world of glamour and excess. In the late 60's, people used the phrase *beautiful people* to make fun of the famous, powerful, and rich.

Before the class, write the song line from the top of p. 16 on the board with all the vowels missing:

B_ _ _t_f_l p_ _pl_. Dr_p t_p, d_s_gn_r cl_th_s. Fr_nt r_w _t f_sh_ _n sh_ws.

As sts arrive in class, ask them not to open their books, and start the class by asking them to sit in pairs and look at the board. Tell them that this is the song line from the lesson and ask: *What's missing in this song line?* Encourage sts to answer. Help them notice that all the vowels are missing in the song line. Then, have them work in pairs to complete it. When all pairs are ready, ask: *Can you identify this song? Can you sing this line?* Encourage sts to answer and sing the song line if they want to. Finally, allow them to open their books on p. 16 to check the actual song line.

2.1

♪ **Song line:** *And I got my hands up, They're playing my song, I know I'm gonna be ok, Yeah, it's a party in the USA.*
Song: *Party in the U.S.A.*, released in 2009
Artist: Miley Cyrus (American)
Lesson link: countries
Notes: This was the lead single from Cyrus' first EP, *Time of Our Lives*. This EP was only sold at Wal-Mart stores together with her clothing line, Max Azria. Her provocative dance moves when performing this song at the 2009 Teen Choice Awards caused controversy because of her age and the age of her young fans.

At any time during the lesson, have sts read the song line at the top of p. 19, and ask: *Do you know this song? Can you sing this line?* Encourage them to answer and sing the song line if they want to. Next, ask: *Can you identify the link of the song line with the lesson?* Have sts work in pairs and tell them to scan the whole lesson and try to identify the link of the song line with the lesson. Allow sts some time to do this, and then check that they realize the link is *countries* (in this case, the U.S.). Then, ask the pairs to come up with as many songs that mention countries as possible. Explain that they can search the web to find the songs, but they must be able to sing or hum the part where the country is mentioned if they want to score a point. Allow sts a few minutes to do this and, when they're ready, have pairs present their songs to the class. The pair with the most songs mentioning countries is the winner.

2.2

♪ **Song line:** *Bad things, It's a lot of bad things, That they wishin' and wishin', They wishin' on me, Bad things.*
Song: *God's Plan*, released in 2018
Artist: Drake (Canadian)
Lesson link: adjective order
Notes: *God's Plan* is an orchestral melodic track that has a bouncy flow. This song was one of two in Drake's EP *Scary Hours*, and it is considered more commercial than the other song in the EP, *Diplomatic Immunity*.

Before the class, write the song line from p. 21 with mistakes in the adjective order for sts to spot:

Things bad, It's a lot of things bad, That they wishin' and wishin', They wishin' on me, things bad.

As sts arrive in class, ask them not to open their books. Start the class by having sts work in pairs to try and identify the mistakes in the song line on the board. Explain that there are three mistakes related to the topic of the lesson, and that they have to race the other pairs to correct them. When the first pair is ready, they say "Stop!", and then come to the board to correct the mistakes in the song line. Encourage the other pairs to say if they agree with the proposed corrections. Note that, since sts haven't yet seen adjective order (they will in this lesson), it might be difficult for them to spot the mistakes. If nobody knows the song, and no sts find the mistakes, allow them to open their books and read the song line at the top of p. 21 to check. Finally, tell them that in this lesson they will learn more about adjective order.

♪ 2.3

Song line: *You are the dancing queen, Young and sweet, only seventeen.*
Song: *Dancing Queen*, released in 1976
Artist: ABBA (Swedish)
Lesson link: numbers
Notes: According to ABBA's website, this song was originally created as a dance song. Its working title was *Boogaloo*. The band manager, Stig Anderson, came up with the final title, *Dancing Queen*.

Before the class, search for a video or audio clip of the song line at the top of p. 23. As sts arrive in class, ask them not to open their books. Start the class by explaining that you will play a clip of the song line from this lesson, and they have to write down what they hear. Play the clip, and allow sts to write it down. Play it two or three times, as necessary. When all sts are ready, have a volunteer come to the board to write down their version of it. Encourage the other sts to correct them and change anything that they believe is not correct. When they are all happy with the version on the board, allow them to open their books on p. 23 to check. Finally, ask: *What was the most difficult thing for you to understand?*, and encourage sts to share their opinions.

♪ 2.4

Song line: *Are we human, or are we dancer? My sign is vital, my hands are cold, And I'm on my knees looking for the answer.*
Song: *Human*, released in 2008
Artist: The Killers (American)
Lesson link: verb *be*
Notes: This song talks about moral decay in society. When asked about the message of the song, The Killers' frontman replied that "it's a mild social statement, and I'm leaving it at that." He ended by saying that he didn't want to be a preacher.

At any time during the lesson, have sts look at the song line at the top of p. 25. Ask: *Do you know this song? Can you sing this line?* Encourage sts to sing the song line if they want to. Next, have sts work in pairs to find the correct number of verb *be* occurrences in the song line (there are five), and say how many are in the affirmative, negative, and interrogative (questions). Allow sts a few minutes to do this, and tell pairs to raise their hands when they are ready so you can take note of the order. When all pairs are ready, have the first pair say their answers and check. If they're right, they are the winners. If not, move on to the second finishing pair until you have a winner with the correct answers.

Songs

♪ 2.5

Song line: *We're up all night to the sun, We're up all night to get some, We're up all night for good fun, We're up all night to get lucky.*
Song: *Get Lucky*, released in 2013
Artist: Daft Punk (French) feat. Pharrell Williams, Nile Rogers
Lesson link: Review verb *be*
Notes: This song broke Spotify's streaming record on the day it was released. It achieved the highest number of streams in both the UK and the U.S. This was also Daft Punk's first UK number one single. Their previous best was *One More Time*, released in 2000, which peaked at number two.

As sts arrive in class, ask them not to open their books. Organize them into four groups and explain that they will play *Telephone* with the song line of the lesson divided into four equalsized parts:

We're up all night to the sun / We're up all night to get some / We're up all night for good fun / We're up all night to get lucky.

Explain that each group will be working with one quarter of the song line, and that by the end of the activity, they will have to put the four parts together to guess what the actual song line is. Line the groups up facing the board and give the first student in the line a marker to write on the board what they hear when the last student in their group whispers their part to them. Start reading the groups' corresponding song line parts to the last student in each line, so that they can pass the message ahead, trying to keep the original message as much as possible. Since this is a Starter level, say the chunks in a clear and paced manner for sts to better understand. When the sentence gets to the first student in each line, they have to write what they heard on the board. Then, have sts read the whole line together and ask: *Can you recognize the original song line?* Finally, have sts open their books on p. 27 to check the actual song line.

♪ Writing 2

Song line: *Maybe I'm crazy, Maybe you're crazy, Maybe we're crazy, Probably ooh hmm.*
Song: *Crazy*, released in 2006
Artist: Gnarls Barkley (American)
Lesson link: *crazy* (adjectives)
Notes: This song is about losing your mind and diving into insanity. Cee-Lo Green explains that when he wrote this song he was going through a divorce, and had other personal issues. But, according to him, it was a good opportunity to be expressive.

Before the class, write the song line from the top of p. 28 on the board, with gaps where the verb *be* appears:

Maybe _____ crazy, Maybe _____ crazy, Maybe _____ crazy, Probably ooh hmm.

As sts arrive in class, ask them not to open their books. Start the class by having them look at the song line you wrote on the board. Explain that this is the song line from the lesson, but there are three gaps to complete. Sts work in pairs. Allow sts a few minutes to do this and, when they're ready, have volunteers come to the front of the class to complete the gaps. As they do this, encourage the other sts to correct anything they believe is incorrect. Finally, allow them to open their books on p. 28 to check.

♪ Review 1

Song line: *I am a giant. Stand up on my shoulders, tell me what you see. I am a giant. (We'll be breaking boulders underneath our feet.).*
Song: *Giant*, released in 2019
Artist: Calvin Harris (Scottish) feat. Rag 'n' Bone Man
Lesson link: verb *be*
Notes: The song is about feeling like a giant, with more confidence and power, when one has the support of a friend / lover. But curiously, both Calvin Harris and Rag 'n' Bone Man are about 1.95m tall, and as such are close to being "giants" themselves.

Before the class, write the song line from the top of p. 31 on the board, but with all the vowels missing:

_ _m _ g__nt. St_nd _p _n my sh__ld_rs, t_ll m_ wh_t y__ s__. _ _m _ g__nt.

As sts arrive in class, ask them not to open their books. Start the class by having them look at the board and ask: *What's missing in this song line?* Encourage sts to answer. Expect them to notice that all the vowels are missing in the song line. Then, have them work in pairs to complete it. Allow sts a few minutes to do this and, when all pairs are ready, ask: *Can you identify this song? Can you sing this line?* Encourage sts to answer and sing the song line if they want to. Finally, allow them to open books on p. 31 to check the actual song line.

♪ 3.1

Song line: *I want to be the one to walk in the sun, Oh girls they want to have fun, Oh girls just want to have fun.*
Song: *Girls Just Want to Have Fun*, released in 1983
Artist: Cindy Lauper (American)
Lesson link: *want to*
Notes: This was the song that made Cindy Lauper famous. It gained recognition as a feminist anthem in the 80's, and was a huge part of that decade's culture. In 1985, Sarah Jessica Parker, starred in a movie with the same name and with this song in its soundtrack.

Before the class, search for a video or audio clip of the song line at the top of p. 33. As sts arrive, ask them not to open their books. Start the class by explaining that they will listen to an audio or video clip of this lesson's song line, and they have to write down what they hear. Play the clip two or three times as necessary and, when they are ready, have them compare in pairs and discuss what they wrote down. Explain to sts that they should reach an agreement about the correct version. Next, have a volunteer pair come to the board to write down their song line. Encourage the other pairs to correct anything they think should be corrected. Finally, have sts open their books to check and ask: *What was the most difficult part to understand?* Encourage sts to share their opinions with the whole class.

♪ 3.2

Song line: *Whether you're a brother or whether you're a mother, You're stayin' alive, stayin' alive.*
Song: *Stayin' Alive*, released in 1977.
Artist: Bee Gees (Australian)
Lesson link: family
Notes: This song features the opening credits of the movie *Saturday Night Fever*, from 1977, while Travolta walks on the streets of New York City. This movie represented the disco era and, as such, *Stayin' Alive* became directly associated with disco.

Before the class, write the song line from the top of p. 35 on the board, with five mistakes in it for sts to spot:

Songs

Whether I'm a father or whether she's a daughter, We're stayin' alive, stayin' alive.

As sts arrive in class, ask them not to open their books. Start the class by having them work in pairs to try and identify the mistakes in the song line on the board. Explain that the song line you wrote on the board has five mistakes, two of which are directly related to the topic of the lesson (family), and three related to what they have learned in previous lessons (verb *be*). They have to race the other pairs to correct them. When the first pair is ready, say *Stop!* and come to the board to correct the mistakes in the song line. As they do so, encourage the other pairs to say if they agree or not with the proposed corrections. Note that, since sts haven't yet seen family vocabulary (they will in this lesson) it might be difficult for them to spot the mistakes if they don't know the song well. If nobody knows the song and sts cannot find the mistakes, allow them to open the books and read the song line at the top of p. 35 to check.

3.3

Song line: *Do you really want to hurt me? Do you really want to make me cry?*
Song: *Do you really want to hurt me?*, released in 1982
Artist: Culture Club (British)
Lesson link: simple present questions
Notes: Singer Boy George came up with the lyrics of this song. He later admitted that it was about his relationship with the drummer Jon Moss. He explained that they had an affair for about six years, which was kept hidden, and he often felt hurt and emotional because of this.

At any time during the lesson, have sts read the song line at the top of p. 37, and ask: *Can you recognize this song? Can you sing this part?* Encourage sts to answer and sing the song line if they want to. Next, ask: *Can you identify the link of the song line with the lesson?* Encourage sts to work in pairs to scan the pages of the lesson and find the link. Allow them a few minutes to do this, and, when they're ready, have them share their answers. They should be able to identify that the questions *Do you really want to hurt me?* and *Do you really want to make me cry?* connect with the lesson because these are simple present questions. Then, have sts work in pairs to make a list of other famous song lines that use questions in the simple present. When they're ready, have them share their lists with the whole class. The pair with the most song lines using simple present questions is the winner. Remind them that they should be able to sing or hum the part with the questions in the songs from their lists.

3.4

Song line: *Oh, whatever it takes, 'Cause I love the adrenaline in my veins, I do whatever it takes, 'Cause I love how it feels when I break the chains."*
Song: *Whatever It Takes*, released in 2017
Artist: Imagine Dragons (American)
Lesson link: simple present
Notes: In this song, Dan Reynolds is striving to be the best he can be, despite the obstacles. The song is about recovering from past pain. It is about overcoming the self-confidence issues he has had since he was young.

Before the class, write the song line from the top of p. 39 on slips of paper (one per pair or trio), and cut each of the slips into five pieces or more for sts to assemble (the higher the level of the sts, the more pieces you should cut the song line into). As sts arrive in class, organize them into pairs or trios, and ask them not to open their books. Start the class by giving each pair or trio the song line of this lesson cut into pieces. Tell them that they have to work together to put the pieces in order, so as to form the song line of the lesson. Tell the pairs or trios that, when they are ready, they should raise their hands and wait for the others to finish. When all sts are ready, have them read their version of the song, in order to compare their version with those of the other pairs or trios. Finally, allow sts to open their books at p. 39 to check the actual song line and compare it with their versions.

3.5

Song line: *We are young we run free, Stay up late, we don't sleep, got our friends, got the night we'll be all right.*
Song: *We'll Be Alright*, released in 2010
Artist: Travie McCoy (American)
Lesson link: simple present
Notes: This is a fun song about not caring or worrying about what other people think. It's about ignoring your insecurities. This song samples UK rock band Supergrass' *Alright*, which was a number two hit in the UK in 1995.

As sts arrive in class, ask them not to open their books. Organize them into four groups and explain that they will play *Telephone* with the song line of the lesson divided into four similar-sized parts:

We are young we run free / Stay up late, we don't sleep / got our friends, got the night / we'll be all right.

Explain that each group will be working with one quarter of the song line, and by the end of the activity they will have to put the four parts together to guess what the actual song line is. Line the groups up facing the board and give the first student in the line a marker for them to write what they hear on the board when the last student in their group whispers their part to them. Start reading the groups' corresponding song line parts to the last student in each line, so that they can pass the message ahead, trying to keep the original message as much as possible. Since this is a Starter level, say the chunks in a clear and paced manner for sts to better understand. When the sentence reaches the first student in each line, they have to write what they heard on the board. Then, have sts put the four parts of the song line together and ask: *Does this look similar to the original song line?* Finally, have sts open their books on p. 41 to check the actual song line on the page.

Writing 3

Song line: *You don't know you're beautiful. Oh, oh. That's what makes you beautiful.*
Song: *What Makes You Beautiful*, released in 2011
Artist: One Direction (British)
Lesson link: what makes people beautiful – we're all different, but all beautiful
Notes: This song became the fastest selling single in 2011 when it was launched. It sold 153 thousand copies just a week after it had been released. It was voted the Best British Single at the 2012 BRITS Awards.

Before the class, write the song line from p. 42 on the board with a few pronunciation-related mistakes in it for sts to try and identify. The idea is that the pronunciation of the substituted words (in bold) is similar to that of the original words. Here are some possible mistakes you could include:

*You don't **no your** beautiful. Oh, oh. **Dad's** what makes you beautiful.*

As sts arrive in class, ask them not to open their books. Start the class by having them look at the song line on the board and ask: *Do you know this song? Can you sing this part?* Encourage sts to answer and sing the song line if they want to. Next, tell them that they have to work in pairs to identify the mistakes in the song line on the board. Explain to sts that the song line on the board has three pronunciation-related mistakes (depending on how many mistakes you choose to include) and that they have to race the other pairs to spot all of them. When the first pair is ready, they say *Stop!* and come to the board to correct the mistakes in

Songs

the song line. As they do this, encourage the other pairs to discuss and suggest any other corrections in case they don't agree with any of the proposed corrections. Finally, allow sts to open their books on p. 42 to check.

4.1

🎵 **Song line:** *This the part when I say I don't want it, I'm stronger than I've been before, This is the part when I break free.*
Song: *Break Free*, released in 2014
Artist: Ariana Grande (American)
Lesson link: pronunciation of /ɪ/, /iː/ and /ð/
Notes: In this song, Ariana Grande celebrates the fact that she is now independent from a past love she had. This song has an awkward lyric in which she says *Now that I become who I really are* written in order to rhyme with the previous line. Grande blames Max Martin, not herself, for bending the grammar rules of English.

Before the class, search for a video or audio clip of the song line at the top of p. 45. As sts arrive, ask them not to open their books. Start the class by telling them that they will listen to an audio or video clip of this lesson's song line, and they have write down what they hear. Then, play the clip two or three times as necessary and, when they are ready, have them work in pairs to compare what they have written down. Explain to sts that they should reach an agreement about the correct version in case they have different understandings of what has been said in the song. Next, have a volunteer pair come to the board to write down what they believe is the correct song line. As they do this, encourage the other pairs to correct anything that they believe should be corrected. Finally, have sts open their books to check and ask: *What was the most difficult part to understand?* Encourage sts to share their opinions.

4.2

🎵 **Song line:** *I'm waiting for it, that green light, I want it, Oh, I wish I could get my things and just let go.*
Song: *Green Light*, released in 2017
Artist: Lorde (New Zealander)
Lesson link: green (colours)
Notes: The song finds the singer coping with her first real heartbreak, which left a clear mark on her. She is metaphorically waiting for the traffic light to turn green so she can remove the guy from her mind and get on with her life.

Before the class, write the song line from the top of p. 47 on the board with all the vowels missing:

_'m w_ _t_ng f_r _t, th_t gr_ _n l_ght, _ w_nt _t, _h, _ w_sh _ c_ _ld g_t my th_ngs _nd j_st l_t g_.

As sts arrive in class, ask them not to open their books. Start the class by having them look at the board and ask: *What's missing in this song line?* Expect them to notice that all the vowels are missing in the song line. Then, have them work in pairs to complete it. Allow sts a few minutes to do this, and, when all pairs are ready, ask: *Can you identify this song? Can you sing this line?* Encourage sts to answer and sing the song line if they want to. Finally, allow them to open their books on p. 47 to check the actual song line.

4.3

🎵 **Song line:** *You're dangerous cause you're honest, you're dangerous 'cause you don't know what you want.*
Song: *Who's gonna ride your wild horses?*, released in 1991
Artist: U2 (Irish)
Lesson link: honest
Notes: Bono wrote this song based on what U2's guitarist, The Edge, was going through while separating from his wife after seven years of marriage. Bono was the best man at The Edge's wedding, and watching his friend go through the divorce inspired the lyrics.

Before the class, copy the song line from the top of p. 49 onto two pieces of paper. As sts arrive in class, ask them not to open their books. Start the class by organizing them into two teams and place them as far apart in the classroom as possible. Then, choose one student in each group and give them one of the pieces of paper each. They must not show the piece of paper to the other members of their team. They are going to mime the whole song line for their team to guess it. Next, allow the miming sts a few minutes to think of a good way to mime the whole line, and remind them that they can do so in chunks, as it will make things easier for them. They cannot say a word or show the paper to their team. When a team is ready, they should raise their hands and wait for the other team to guess the complete line. When both teams are ready, allow the first one to finish to read their line. If they got it right, they are the winners, if not, the other team has their chance. Finally, allow sts to open their books on p. 49 to check the actual song line.

4.4

🎵 **Song line:** *No one knows about you, about you, And you're making the typical me break my typical rules, It's true, I'm a sucker for you.*
Song: *Sucker*, released in 2019
Artist: Jonas Brothers (American)
Lesson link: typical
Notes: This song was released in 2019, six years after Jonas Brothers announced their split. The song *Sucker* made the trio's reunion public. In this song, they are so obsessed with a girl that it makes them do crazy things. But even so, they are proud of being suckers for love.

Before the class, write the song line from the top of p. 51 on the board with a few pronunciation-related mistakes for sts to try and identify. Here are six possible pronunciation-related mistakes:

"**Know** one **nose** about you, about you, **End your** making the typical me **brake** my typical rules, Its true, I'm a sucker **four** you."

As sts arrive in class, ask them not to open their books. Start the class by having them look at the song line on the board and ask: *Can you recognize this song line? Can you sing this line?* Encourage sts to answer and sing the song line if they want to. Then, explain that the song line on the board has X mistakes (depending on how many you choose in include), and they have to work in pairs to identify the mistakes. Explain to sts that the mistakes are pronunciation-related and that they have to race the other pairs to spot all of them. When the first pair is ready, they say *Stop!*, and come to the board to correct the mistakes in the song line. As they do so, encourage the other pairs to say if they agree or not with the proposed corrections. Make sure sts realize that the words used in the original version have a very similar sound, but completely different meaning, to the ones you wrote on the board.

Songs

4.5

🎵 **Song line:** *Tell me somethin', girl. Are you happy in this modern world? Or do you need more? Is there somethin' else you're searchin' for?*
Song: *Shallow*, released in 2018
Artist: Lady Gaga (American) feat. Bradley Cooper
Lesson link: modern world & searching for something lost
Notes: This duet was recorded for the remake of the classic movie *A Star Is Born*. In this remake, Gaga plays the role of rising star, Ally, while Bradley Cooper is the well-known musician, Jackson Maine. Jackson becomes Ally's mentor and lover.

Before the class, write the song line from the top of p. 53 on slips of paper (one per pair or trio), and cut each of them into four pieces or more for sts to assemble. As sts arrive in class, ask them not to open their books. Organize them into pairs or trios and start the class by explaining that each pair or trio will receive a song line cut into pieces, and they have to put the pieces in order to form the song line of the lesson. When all sts are ready, have them read their version of the song line, and compare with those of the other pairs or trios. Finally, allow sts to open their books on p. 53 to check the actual song line and compare it with their versions.

Writing 4

🎵 **Song line:** *Yeah, I left my wallet in El Segundo, Left my wallet in El Segundo, Left my wallet in El Segundo, I gotta get it, I got-got ta get it.*
Song: *I Left My Wallet In El Segundo*, released in 1990
Artist: A Tribe Called Quest (American)
Lesson link: lost property
Notes: El Segundo is a city in California and the song is about Q-Tip accidentally forgetting his wallet at a restaurant there after being distracted by an attractive girl.

At any point during the lesson, have sts read the song line from p. 54 and ask: *Do you know this song? Can you sing this line?* Encourage them to answer and sing the song line if they want to. Then, ask: *What is the link of the song line with this lesson?* Sts work in pairs to scan the Writing page to try and find the link of the song line with the lesson. Allow them a few minutes to do this and, when they are ready, have them share their ideas with the whole class. Hopefully they will be able to identify that, just like the writing lesson, the song line talks about lost property. Next, have the pairs make a list of all songs they can remember that talk about lost things. Explain that they can search the web for the songs, but they must be able to sing or hum the corresponding part of the song lines they put on their lists. Allow them a few minutes to come up with their lists. Finally, have the pair with the most song lines in their list share them with the whole class. If they can either sing or hum all song lines in their list, they are the winners.

Review 2

🎵 **Song line:** *So, so what, I am a rock star, I got my rock moves, And I don't want you tonight.*
Song: *So What*, released in 2008
Artist: Pink (American)
Lesson link: jobs
Notes: In this song, Pink makes reference to her relationship with motocross racer, Carey Hart. They divorced after a rumored infidelity. In *So What*, Pink decides to enjoy being famous without attachments instead of showing sorrow for the break up.

As sts arrive in class, ask them not to open their books. Start the class by telling them that they will play *Telephone* with the song line of this lesson. Organize sts into three teams lined up facing the board, and divide the song line from p. 57 into three parts. Each team will work with one part of the song line:

So, so what, I am a rock star / I got my rock moves / And I don't want you tonight.

Next, give the first student in each line a marker. They will need it to write what they hear on the board. Start by whispering the first part of the song line to the last student in the first team. Explain that they should then whisper what they heard to the next student in line until it gets to the first student in their team, who has to write down what they understood on the board. Do the same with the other teams and, when they're ready, ask: *Can you recognize this song?* Encourage them to guess and share their opinions based on what they heard in the *Telephone* game. Then, have sts open their books on p. 57 to check the actual song line. Finally, ask: *Do you know this song? Can you sing this line?* Encourage sts to answer and sing the song line if they want to.

5.1

🎵 **Song line:** *'Cause I don't care, when I'm with my baby, yeah, All the bad things disappear, And you're making me feel like maybe I am somebody.*
Song: *I Don't Care*, released in 2019
Artist: Ed Sheeran (British) feat. Justin Bieber
Lesson link: things that are bad for you
Notes: In *I Don't Care*, Ed Sheeran is at a party he doesn't want to be at, and where he doesn't seem to fit in because people are wearing formal clothes, which he isn't used to. His partner puts him at ease.

Before the class, write the song line from p. 59 on slips of paper (one per pair or trio), and cut each of the slips into five pieces or more for sts to assemble (the higher the level of the sts, the more pieces). Make sure the pieces can be assembled in various different ways and still make sense. As sts arrive in class, organize them into pairs or trios and ask them not to open their books. Start the class by explaining that each pair or trio will receive a song line cut up into a number pieces. Explain to sts that they have to work together to put the pieces in order, so as to form the song line of the lesson. Remind them that they cannot open their books or search the web for the lyrics. Tell the pairs or trios that, when they are ready, they should raise their hands and wait for the others to finish. When all pairs or trios are ready, have them read their version of the song line and compare with the other pairs or trios. Finally, allow sts to open their books on p. 59 to check the actual song line and compare it with their versions.

5.2

🎵 **Song line:** *I love it when you go crazy, You take all my inhibitions, Baby, there's nothing holding me back.*
Song: *There's Nothing Holdin' Me Back*, released in 2016
Artist: Shawn Mendes (Canadian)
Lesson link: love
Notes: In this song, Shawn Mendes sings about a relationship that helps him feel free and be himself. The girl in the relationship makes him feel so good that he stops feeling self-conscious and wants her to take him to places he's never been.

As sts arrive in class, ask them not to open their books. Start the class by telling them that they will play *Telephone* with the song line of this lesson. Organize sts into three teams lined up facing the board, and divide the song line from p. 61 into three parts. Each team will work with one part of the song line:

I love it when you go crazy / You take all my inhibitions / Baby, there's nothing holding me back.

Songs

Next, give the first student in each line a marker. They will need it to write what they hear on the board. Start by whispering the first part of the song line to the last student in the first team. Explain that they should then whisper what they heard to the next student in line until it gets to the first student in their team, who has to write down what they understood on the board. Do the same with the other teams and, when they're ready, ask: *Can you recognize this song?* Encourage them to guess and share their opinions based on what they heard in the *Telephone* game. Then, have sts open their books on p. 61 to check the actual song line. Finally, ask: *Do you know this song? Can you sing this line?* Encourage sts to answer and sing the song line if they want to.

5.3

♪ **Song line:** *I wanna rock n roll all night and party every day.*
Song: *Rock and Roll All Nite*, released in 1975
Artist: Kiss (American)
Lesson link: free time activities
Notes: Kiss members Gene Simmons and Paul Stanley wrote this song as an anthem for all their fans. They wanted a song that could become a symbol for their fans who wanted to "rock and roll all night". This song was featured in more than five different soundtracks for movies, including *Why Him* in 2016, and *Gulliver's Travels* in 2010.

Before the class, search for an instrumental (without vocals) audio clip of the song line from p. 63. Alternatively, you can hum the song line without singing the lyrics. As sts arrive in class, ask them not to open their books. Start the class by explaining that sts will work in pairs to write down the song line of this lesson just by listening to an instrumental version. Explain that this is a very famous song, and that they will almost certainly recognize it, so it should be fairly easy for them to identify. Next, divide the class into pairs and start humming or playing the instrumental track. Sts write down the lyrics of the song line. When all pairs are ready, have a volunteer pair come to the board to write it down. Encourage the others to correct anything they believe is incorrect. Finally, ask: *Do you know this song? Can you sing this line?* Encourage sts to answer and sing the song line if they want to.

5.4

♪ **Song line:** *Only hate the road when you're missing home, Only know you love her when you let her go, And you let her go.*
Song: *Let Her Go*, released in 2012
Artist: Passenger (British)
Lesson link: love and hate
Notes: This was the second single to be released from the album *All The Little Lights*. It was also the singer's first international success, reaching the top on the charts in several countries.

Before the class, search for a video or audio clip of the song line from p. 65. As sts arrive, ask them not to open their books. Start the class by explaining that they will watch / listen to an audio / video clip of the song line of this lesson, and they have write down what they hear. Then, play the clip two or three times and, when they are ready, sts work in pairs to compare what they have written down. Next, have a volunteer pair come to the board to write down what their version of the song line. As they do so, encourage the other pairs to correct anything that they believe is incorrect. Finally, have sts open their books to check the actual song line on p. 65 and ask: *What was the most difficult part to understand?* Encourage them to share their opinions.

5.5

♪ **Song line:** *Anything you want, you got it. Anything you need, you got it. Anything at all, you got it. Baby!*
Song: *You Got It*, released in 1989
Artist: Roy Orbison (American)
Lesson link: anything
Notes: Tragically, Roy Orbison died from a heart attack in December 1988 and did not manage to see the release and success of this song when it peaked at number nine in the U.S. in April 1989.

Before the class, write the song line from p. 67 on the board with a few mistakes in it for sts to try and identify, e.g.

"**And he think you're one**, you got it. **And he think you're in**, you got it. **And he think** at all, you got it. Baby!"

As sts arrive in class, ask them not to open their books. Start the class by having sts look at the song line on the board and ask: *Can you recognize this song? Can you sing this line?* Encourage sts to answer and sing the song line if they want to. Next, have them work in pairs to identify the mistakes in the song line on the board. They should race the other pairs to spot them all. Tell the first pair to say *Stop!* when they're ready, and come to the board to correct the mistakes in the song line. Encourage the other pairs to say if they agree or not with the corrections and to add any other corrections necessary. When sts are ready, they open their books on p. 67 in order to check the actual song line on the page. Finally, ask: *What is the link of the song line with the lesson?* They should be able to identify that the link is the word *anything* in the question title of the lesson.

Writing 5

♪ **Song line:** *I hate you I love you, I hate that I want you, You want her, you need her, And I'll never be her.*
Song: *I Hate U I Love U*, released in 2016
Artist: Gnash (American) feat. Olivia O'Brien
Lesson link: hate and love
Notes: This song is about the aftermath of a separation where both people involved still miss each other. Olivia O'Brien released a solo version of the song in March 2016. Her version was called *Hate U Love U*.

Before the class, write the song line from p. 68 on slips of paper (one per pair or trio), and cut each of them into four pieces or more for sts to assemble (the more advanced your sts are, the more pieces you should cut.). Make sure that the pieces can be combined in different ways and still make sense. As sts arrive in class, ask them not to open their books. Organize them into pairs or trios and start by explaining that each pair or trio will get the song line cut into pieces. They have to put the pieces in order to form the song line of the lesson. When all sts are ready, have them read their version of the song line to compare with other pairs or trios. Finally, allow sts to open their books on p. 68 to check the actual song line and compare it with their versions.

Songs

Review 3

♪ **Song line:** *Hey now, you're an all-star, get your game on, go play, Hey now, you're a rock star, get the show on, get paid.*
Song: *All Star*, release in 1999
Artist: Smash Mouth
Lesson link: playing games
Notes: This song has been featured in several movies and TV shows, most notably the 2001 movie, *Shrek*. Many Internet memes have also been created based on this song, to which the band has responded by saying that they "like the attention, even though it's a bit of a goof!"

As this is the last song in Starter, and the theme is *playing games*, have sts play Capture the Castle in teams and see which team can complete the game first. Then, give each team a unit of the book to look at and write a quiz on based on the vocab and grammar of that unit. Check the questions, then give each team's quiz to another team to play.

As an end-of-term treat, you could play the whole song for sts and have them sing along, or, alternatively, play the movie, *Shrek*, which features this song on its soundtrack!